Disaster Operations
and Decision Making

Disaster Operations and Decision Making

Roger C. Huder

WILEY

A JOHN WILEY & SONS, INC., PUBLICATION

Library of Congress Cataloging-in-Publication Data:

Huder, Roger C.
    Disaster operations and crisis decision making / Roger C. Huder.
        p. cm.
    Includes bibliographical references and index.
    ISBN 978-0-470-92793-9 (hardback)
    1. Emergency management. 2. Crisis management. 3. Decision making. I. Title.
    HV551.2.H83 2012
    363.34'8—dc23   2011033615

Printed in the United States of America.

10 9 8 7 6 5 4

Dedication

To my wife Tricia for her support and patience through the years.

Contents

Preface

Political Decisions Have Operational Consequences, Operational Decisions Have Political Consequences

All disasters are political. And as political events they have all the complications that a political event creates. Everything you do and everything you are told to do will eventually be seen through the prism of self-interest by those inside and outside your organization. The press will emphasize what is going wrong and not what is going right. The strengths and weaknesses that exist in your community's organization will be exposed and magnified by the stresses of the demands that will be made on them. Personnel in your organization will not be up to the challenges at hand. Some will freeze, while others will not show up, choosing to stay with family. There will be promotions on the spot based on personal actions as well as demotions and even firings. On top of all of that is the fact that you are in charge of nothing but responsible for how all the organizations in your community work together and will be judged by their performance. In other words, being an emergency manager during a disaster is one of the most difficult positions anyone can possibly imagine and one of the most important. How well you juggle all of these factors will determine the eventual impact an event has on your community. Because once a disaster occurs, it will continue to impact your community until you get it under control and begin to repair the damage.

How good a job you do will be determined long before a disaster strikes. It will be decided in meetings, offices, and the hallways of your community. It will depend on establishing yourself as a leader and having the ability to maneuver through a bureaucracy to accomplish what you need to do to prepare your community. This process can be a long one with few rewards. I watched appointed officials around me make the decisions they were appointed to make then fired for making them when the political climate changed. I watched as officials did what they were told by those who had appointed them and then, when a scapegoat was needed, not only were they fired but were blamed for their decisions. It is easy to lose sight of what it is you are trying to accomplish and why you are struggling through this maze. I had to develop a way to remind myself of whom I was fighting for in the midst of office battles over the years. I eventually came up with a rule that I tried to use as a guiding principle.

This book is written in the spirit of that principle that I came to call the "the little old lady rule." I had come from the street as a hands-on first responder, where my decisions and their consequences were immediately apparent. I knew immediately if I had made the right decision. I needed something that grounded me in that same way in the conference rooms and offices.

The Little Old Lady Rule

Somewhere in my community there sits a little old lady who has paid her taxes for the last fifty years. She had never required more from my jurisdiction than to pick up her garbage, pave streets and sidewalks, and provide her with utilities, the simple services any community provides to everyone. Now in the midst of a disaster she will need more than the simple service, her home and even her life are in jeopardy. She has no retinue of lobbyists knocking on the doors of elected officials to make sure her interests are served. She is depending on me. So the rule is that what is best for the little old lady is best for the community. She is a reflection of all of those who trust us to be there to make the decisions that are best for her and all of those like her.

If you do what is right for that little old lady, then you will be doing what is right for the community as a whole. All that you can do as an emergency manager is to make decisions that are best for the entire community no matter how difficult or politically unpopular they may be. The rule holds true in any jurisdiction no matter its size. It helped me make the decisions that I thought were best for the community as a whole, because she represented the people who depended on us the most. And the right decision for her was the right decision for the community.

The rule by no means made some of the decisions easier or even popular, but it provided me with a bottom line and a core belief. There were decisions based on this rule that I made long before any disaster threatened that were unpopular with everyone from the labor unions to the administration. The rule never made the decision-making easier or less controversial or politically less volatile, but if I was going to be fired I wanted to be fired for doing what I thought had been best for that little old lady and everyone she represented.

I did not always win those battles before, during, or after events, but the rule worked because I always felt that I had made the best decision I could for the community. In disaster response that is the best you can ever hope for. This book is written in the spirit of the "little old lady rule." My hope is that it gives the reader some tools and approaches to the challenges any disaster presents. If it does that, then I will have been true to the rule.

ROGER C. HUDER

Introduction

Disasters are stressful to any organization and to the personnel who populate them. Some participants will be up to the task and others will not. There will be promotions, demotions, and even firings in the midst of the response. The only way to provide the best possible response to a disaster is to create a structure for information gathering, deciphering, and prioritizing in the midst of such stress. Only then can good decisions be made and implemented.

In the four phases of emergency management, mitigation, preparedness, response, and recovery, much emphasis has been placed on the first two. This book is about the first critical hours and days of a disaster response. It is about how decisions are made and how to train and build the teams you need to respond to any event. It is also about putting into place the systems needed to support that disaster-response team.

The tenets in this book are based on over 30 years of experience in emergency response and emergency management. I have adapted some relevant military operational procedures. All of this is accomplished within the framework of the Incident Command System (ICS) and the National Incident Management System (NIMS).

DISASTER OPERATIONS

Disaster plans are based on assumptions. Those assumptions are static snapshots of a community and its resources at the time the plan is written. Much can change in the time between the writing of a plan and the implementation of that plan during a disaster. No plan, no matter how well written, can ever completely prepare a community for a disaster; the best way for a community to prepare is to have a well-trained disaster-response team.

When a disaster strikes, it is like dropping a pebble in a pond. The impact ripples through the community just as the pebble created ripples across the surface of the pond. The longer it takes for a community to manage the disaster, the greater the disaster's impact on the community. There are many more problems needing attention than there are resources to apply to these problems. It is vital that local authorities be organized and capable of applying available resources as efficiently as possible to the most critical problems. It is vital that local officials be as efficient as they can possibly be during the first 72 hours after a disaster because it will take that long for serious outside resources to reach them. The emergency-management community needs to get better at what the military calls the operational art.

THE OPERATIONAL ART

The military has an old saying, "no plan survives first contact with the enemy." To properly implement their plans, the military talks about the "art of operations." It recognized that fighting a war is not merely the simple execution of a well-designed plan; instead it was a process of adapting the plan to an ever-changing environment once the battle had begun. The military set about to train their commanders to have a suppleness of thinking that produced the needed flexibility. This philosophy of adaptation to a changing environment mimics the challenges faced during a disaster.

Prior to the first Gulf War in Iraq in 1991 the United States had not engaged in a conventional military conflict of similar proportions since World War II. Yet commanders were able to perform as if they had been fighting similar wars for the preceding 50 years. This occurred because the military recognized that during their training commanders would draw up a detailed plan for an operation but could not implement the plan. The first contact with an actual thinking enemy frequently defeated the best plans.

Emergency management is in exactly the same position today. Thousands of human hours each year are devoted to the development of detailed response plans to hurricanes, floods, tornados, and terrorist attacks, yet implementing those plans falls far short of the effort put into them. There are many reasons for this, but the primary reason is that there is no set of basic emergency-response principles that shapes a community's response to a disaster. Principles that can take the plans that were developed, adapt them to the incident, and save lives and property. ICS and NIMS both are powerful tools to carry out operational decisions, but they are not, nor were they ever intended to be, operational templates. They are a structure a community can use to build a response organization to fit a disaster, but they do not do the job by themselves.

Until this century military commanders might fight one war during their career. Yet they had to have the skills to get it right the very first time. It was a career maker or breaker. The same is true in emergency management. Emergency managers may have only one chance to implement a career's worth of planning and training. The consequences of their actions for their career and community are just as dire as for the military commanders.

THE MILITARY LEARN FROM US

The military wanted to improve their ability to train their officers for command. To do this they knew they needed to provide training that was focused on the skills they needed to make command decisions in combat. This training had to provide their commanders with experiences that would translate to the battlefield. To determine the types of training and simulations needed to develop these skills, they first had to determine how people under the stress of time and disaster made decisions.

The United States Army Research Institute for Behavioral and Social Sciences decided that the group of individuals who most closely resembled military commanders were firefighter officers and incident commanders.

The study determined that individuals under the pressures of time and the responsibility for people's lives made decisions in a very different way they than had been expected. The military then used this discovery to shape not only their training but to build a whole new approach to fighting wars called maneuver warfare. We in emergency management should do the same. We need to recognize how decisions are made, then create an operational structure and infra-structure to carry out those decisions. ICS and NIMS provide the structure, but we need an operational infrastructure.

Currently we plan well and perform poorly. This book is about the implementation of operations in the context of a disaster. After a disaster the media is obsessed with whether there was a plan for a specific type of event. There are endless questions about whether a plan took this or that into consideration. We in the industry fall into the trap of trying to produce plans with every possible contin-gency and permutation "planned for." Yet the realities of war and disaster response have repeatedly shown that the old military adage remains true.

NO PLAN SURVIVES FIRST CONTACT WITH THE ENEMY

I would argue that we have seen exactly the same type of situation emerge time after time. From Hurricane Andrew, when Metro Dade's emergency manager Kate Hale asked, "where's the cavalry?" to Hur-ricane Katrina, where thousands of victims were left stranded while the nation watched on television to the BP oil spill—all demonstrate the adage.

GOOD PLANS DO NOT EQUAL A GOOD RESPONSE

We must go beyond critiquing our response to disasters by looking at our plans to determine whether a community was ready and able to respond. We must begin to understand that response is a product of planning and the development of a functioning operational infra-structure within a community. One without the other guarantees a slow and poor response. To build such an infrastructure, you must understand how decisions are made in a crisis, then build the infra-structure, policies, and procedures to support that decision-making paradigm.

HOW TO USE THE BOOK

The author strongly suggests that time be spent in understanding crisis decision making. The basic understanding of how people make decisions in a crisis is the basis for the rest of the chapters. The processes and suggested policies all evolve out of the decision-making process. If an emergency manger has that understanding and has placed the needed operational infrastructure in place, then he or she can expect to have built the kind of organization needed to respond to any crisis. This book is meant to be a reference, resource and hopefully a starting point for a new discussion about the operational side of disaster response.

CHAPTER 1

The Emergency Manager: Leading in a Crisis

Leading during a disaster is not easy. How you perform will matter in profound ways across your community. Many will measure their lives in terms of what they were like before and after the event. Perform badly and people will suffer physically and economically; perform well and it will lessen the impact of the disaster on their lives.

Emergency managers rarely speak from a position of power. Instead they are typically layers down from the seats of power in the jurisdiction. Yet when a disaster occurs, it will be their job to step to the forefront and lead a group of people who are not used to working together, who are under tremendous pressures to accomplish the seemingly impossible task of restoring normality as quickly as possible. This is all done under the scrutiny of the press, outside agencies, and the public.

If operations go well and the community returns to normality in a timely fashion, the elected officials will garner all the credit. If operations do not go well, the emergency manager will be blamed and set up as the scapegoat. Yet being an emergency manager in just such a situation can be one of the most challenging and gratifying jobs around. Knowing that you have led your community back from devastation to recovery provides a profound sense of accomplishment. But the kind of leadership needed to accomplish this does not come with a job title. It must be earned over time.

How effective a leader an emergency manager is during a crisis is not determined when the disaster occurs. It is determined long before a disaster strikes by the relationships the emergency manager establishes within the community. An emergency manager holds a unique position within the bureaucracy. He or she is responsible for the response of the entire community to a disaster. Yet he "owns" no single resource needed to accomplish this goal. He must influence departments, agencies, and people across organizational lines of authority if he is to accomplish his job. The ability to develop this kind of cooperation among a volatile mix of organizations and people under stress does not suddenly emerge. The stage is set long before a disaster threatens.

It involves a lengthy process to lay a groundwork of expertise, trust, policies, and procedures. Through this preparation an emergency manager will be able to overcome the chaos that follows a disaster. The process requires patience, courage, expertise, and a stubbornness to overcome the organizational resistance that is natural in any bureaucracy. It is absolutely essential if an emergency manager is to lead the community's efforts.

Disasters require an unprecedented and completely unique level of coordination both within the community as well as with outside agencies. Not only are everyday lines of authority broken into entirely new organizational structures, but also the organizations themselves and the individuals who run them must work together to accomplish a completely new set of tasks under the added pressure of time and public scrutiny.

This is a new organizational paradigm that calls for a new type of leadership role. A role where the emergency manager has no "official" power over these various organizations, yet his leadership is accepted and recommendations are followed. This new leadership style requires that the emergency manger make recommendations to officials who are their superiors. They must speak truth to power, a skill that comes from trust and is developed over time.

Leonard J. Marcus and Barry C. Dorn of Harvard University, with Joseph M. Henderson of the U.S. Centers of Disease Control and Prevention, discuss this leadership style at length in their groundbreaking 2005 paper "Meta-Leadership and National Emergency Preparedness." The key points of the paper are distilled into an executive summary, "National Preparedness and the Five Dimensions of Meta-Leadership of the National Preparedness Leadership Initiative," a 2007 Joint Program paper by the Harvard School of Public Health and the Kennedy School of Government at Harvard University. There are five major points emphasized in this leadership style.

Meta-Leadership

1. A meta-leader has the ability to instill confidence in other leaders within his community through his expertise or "frame of reference." He is able to present the correct "choice points" so the best decisions for the organization and community are made.

2. A meta-leader has situational awareness; with often incomplete information he creates a broad frame of reference for the team as a whole, thereby presenting the team with the proper choices at the proper point in time. The leader is able to chart and present the progress of those decisions so a continuous situational awareness is retained even in a fast-moving and confusing environment.

3. Meta-leaders lead their silo—they develop subordinates into similar leadership roles within their spheres of responsibility so they have a team of people who foster the same types of relationships with their counterparts.

4. Meta-leaders lead up—they guide their bosses. Not by political manipulation or bureaucratic maneuvering but by becoming a "fair witness" by speaking the truth to power from a point of accepted expertise and not self-interest. If a leader trusts a subordinate to give recommendations that are in the community's best interest, then he will follow those recommendations. During a disaster what is best for the community as a whole is best for the any elected or appointed official.

5. A meta-leader leads cross-agency connectivity. Long before a disaster strikes, a meta-leader establishes relationships of mutual respect with other departments, bureaus, and agencies by respecting the expertise of these individuals and the need for that expertise during a disaster. The emergency manager clarifies their roles and establishes relationships that will function during a disaster.

These five tenets are the guiding principles for emergency managers if they are to become effective leaders during a disaster.

HOW TO BECOME A CRISIS LEADER

This roadmap for an emergency manager to create a place in the community had not been articulated when I began my career in emergency management. Prior to the landmark disasters that came to define emergency management—Hurricane Hugo, Hurricane Andrew, 9/11, and Hurricane Katrina—emergency management was a sleepy backwater in a busy bureaucracy. Resources were scarce or nonexistent; little attention and just plain indifference surrounded the job. Despite my jurisdiction being located in Florida, it had been over 30 years since a hurricane directly struck our community, and the intuitional memory of its effects had been lost. The city was unprepared and complacent about any disaster, much less a hurricane.

Yet it became my job to prepare my city for such eventualities. With no models to follow I approached the job using strategies that seemed to make common sense. Without knowing it I used meta-leadership tenets as defined by Marcus, Dorn, and Henderson in their groundbreaking paper to crave out a respected leadership role in disasters and disaster preparedness.

The meta-leadership definition distills years of my own lessons learned. This style of leadership is not one that will be bestowed on the emergency manager upon his appointment; rather it is one that will be earned by creating such a role in an existing organization. It will require time, effort, and patience. It is not an organizational style that will necessarily be rewarded. The value of the role will only become apparent when a disaster or crisis threatens.

Ideally an emergency manager would report directly to the most senior elected official of a community. More typically the office of emergency management is buried in another department. In my case it was the fire department. Fire departments are one of the more common departments for emergency management at the local level, but it can be located in almost any department. At the writing of this book the Florida Division of Emergency Management is under the Department of Community Affairs. The placement of most offices of emergency management under another department and not in direct control of the jurisdiction's response resources is the reason the meta-leadership model works so well for any emergency manager.

The fire chief had the official title of emergency manager for the city, and he reported to the mayor. I worked directly for him, and it was with his voice that I spoke when I went to meetings or coordinated with other departments. To be able to represent an appointed official, you must develop a good working rapport. When the chief appointed me as the emergency manager, he added it to two other jobs I already performed for him.

There is no set model across the county; it will vary from state to state. In Florida counties are required to have an emergency manager. Cities are not required to do so, but depending on their size some feel the need to have one. Unless they are required to have one, most communities do not have the money to fund a full-time emergency manager. So, as in my case, it is given to someone as a second responsibility.

Once he appointed me I was able to spend enough time discussing emergency management with him to develop an approach that we both felt comfortable with. That did not mean we spent a large amount of time on the subject; he expected me to spend the time needed to accomplish the tasks, then brief him on the progress. Planning and developing relationships with other departments was up to me. He literally had other fires to put out as well as budgets, the union, and the administration all competing for his time. No matter what department an emergency manager works for, it is critical that he develop a working trust with the head of that department. It also must be known that the manager represents the department head on the subject. It provides him with the cachet needed to begin developing the needed relationships.

While being a designee was important, it was only the first step. It did not give me the respect as a leader with other departments that would be needed during a crisis. That level of respect was going to have to be earned over the next months and even years. This lack of respect is not out of pettiness; instead it came from a realization that should a disaster strike, the careers of these officials would be on the line. Until I proved myself as a trusted advisor, they would be reluctant to take recommendations from someone when their performance and their department's performance would be so closely scrutinized. That respect would have to be earned.

BECOME THE EXPERT

Part of the answer to becoming a crisis leader in your community is to become the authority on disasters and how to respond to them. If you are appointed, you must have credentials, but that does not necessarily make you an expert in the eyes of others in your community. You become an expert in the eyes of others by continuing to learn, by striving for more certifications and education. The continued pursuit of additional education and training creates the image of someone truly interested in their subject matter.

But simply accumulating more training, education credits, and degrees is not enough. You must go above and beyond what may be considered normal qualifications. One way is to read as much about the histories of disasters as you can lay your hands on. (See the reading list in this book for some good titles to start with.) History is context. Look for detailed histories filled with firsthand accounts that are rich in detail. The kind of detail that can be translated into specific impacts a similar event would have on your community. These details will become recognizable issues for your community that you will be able to use to plan and emphasize during training. These historical details will make the training more compelling and relevant.

A couple of excellent examples that should be on every emergency manager's reading list are *The Great Influenza* by John M. Barry and *City on Fire* by Bill Minutaglio. *The Great Influenza* is a richly detailed account of the pandemic that ravaged the world in 1918. It describes specific details of its impact on society and the disruption it caused in cities across the world. The authors go into the particulars of how some cities took precautions and were able to ameliorate the impact of the disease, while others did not take those same precautions, with terrible consequences. It was a source of more useful information than any other during the Bird Flu and Swine Flu scares.

City on Fire details the explosions of two cargo ships carrying ammonium nitrate in the Texas City harbor just after World War II. The devastating effects are the closest you will ever come to understanding the impact of terrorist use of a tactical nuclear weapon on a U.S. city. This book should inform any emergency manager responsible for developing plans for such a contingency.

Another rich source of information are the reports of lessons learned created after major disasters. They are not consistently produced, but there are some excellent resources with the kind of detail that will provide you with rich information. The Internet is your primary source for these reports; searching on the type of disaster will bring up a range of sites that can be farmed for what you need. Find them, read them, print then out and start a library. If they are detailed enough to include timelines, and specific minute-by-minute accounts, they are an excellent source of ideas and information for the creation of exercises and training.

When you teach a class or lead an exercise, referring to specific problems or consequences in previous disasters only adds weight to your point. It also quiets the "that would never happen" skeptics who always seem to be included in any audience. So when they question an issue or problem because it could not really happen, you can simply quote the source and explain why you included it in your training. This is also a tactic that works well in meeting rooms as you fight for money and resources; few can argue with actual events. Your knowledge of past disasters also reinforces your role as an expert.

Whenever you use an example from a previous disaster, make sure you make the point that our society is becoming more and more fragile and susceptible to to disruptions caused by a disaster. Any disruptions in power will be magnified significantly. An example is included in a study done by the Urban Institute of the University of North Carolina at Charlotte on the effect of Hurricane Hugo on that city. They found that 80 percent of the businesses in the city had been severely or moderately affected by the hurricane. The top cause of this damage was loss of electrical power. Something as simple as the long-term loss of power leads to severe impacts on businesses and emphasizes the fragility of today's society and the fact that the historical impact will be magnified by the complexity and interdependence of today's world.

While you should read widely about disasters, do concentrate on your community's most common or direct threat. In Florida our most common threat is, of course, hurricanes. So I became a weather geek. I read everything I could on hurricanes and the affects they had on communities. I taught myself how to read the hurricane products created by the National Hurricane Center. I found some of the earliest software online that showed the modeling of the storms and how the forecasters used them to make their forecasts. I started tracking storms long before anyone else. I was constantly trying to get smarter about storms, their histories, and the effects on the community. This was after Andrew but before the constant barrage that seems to have attacked the state in the last few years. As I mentioned earlier, a storm had not affected my community in over 30 years. This meant there was no intuitional memory of what that would mean in terms of damage and disruption of services. The same holds true for almost any type of recognizable threat to your city, county, or state. It is your job to learn as much about the possible impact as you possibly can.

For my trouble I was called everything from somebody justifying my position to "Chicken Little." It was not until the first storm threatened our community and I briefed the senior staff that the importance of what I had emphasized become apparent. I briefed the staff on the projected course, what the impact might be, and as of the current forecast when they could expect to feel the first effects from the storm. I made recommendations about the preparations that should be made by each department and set a time frame for the next update.

At the end of the meeting one of the senior public-works administrators came up to me and said, "That was the briefing I had always hoped to receive before a storm." The various department heads were able to make the best decisions about preparations they would have to make and when they would have to make them.

By becoming the recognized expert who is truly interested in the field you have chosen and can be depended on to deliver timely information to decision makers, you can carve out an important role in your community. If you get drawn into the day-to-day bureaucratic infighting, you will be seen as just another official jockeying for position. If you are going to direct the disaster operations for your city, you must be seen as a impartial advisor and expert.

BECOME A TRAINER

The role of trainer is critical in establishing your leadership authority in your organization. Develop classes aimed at the specific audiences in your community—fire, law enforcement, public works, etc. Teach the classes using emergency-management needs as a lever to build two-way communications of ideas and expertise. Understand that you are standing in front of subject-matter experts in their fields; respect their knowledge because you are going to need it during a disaster. As you teach the classes, involve them by asking them as a police officer, firefighter, or public-works expert what they see as issues or solutions to the problems presented. Involve them and respect their input because, depending on the disaster, you will need them to take a lead role in the response. Specific types of disasters require some very specific skill sets, and you as an emergency manager will have to work closely with the needed subject-matter experts.

Develop a series of classes for the various departments individually and together to build disaster-response expertise. These classes should lead up to a full emercency-operations center (EOC) exercise with all of the various departments in attendance. The objective of this exercise is to bring together the various individual skills sets and begin to build a team. As you plan the exercise, make sure it is understood that this is not a test of their skills. This is a learning experience for everyone. This is very important. Professionals with years of experience do not like to be put in a position of being tested like a school kid. Instead, emphasize the need to pull all the various "experts" together to allow them to practice their new skills. At the end of the exercise hold an informal "hot wash," a give and take about what went right and wrong. Do not stand in front of them and point out their mistakes. Instead, ask them what they thought about the exercise and what they thought went right and wrong. You will find they will be harder on themselves than you ever would be and have insights you had missed.

Since hurricane season has a specific beginning calendar date, it provides an ideal excuse for an exercise. We convinced the administration to have a hurricane exercise to raise awareness and prepare for the upcoming season. I researched lessons learned from Hurricanes Hugo and Andrew and drew up a timeline and scripts of problems for each department. We sent out reports of the training hurricane's approach for several days. Each day the reports of the storm escalated as it approached the coast. I led a class on EOC procedures the day before the exercise to make sure all participants were comfortable in their roles. I borrowed radios so controllers could report problems as if from the field just as they would in a normal storm. I had off-duty dispatchers give situation reports and pass on problems just as they would during a normal storm.

The exercise was a success, and the participants felt as if they had received good training that would translate to a real emergency. The hot wash after the exercise produced a very useful list of deficiencies that needed addressing. The exercise was a success.

Not long after the exercise a real tropical storm struck our area of the state. We geared up for real. The storm turned out to be a minor one, but everyone felt more confident in his or her roles. Afterwards I received what I thought was one of the biggest compliments of my time as emergency manager. One of those who had participated both in the exercise and the storm response said, "Your exercise was harder. The storm was a piece of cake." That one well-planned exercise went a long way to validating my role within the community.

BECOME A FACILITATOR

Each department in your community will need to develop its specific section of the comprehensive emergency management plan (CEMP) for your jurisdiction. Do not simply ask a department to develop a plan to include in your overall plan and then leave it without some guidance. Hold planning sessions with each of the department's staff given the responsibility to produce this document. Explain that you are there for two reasons, to help with any questions about how the plan might fit within the larger document and, just as important, to learn as much as you can about how their department works. Understanding how your community's critical infrastructure works is a vital piece of knowledge for an emergency manager. You do not have to become an expert in all the fields, but you do need to understand each department at a systems level. Assist in the development of their expected action guides (EAG). (See Chapter 3.) Establish relationships within the department with the midlevel personnel. These are the individuals who make the department work every day. They will be the ones with the responsibility to hold it together during a disaster.

The purpose of this role is twofold: to assure that the departments within your community have a plan that works within the CEMP and to establish you as a fair advisor. By this I mean someone whose agenda is the protection of the community and not a personal one. It also establishes you as someone who is interested in their departments' particular problems and who wants to assist them in their efforts and by doing so to accomplish the overall goal of preparedness for your community.

This is a difficult and politically sensitive line to walk. Some departments are very insular and resistant to outside "intrusion." You may need an ally to gain access. In my case the city manager let it be known that she expected departments to cooperate with the development of the plan. Once it became known that I had her blessing, many doors opened. While you may be able to walk in that door, it will still be up to you to establish the relationships needed. All of the critical response departments have very specific cultures and skill sets, and acceptance in each will be a challenge. If you can gain access and facilitate at least parts of their planning process, you will have accomplished enough to build a working relationship.

USE IT OR LOSE IT

If you have managed to jump the hurdles and have the beginnings of a community-wide emergency-management team the next step is to move from training to actual activations. A disaster does not have to occur to have an excuse to bring at least some of the team together. A major special event takes a lot of coordination between law enforcement, traffic, vendors, and the venue staff. Open a makeshift emergency operations center as a convenience to those managing the event. The cross-departmental communication will lay the groundwork for a disaster response. Take advantage of every opportunity to show how emergency management would work, and you will begin to build a team before the disaster strikes. It can also provide some unexpected benefits.

During the Florida wildfires of 1998 our city was never threatened. The state was burning around us, but my county was never affected to the extent that others were by the fires. So we, along with other fire departments within the county, became a resource for manpower and equipment through mutual-aid pacts across the state. The city eventually had units and personnel in five different counties. This was not strictly an emergency-management problem given the fact that only one department was affected, but we were able to take advantage of the situation to demonstrate the importance of city-wide coordination.

The fire chief had me establish a makeshift EOC in a conference room to track our units and manpower around the state. We moved some computers into the room, set up projectors, and began to put together a picture of where and what our units were doing. We used fire-department personnel to staff the room and to coordinate the city's efforts. When the mayor wanted a briefing on the situation, the chief brought her to our thrown-together EOC. She was impressed. Impressed enough to give us permission to establish a mini-EOC in that conference room permanently.

We secured a State of Florida grant that allowed us to equip our new mini-EOC with projectors, TVs, computers, and office furniture. Once everything was installed, we realized that it made the perfect wired class or conference room. We made it available to any department needing a room with multimedia capabilities. It was used for classes and presentations from then on by a number of different departments. When we were threatened by hurricanes, it was ready for use for our briefings. The mini-EOC established the need for a larger, more complex facility to serve everyone and led the city to build a permanent EOC in the city's new combined communications operations center.

When you are able to activate your system, even if it includes only part of the team, it establishes your role in the community and provides practice for the larger events. Our room became well known because of its use for classes and presentations. On 9/11 it was filled with people from all departments watching the feeds for all of the media outlets, both local and national. I eventually had to ask them to leave to prepare for the mayor, but it had done its job by establishing the need for a central point for information for the city. The same would hold true for any jurisdiction.

ULTIMATE GOAL

I started this chapter by explaining how establishing a meta-leadership role within your community is vital to accomplishing your job as an emergency manager. The meta-leadership model includes situational awareness as one of its strengths. This situational awareness should be developed so that it is shared with the community as a whole. Given the vast amount of information needed to manage a disaster, creating an understandable frame of reference that reflects the situation requires the construction of a system that feeds the proper information to the proper personnel at the proper time. This type of system is difficult to be turned on like a light switch when a disaster occurs. Instead, the infrastructure within a community must be there and working. Once you have established yourself as a meta-leader within your community, you must begin to make emergency management part of the community's everyday operations.

Emergency management, if it is to truly function as needed during a disaster, must create a functionality and role that establishes its visibility and value in the community daily. We cannot simply sit in a corner and write plans and provide training and then expect to step into the role we must fill during a disaster. We need a daily role. The local law-enforcement agency, fire department, information systems, traffic control, and public works all have specific and well-defined roles. Their responsibilities and the reason for their existence and funding are accepted without question; the only real arguments concern the extent of their funding. This is not true of emergency management. Even today post-9/11 and Katrina most offices of emergency management are understaffed and underfunded.

There is a role that is emerging in many communities that needs to be filled. Technology has emerged to the point that geographic information systems (GISs), global positioning systems (GPSs), digital radars, and a myriad of other technologies are affordable and available to communities. These technologies allow a community to track in real time everything from traffic to the location of each law-enforcement patrol car and fire-engine company. If properly coordinated they can be used for real-time decision making in daily community operations. It would amount to a city or county operations center with feeds from law enforcement, fire, traffic, and public works all coalescing in one place. In this age of terrorism and increased security I would call it the Warning Point. (I will explain in a minute where I stole the idea and name.)

Emergency management would be in charge of running and disseminating the information as needed. Should a disaster strike, all the technology needed to run the Warning Point would then be available and already in use for the response. It would be collocated with the EOC, and all you would have to do is to turn on the EOC lights. There are two real-life examples that if combined would fulfill the concept of the Operations Center/Warning Point.

The State of Florida established a State Warning Point as the clearinghouse and situational-awareness center for all major incidents within the state. The state established a set of minimum standards for each incident report that were trigger points so that only the most serious would be reported. The point of the effort was to have an on-going understanding of all the major emergencies in the state that could impact a county, region, or even the state as a whole. The following is a list of the incidents needing reporting.

The State of Florida Warning Point Incidents to Report

Aircraft Incident	Nuclear Power Plant Drill/Event
Animal Disease	Biological Threat
Bomb/Threat	Petroleum Spill
Drinking Water Facilities	Radiological
Energy Emergency	Railroad
Environment Crime	Search and Rescue
Fire-Brush/Forest	Security Nonspecific
Fire-Major Structure	Severe Weather
General	Sinkhole
Hazardous Materials	Transportation
Wastewater	Migration/Immigration

The Warning Point is an effort to not only maintain statewide awareness of all significant incidents but to exercise the system, to keep the communication lines open to the counties all of the time so they could establish lines of communication within their own response community. It is manned 24 hours a day, 7 days a week. It provides totals of the types of incidents and their status on a daily basis. Trends can be followed and progress can be tracked on state-wide issues.

A county or city emergency-management office could serve as just such a Warning Point for its jurisdiction with no extra equipment or technology; all that would be needed is the establishment of a set of priorities for which incidents are reported by each department each day. A report could be generated each shift or day of the major incidents within the city and disseminated to all departments. This could be accomplished by a set of Core Liaisons (see Chapter 10) assigned to the Office of Emergency Management (OEM). Or it could be accomplished informally with the right relationships and the right political climate. This simple report would begin to establish emergency management as part of the day-to-day operations of a jurisdiction. The final goal would be a significant and long-term project but one that I think is worth the time and effort to take on given its power for the community.

I saw what the future should look like in the late 90s when I was sent to Houston, Texas, to research an upcoming project. Houston TranStar is a consortium of four government agencies to provide transportation and emergency-management services to the Greater Houston area. It is made up of the Texas Department of Transportation, Harris County; The Metropolitan Transit Authority of Harris County; and the City of Houston. It lists as its two main goals traffic management and emergency management.

TranStar leverages the multiple traffic technologies to manage and monitor traffic around Harris County and 50 miles to the coast through sensors and cameras. Emergency management has its EOC above and overlooking the operations floor. It has its own technology that includes an automated flood warning system, Doppler radar imagery, satellite weather maps, road flooding warning systems, and the regional incident management system.

To walk onto the operations floor is to feel as if you have entered into the war room at the Pentagon. It is two stories high with an open architectural plan with something on the order of 50 separate desks with operators sitting at each. The front of the room has floor-to-ceiling display screens with constantly changing views of the traffic throughout the metropolitan area. If an accident is reported or detected by cameras or other technology before being reported to the authorities, the cameras will stop their random views and focus on the accident and the surrounding traffic.

FIGURE 1.1   The TranStar operations floor with representations from numerous local agencies. *Photo courtesy of TranStar.*

FIGURE 1.2 Law Enforcement officers coordinate with transportation officials. *Photo courtesy TranStar.*

Figure 1.3 Emergency Management officials coordinate with other agencies. *Photo courtesy of TranStar.*

Representatives from the various traffic agencies; the road rangers who respond to non-accident-related problems; the relevant police, fire, and EMS agencies; and even the local radio station providing local up-to-the-minute traffic reports all are aware of the incident at the same time. Everyone needed to manage the problem sits in the same room and has the same situational awareness of the events so they can begin to take the appropriate action together.

In 2009, according to their annual report, TranStar managed 14,527 incidents and 138,000 operator-activated messages for everything from traffic alerts and rerouting to amber, silver, and blue alerts.

It costs an estimated $27.7 million a year to run, but TranStar estimates that the benefits in better, faster, and more efficient traffic and incident management translate into a $274 million saving or 9.9 to 1 benefit-to-cost ratio per year. TranStar took years of effort and team building to accomplish, but it stands as the first generation of community operational centers. It allows leaders to run day-to-day operations more efficiently and also to more effectively manage any disasters that may strike. It should be the goal for every emergency manager.

Figure 1.4 Transportation officials keep a close eye on traffic flow. *Photo courtesy TranStar.*

CONCLUSIONS

This chapter is an effort to give someone new to emergency management or even an experienced emergency-management professional a blueprint of how to establish oneself as a meta-leader and crisis manager in his or her community. Emergency management as a profession is still in its infancy. It roots go back only to the 1970s and the formation of Federal Emergency Management Agency (FEMA) as a separate federal agency. No one today can point to a clear career path. Instead, there are a number of ways to enter the profession and as many different interpretations of what the job entails.

My career path was a real-life example of what the Harvard Study has so clearly defined. While it was first identified in the rarified atmosphere of a university, its outline of the needed skills of a meta-leader are a perfect outline of the skill set an emergency manager should possess:

- Become an expert not just through certification, education, and classes but through any and all means you can find to learn about disasters.
- Have a continuous working situational awareness of your community's threats and disasters.
- Lead up by becoming a trusted advisor to leaders within your community
- Lead across all professional silos by developing yourself as an expert, trusted advisor, and facilitator to other departments.
- Develop subordinates who are also meta-leaders and expand your office's ability to lead during a disaster.

Mine was not the only path to become an emergency manager, but it holds lessons for everyone. I was not connected politically when I was assigned the job, nor did I have specific expertise. I just had an interest. If you are lucky enough to be appointed as an emergency manager, it does not mean that the authority and respect will naturally follow. Use the meta-leader example as your guide to become a real crisis leader in your community so that if you are faced with a true disaster you have the skills and relationships needed to perform your job to the best of your ability in very difficult times with lives and property on the line.

CHAPTER 2

Crisis Decision Making

"Bureaucracy depends on routines and schedules and papework...If done right the modern world could not exist without bureaucracy. The only trouble with that is at the time of disasters when you need innovations and doing things differently...they can't maneuver, the can't integrate... organizations, in a sense, fall down."

—Dr. Enrico Quarantelli, University of Chicago, quoted in *A Paradise Built in Hell* by Rebecca Solnit

Disasters are different. They require a different decision-making process for a successful response. This process is in many ways a complete reversal of the way people normally make decisions. This process is not intuitive to someone who has spent their career in a normal analytical decision-making environment. In fact, unless crisis decision making is taught, people will not be able to change their long-held and successful way of making decisions and rise to the occasion. Yet how people make decisions in a dynamic, uncertain, and stress-filled environment is understandable and can be taught. It must be a part of the preparation of your disaster-response team, or it can significantly impact your team's ability to perform. As an emergency manager you must be confident that a team of personnel is trained to perform in the chaos of a disaster response. You cannot assume everyone will adapt to the challenges faced during an incident.

The Frozen Bureaucrat

During a response to what eventually would become a very minor tropical storm, we had opened our emergency operations center for the first time. We had just had a full-scale exercise in the EOC with all the Emergency Support Functions at their positions weeks before the storm. We had given all the participants classes on EOC operations before the exercise, and then during the exercise we were there to coach them through the process. So the emergency management staff (two of us) felt we had prepared the team to the best of our ability.

As the storm began to threaten, we activated the EOC and called in all the personnel assigned to the Emergency Support Functions (ESF) to staff their positions. Given that this storm occurred only a few weeks after the training, we were confident that our team members felt comfortable in their roles.

Some shelters in the county were opened for people with special needs and those in mobile homes, given the projected wind speeds. Our public information line received a phone call from someone in one of the trailer parks in the city, wanting to know if shelters were open and if there was transportation to those shelters.

Given the small number of people needing shelter, the county was providing bus service. Since we were a municipality and shelter management is a county responsibility in our state, I gave the message to the person managing ESF #6, mass care, and asked him to contact his counterpart in the county EOC. He was to call and let the county know someone needed assistance to a shelter and the location of that individual.

I moved on to the next problem. I returned to ESF #6 approximately half an hour later to see how things had gone and asked what he had found out. He had not done a thing. He had not called the county, even though the phone number was posted less than a foot in front of him on the wall. He had not contacted the person who had called. He had been frozen in place by a simple request.

This was a respected middle manager in the city who was responsible for a large number of personnel and a budget. Yet he could not make a phone call. He had never called another jurisdiction, especially the county, without going through his boss and not without a significant amount of justification as to why he needed to contact the county. So when placed in a position of having to do just that, he froze in place, unable to take such a large step. I picked up the phone and in two short calls had the answer and arranged for the caller to be picked up.

It is difficult to put people in entirely new decision-making environments and have them perform well. They must be placed in a structured environment with well-defined role, job aids, and directions or you will end up with a frozen bureaucrat in a much more serious situation.

HOW WE MAKE DECISIONS

Normal decision-making is identified as a "rational choice strategy (Janis and Mann, 1977)." The decision maker examines the problem through a range of options that could each be the proper decision. The risks and rewards of each of those alternatives are weighed, while other options that may have been overlooked are still being considered. Finally, the best options are compared and discussed. A final decision is made and implemented. A rational and reasonable choice has been made.

The advantages of this type of decision making are obvious. It is reliable and repeatable. It allows all aspects of the problem to be examined and compared. It produces decisions that are by and large the proper ones. The process can be examined after the fact for weaknesses of analysis or missed alternatives. The process uses information normally produced and understood by an organization. Finally, the system lends itself to the use of existing organizational structures and bureaucracies.

In studies done when time constraints were added, scientists found that individuals were unable to use the standard analytical evaluation of all the possible solutions to the problem. There simply was not enough time to go through the process normally necessary to make decisions. The drop in their ability to make the proper decisions was significant. As Professor Quarantelli said in the epigraph to this chapter, it is what our society is built upon. Yet it will not work during a disaster.

A disaster is like a battle in the demands it makes on decision makers. It has all the aspects of a battlefield environment—inadequate information, time constraints, changing conditions, and high stakes. It even creates the most difficult problem of all, the "fog of war." The fog of war is a phrase originally coined by the military theorist Carl von Clausewitz. It simply means the lack of a clear picture of what is happening before you. More than one general has lost a war because of this fog obscuring the realities of a critical battle. If you want examples of the "fog of war" in disasters, read any of the books or studies about Hurricane Katrina and the operations during that catastrophe.

Unless you can learn to deal with this ambiguity, you cannot be a good leader in war or during a disaster. The army understood the challenges of such an environment and tried to train its commanders in how to make decisions in the chaos and confusion of battle. In the 1980s army analysts had spent ten years and millions of dollars studying decision making, then developing training and decision aids from this research in an attempt to prepare commanders. Despite these efforts the army was not satisfied; researchers had seen little improvement in the commanders' decisions and were looking for a new approach. So the army commissioned a study of decision making under time constraints.

Dr. Gary Klein, a research psychologist, won the grant. Dr. Klein chose the fire service as the best example of making critical decisions under strict time constraints, with lives and property hanging in the balance. The researchers interviewed a number of experienced firefighters; they were asked to identify one incident that presented a particular command "challenge" or was "non-routine in some way." They rated the incidents according to the risk to the building (economic), risk to civilians, or risk to the lives of firefighters. Every incident was rated high risk in at least one category.

KLEIN'S FINDINGS

The study produced some surprising results. "In almost no case studied did a fire ground commander even report making a decision…in terms of comparing options."(1) Instead of examining the situation and then producing a set of options, the commanders worked from a very different mindset.

The commanders worked from a situational awareness or mental model of the incident. The situational awareness or mental model was an accumulation of all the previous fires of similar types that the commander had seen. Once he recognized the type of incident, then he implemented the tactics necessary for that type. Yet this was not a simple equation on the order of if X occurs, then do Y; it was a much more dynamic process.

The fire ground commanders recognized a fire as one that was similar to another they had faced earlier in their careers. They did this by identifying the cues and clues that each fire created. These markers could be anything from building construction to the color or amount of smoke. Once identified, the commanders compared them to previous fires and, if there were a close match, they had a course of action that had proven successful in the past. Yet once they had decided on a course of action, the commanders did not assume they had made the correct decision. They continued to monitor the fire and the operations for the feedback that would signal to them that the decision was the correct one. If they did not identify these changes in the fire, then they immediately began to reconsider their decisions and look for information they might have missed or conditions that were not initially apparent. This cycle of initial decision making, then monitoring for confirmation of the proper set of actions, created a successful and flexible decision-making process that met the challenges of a dynamic and confusing environment.

Klein also found that these commanders were constantly learning by sharing stories with other commanders and firefighters. This "talking fire" is a tradition in the fire service. No two fires are alike. You can always learn from a fire, no matter how routine, even if it is a tiny detail. That detail could one day turn out to be a life or death detail on another fire. Dr. Klein describes it as "experience counts," but experience can be gained in a number of different ways—everything from "talking fire" to studying the lessons-learned reports from other major fires around the country.

As a firefighter who spent 26 years on the fire department I can attest to the need for constant learning. Every time I began to feel overconfident as if I had it all wired and was ready for anything, the "street," as I used to call it, always had something so outside of my experience that it made me step back and take a deep breath before I dove in and tackled the incident. If someone is to become a good decision maker in a crisis, they must work at it constantly and be open to learning from any and all sources. Klein's model was adopted by the military, and it led to a whole new generation of training techniques and tools for military commanders.

Dr. Klein expanded his research to a number of different fields, and he found that decision makers in very different types of industries from airline pilots to nurses and physicians all shared these common traits. This type of decision making was common across many very different professions, reinforcing its value as a tool with many different applications.

One of my own experiences in crisis decision making is a good example of the first concept that must be understood. It occurred over 30 years ago when I was a young and inexperienced paramedic. It was in March 1979.

The Apartment Fire

I was riding on a rescue truck as one of the first group of paramedics in our department. We were firefighters as wells as paramedics, so our job during building fires was search and rescue. We received a call of an apartment fire at approximately 3 am. We were dispatched with a full complement of engines, towers, and a battalion chief to the structure.

Upon arrival we found a two-story brick building with nothing showing and no one out front to meet us. As I dressed out in my firefighting gear, the engine companies and tower crews began to search for the supposed fire. The crews found nothing except a faint smell of smoke, but no one could determine its origin. As I approached the building, a lieutenant from one of the engine companies indicated that he thought he had found the apartment. The window to the apartment was covered with a residue of smoke.

No one was answering the door, so he and I donned our masks and crawled in through a window. As soon as I entered the apartment, I looked to my left and saw a woman on the floor. I yelled that I had a victim and went to grab her. The tower company forced the front door, and with another firefighter I carried the woman outside where we began CPR. There was almost no smoke in the apartment, so finding a woman not breathing and without a heartbeat was completely unexpected. As we worked on the woman, other crewmembers began to find additional victims. Two children were found both in full cardiac arrest. My partner returned with advanced life-support equipment and drugs to work on the woman. I turned the woman over to him to assess the children. When I stood up the shift chief walked up to me and asked, "What should we do, Roger?"

Normally you want a minimum of one paramedic per code, and at that point we had three. There were only two of us on the scene. Without hesitating I said, "Chief, we will work the mother through Hospital X and we will take the children to Hospital Y. Let Hospital Y know we are coming as soon as the ambulance shows up."

The ambulance arrived on the scene, and the single paramedic in it ran to help my partner with the woman. When I turned around, I was handed a third baby that had just been found and I immediately began CPR. The three of us loaded up in the back of the ambulance and were transported to Hospital Y, where they had three pediatric specialist teams waiting for us. None of the four victims survived. The woman had been doing some ironing and left the iron sitting on an ironing board that had a plastic cover. There had been a small fire involving just the plastic on the ironing board, but the plastics when burned produced very toxic and poisonous smoke. All the victims died of smoke inhalation.

When the chief had asked me what we should do with the victims, he was asking advice from the person with the most medical training but one of the junior men on the scene; normally he would have sought advice from a captain or lieutenant. While I had only been on the department three or four years at that time, he had gone to person with the most medical knowledge.

When I told the chief what we should do, I had no idea where that decision had come from or how I had arrived at it. After the fire I went over and over the decision, trying to determine if it was the right one. The more I dissected the decision, the more I was convinced I had made the right recommendation. Yet I had no idea how I had come to that decision, and therefore I was unsure if I could trust it. As I examined and re-examined it, I found there were several aspects of the decision that made it the correct one.

The very first thing I had recognized was the fact that we simply did not have enough people or equipment to adequately provide the level of care needed for all the patients. If we were going to provide that care, we needed additional paramedics and medical gear. At the time there were four rescue trucks in the city with paramedics, one on the west side of town, one in the center of town (mine), one on the east side of town, and finally one to the north. Each truck was approximately seven to ten minutes away from our location. There were two private ambulances on duty at the time within ten minutes of our location, and one had already been dispatched. It would take the second at least ten minutes to arrive on the scene.

Balanced against those times was the fact that we were only five minutes away from Hospital Y; it was the neonatal center for the area.

Y's staff was the most qualified to manage the three children. We would need to take the mother to another hospital if she was to have the best chance at survival because of the amount of resources three pediatric codes would demand. Hospital X was approximately five minutes away in another direction; it was a much smaller hospital but could easily manage the mother.

So no matter how I looked at the problem I had made the best use of the resources and proximity to facilities given the situation. By sending the children to Hospital Y they were able to pull experienced physicians and nurses to the emergency room to work on them. Three children in cardiac arrest will stress any hospital at three in the morning, but Hospital Y was the best equipped to give the children the best care. Hospital X could handle the woman, and it was almost exactly the same distance away. So all the patients received the best care given the circumstances.

Yet I had no conscious memory of how I worked my way through all of those factors and then told the chief what was the best solution. Without understanding the process I was not sure I could trust how I made the decision. Had I just lucked into the right decision? Where did it come from? I continued to question the decision for years.

It was not until I read Gary Klein's groundbreaking study of fire-fighter incident commanders that I came to understand that I was not unique in how I made decisions or in being perplexed by the process. It goes back to the ability to recognize a similar problem from the past, "a situation, even a non-routine one, as an example of a prototype, so they knew the typical course of action right away."(2)

In my case it was an extension of something that I did constantly through a shift. Rescue 1 was situated so that it would cover for any of the other three rescues should they be busy on a call and a rescue was needed. During any given shift I was constantly monitoring the status of the other rescues as a way of getting a jump on our next call. So I knew where the other rescues were and how long it would take them to respond to our location.

In addition, as paramedics we were required to follow a strict set of guidelines that determined where a patient was to be transported. It was either the closest "most appropriate" facility or in special cases you could bypass the closest hospital to take patients in need of specific types of care to facilities that specialized in those types of care—a burn center, for example. In this case we had three children and the closest hospital was the one that specialized in neonatal care and would have nurses and physicians most qualified to work on the children.

So the decision I made was a more complex and emotion-filled extension of the decisions I made every day on the truck. Klein identifies many factors that go into a decision like this one but emphasizes two: pattern recognition and mental simulation. I recognized the right hospitals for the right patients in the same way as I did each day. It was a decision based on my experience with hundreds of different patients in different parts of the city.

I was mentally able to simulate the response times of the other rescues because I had to cover for them when they were busy. I had put a recognized pattern with a simulation of the response times and come up with the only workable solution. So my decision had been built on the awareness that had become a part of each day as I monitored available resources compared to my own location and proper facility selection by type and severity of the patient. I had not recognized the decision for what it was or why I had come to the correct decision. Now that I did I began to use that knowledge consciously to prepare myself for other difficult decisions.

By understanding that with each decision you make you are building a database of experiences from which you can draw information in the future puts those experiences in a different perspective. You examine each incident more closely and look at what you did correctly and incorrectly. I also found myself reading as much as I could about other incidents with real lessons learned. These also helped in developing the stored knowledge that I could pull from in future incidents. Experience is important, but disasters do not happen with the same frequency as emergency medical service calls or fires. So how does one build a database?

While you cannot expect to experience a number of disasters in your community, you can build your database and solutions by studying other disasters and the lessons learned from them. All forms of exercises from tabletops to full functional exercises that require you to make decisions will add to your knowledge. The key is that you are consciously trying to add knowledge even in situations where you might not expect to find a relevant experience. This is one of the key points that must be taught to those who are not in the emergency-response community.

These professionals have built a subject-matter expertise through their years of experience. That knowledge will translate even in disaster situations. My decision about how to manage the children and mother was based on everyday non-emergency decisions. Yet I was able to apply these seemingly everyday experiences to the single most difficult decision I made while I was in the department. The same is true of those who will be assigned to the EOC; their expertise will apply and be needed by the EOC team.

While an emergency manager will not make split-second decisions, the decisions they will be faced with are very similar to those faced on the street by firefighters or soldiers in battle. You will not have all of the information to make a completely informed decision; instead you will have to recognize a problem as similar to a lesson learned from another disaster and use that knowledge to come up with your own solution. Studying, exercising, and learning all must become day-to-day habits if you are to build the kind of knowledge base that will allow you to be a leader during a disaster. Understanding why that knowledge is important and how you will use it to make decisions is critical to developing your decision-making capabilities.

THE BOYD CYCLE

Once a decision is made during a disaster, the decision maker cannot assume that the decision was the right one. He must continue to monitor the event and the decision for feedback that informs him that the decision that had been made was the correct one. This cycle of decision making and monitoring for additional feedback was first identified by Colonel John Boyd, a pilot in the air force.

Colonel Boyd was a fighter pilot when he first began to study decision making. He impetus was to improve the performance of American fighter pilots against their North Korean foes. What he discovered not only changed how fighter pilots were trained but produced a profound change across the military that created a new theory of fighting wars.

As a fighter pilot himself he began his research into decision making by observing others pilots and their aircraft. Boyd's observations of dogfights between North Korean and United States pilots led to a discovery that eventually changed the way the military trained for and fought wars.

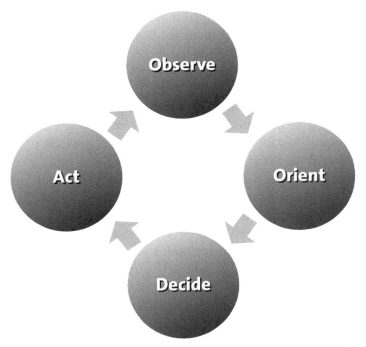

Figure 2.1   Observe, Orient, Decide, Act and repeat the process until the situation is under control.

He found that American pilots had greater visibility of the airspace than their North Korean counterparts. The design of the American aircraft and the cockpit canopy gave the pilots a wider field of vision. As the North Koreans maneuvered their aircraft, the Americans were able to observe the maneuver earlier and were able to react more quickly. When the North Koreans tried to counter their moves, the Americans were again ahead of the curve because they could observe the enemy pilots' reactions earlier. This maneuver/countermaneuver led to an ever-tightening circle of tactics until the American was in a position to shoot down the North Korean. The ratio of American to North Korean victories was close to ten to one. Colonel Boyd called this decision-making process the Boyd cycle or the OODA loop.

Once Colonel Boyd understood what was occurring, he broke it down into its simplest component parts. The loop consisted of observe, orient, decide, and act (OODA). He discovered that American pilots would observe what the enemy pilot was doing in the dogfight earlier, allowing them to orient to that maneuver, determine the best action, and act on that information. But the pilots did not simply make a single decision and win the fight. They then had to observe the enemy reactions to their actions and start the process all over again until the dogfight was won.

The complexity of what was happening in seconds was almost overwhelming to understand in a coherent way. It wasn't until he broke it down into OODA that he was able to provide a simple-to-remember and useful acronym.

The cycle of observation, reaction, and observation was determined to have much wider implications than just aircraft dogfights. Army generals realized that it could be applied to battlefield decision making. Once the military understood that all decisions were based on the OODA loop, they realized that they could then build training, equipment, and strategies to take advantage of this understanding. The military's objective was to be able to observe the enemy commanders' actions quickly enough to react before they implemented their decisions. They were trying to get inside the enemy commanders' "decision cycle." Once inside the cycle, they would be able to disrupt their actions before their troops could carry them out. They were able to break the enemy's OODA loop, thereby winning the battle through the disruption of its decision-making cycle.

The Sixth Sense

It is a simple house fire in a one-story home in a residential neighborhood. The fire is showing in the back in what appears to be the kitchen area. The lieutenant leads his hose crew into the building to the back to apply water on the fire. The crew opens up the nozzle, and nothing happens except the fire roars back at them.

"Odd," he thinks. The water should have more of an impact. They try dousing it again and get the same results. They retreat a few steps to regroup. The lieutenant starts to feel as if something is not right. He doesn't have any clues; he just doesn't feel right about being in that house, so he orders his men out of the building—a perfectly standard building with nothing out of the ordinary. As soon as his men leave the building, the floor where they had been standing collapses. Had they still been inside, they would have plunged into the fire below.

Disasters are not thinking enemies. Instead they are forces of nature or destructive man-made or natural events. While they are not thinking foes, they do produce complex problems worthy of a thinking enemy. So much of the information, infrastructure, response, and other factors affecting operational capabilities have been affected by the disaster that one cannot make a decision without monitoring the situation. Klein's use of fire commanders' experience to explain just such an incidence also illustrates the OODA loop as used in a civilian application.

The lieutenant had used the Boyd cycle without ever realizing it. He had observed the residential fire. He recognized it as similar to many they had found in the past, which allowed him to orient himself to the task. He then decided on a course of action based on his training and experience, but the lieutenant did not stop there. He continued to observe the fire for the feedback that would inform him that his decision had been the correct one. Instead he received none of the usual feedback that would reinforce the fact that he had made the right decision.

First he noticed that the fire had not "darkened down" the way a normal fire would have given the application of 150 gallons of water a minute by a fire attack line. Next he noticed that the fire was "quiet." Fires are noisy, with glass breaking and furniture falling adding to the roar of the flames.

So when the lieutenant did not detect those signs of a correct decision, he knew he had to reorient himself. He reentered the Boyd loop by pulling his crew out of the structure until he was properly oriented to the situation at hand. As soon as he led his crew out of the structure, the floor collapsed; if they had not retreated they would all have been killed. The fire had been in the basement the whole time. His crew had been putting water on the top of the flames from the basement, not on the seat of the fire. Water will have little effect on a fire unless it is applied to the seat of a fire. He ordered his crew to find the basement entrance, and they attacked the fire from the stairs and put it out.

Decisions made in a dynamic, changing environment when it is not clear that all of the relevant facts are known must be closely monitored for feedback to assure the decision maker that she had made the correct decision, just as the fighter pilot could not assume his first reaction to the enemy's maneuvers were the only ones needed to win the fight. An emergency responder or emergency manager cannot assume that the first decision is the correct one. He must continue to monitor the outcomes of the decision and the situation as a whole to determine if the decision was the correct one.

Information breeds decisions.

Decisions generate a need for more information.

THE THREE QUESTIONS SYSTEM

How do your prepare those who will occupy the EOC for this new type of decision making? How do you distill an understanding of what is needed in this new environment? It normally takes years of experience before someone is able to change his or her way of decision making to meet this challenge. There will have to be a simple, easy-to-remember system that focuses their efforts on the right questions and keeps them focused.

The three-question system is just such a simple but easily remembered mantra that can be used to teach people how to approach this huge challenge. Then, when in midst of operations, it provides a framework for their decision making. It consists of just three questions.

What have you got?

What do you need to do?

What do you need to do it?

What have you got? seems like a simple question, but if used properly it forces a person to focus on precisely what is the problem facing him. What is the problem specifically? The problem must be distilled into a single actionable item so it can be addressed with the proper resources and prioritized against other issues and challenges. The person should be able to answer it in just a couple of sentences. There can be no more than three problems prioritized according to the following criteria from each Emergency Support Function (ESF):

- The first priority is life safety and the support of those operations.
- The second priority is critical infrastructure repair such as the repair and restoration of power and water or the clearing of major arteries.
- The third priority is property damage that has an economic impact on the community.

Using these three criteria will focus the efforts on the most important issues. The sheer volume of information pouring into the EOC is the biggest barrier to efficient operation during a disaster. There is simply too much information from too many sources to make good decisions without a system to sort and prioritize it. These priorities can change as time goes on and as incidents are taken care of over time, but in the first hours or even days these priorities can help focus the team on the most critical problems out of hundreds that will confront them.

What do you need to do? As specifically as possible describe the actions that need to be taken to address the problem. It cannot be something as vague as we need to clear the streets. It must be as specific as we need to clear Semoran Street from Conway Road to McCoy Drive of downed power lines and other debris. It is blocking access and slowing the response of emergency units to the building collapse. By being specific the emergency-management team is going to be able to prioritize the requests so the most critical are managed first. In this case, while it is not an operation directly addressing the building collapse, it is certainly having an effect on life-safety operations and therefore is important.

What do you need to do it? Again the ESF must be as specific as possible in the request for equipment and manpower. Personnel cannot just say they need equipment to clear Semoran. They will have to work with field operations and find out specifically what is needed. For example, we need two power crews to manage the downed power lines and three front-end loaders. When the request is specific enough, the representatives from the power company can determine if they have the needed crews or will have to request outside assistance. The public-works representative can also advise if they have the needed equipment or will have to ask for outside equipment.

Once everyone has answered those three questions, then the needs can be prioritized and the needed manpower and equipment can either be assigned immediately or be requested through mutual aid agreements or from local government. Then those specific incidents can be tracked until their needs have been met and the incident can be closed.

The last part of the system is that the questions have to be *repeated* for each of the incidents even after they have received the needed resources. By asking them to repeat the question they are being forced through the OODA loop. The incident responders have to be continually monitored to make sure they have what they need to accomplish the task. New problems or initially unrecognized problems may present themselves, and additional resources may be needed. So the process is forcing the person into the observe, orient, decide, act process over and over to make sure they understands the issues faced in the field.

The Three Questions in Action

What have you got? Equipment, crews, and supplies cannot get to the collapse site easily or quickly, and it is slowing the rescue efforts.

What do you need to do? We need to clear Semoran Street from Conway Road to McCoy Drive of downed power lines and other debris.

What do you need to do it? We need two power crews, two front-end loaders, and two dump trucks to begin at the north end of Semoran.

Repeat: The ESF that had been tasked with these actions must keep in touch periodically with the on-scene personnel to make sure that the problem was being solved.

For example, when contacted the road was not being cleared fast enough. So at the next briefing she would report the following.

What have you got? The street clearing down Semoran is not getting done fast enough. The incident commander (IC) at the scene says that equipment and supplies are still not getting through fast enough.

What to you need to do? We need to clear Semoran faster. The operations at the collapse site are still being slowed.

What do you need to do it? I spoke with ESF #3, and we need three more front-end loaders just to get the debris out of the way. Loading it in dump trucks to be hauled away is taking too much time. We will clear it later.

Repeat: The ESF has checked again with the on scene commander.

What have you got? The IC reports that Semoran has been cleared enough that supplies and equipment are arriving much faster. He now requests that a USAR team be assigned to his location. It appears that this is going to be a much longer operation than originally thought.

What do you need to do? Request a USAR team for the collapse site.

What do you need to do it? I need ESF #9 to request a USAR team from the state.

This example demonstrates how consistently going through the OODA loop with the three questions can meet the needs of an operation over time even as the needs change dramatically. Now another ESF has been brought in whose job is to coordinate the USAR team response and deployment. By continuing to constantly monitor a situation, never assuming that once you've made the right first decision, allows for someone to meet the initial needs, shift the emphasis of the first request as it was discovered to be not enough, and then hand off the incident to another ESF as the problem dictated. Constant monitoring and coordination with the field and the correct ESF in the EOC are precisely the type of decision making and problem solving that must go on if the needs of a disaster response are to be met.

At briefings all reports should be framed using the three-question system. This does not mean that a more detailed discussion of progress should not occur if needed, but by asking the three questions the discussion and decision making can focus on the most critical issues and problems of the response. Structuring the process is the key to using largely untrained personnel during a disaster response. Structuring the decision-making process even with something as simple as the three-questions system can help bridge the gap in training and experience of those involved. By structuring their decision-making process you force them to use the processes needed to make decisions and then monitor those decisions to assure they were the correct ones.

The three-questions system is easy to understand and simple to teach. In fact, even those who have not had training can quickly understand the process and begin to use it. The three questions can be posted around the EOC or even used as a screen saver on all computers. The objective is to focus the actions of those in the room, to cut through the vast amount of information, in order to make the right recommendations, then monitor the incident to make sure the situation has not changed and their needs are still being met.

The three questions force people who are not familiar with the type of decision making and the environment in the EOC to go through a process that will frame their approach to their jobs.

By forcing them through the OODA loop they will be performing a continuous sizing up of the incident and enhancing their own contribution to the overall response. Continuous sizing up leads to a shared situational awareness that is vital for everyone in the EOC.

UNDERSTANDING DECISION MAKING IS IMPORTANT

People are the key to any disaster response. An emergency response to a disaster is made up of ten thousand individual decisions. These decisions add up to an overall response that determines the eventual impact of a disaster on a community. It is critically important that the right decisions are made at the right time. The reality in the vast majority of communities around the country is that the personnel involved in the response are not experienced emergency responders. If they have had any training, it is minimal and given during a single yearly training session. The infrequency of disasters and the demands of their normal responsibilities take precedent over training for what is perceived as a once-in-a-career event.

Communities simply do not have the personnel or money to have a large cadre of highly trained and experienced disaster responders. They must depend on the personnel who make their community work day to day. They come from different organizations, cultures, and job descriptions that have nothing to do with emergency management. Even with training they come to the EOC with different understandings and different expectations of what they will face.

It is up to the emergency manager to prepare his community for a disaster. You must develop a team through training and decision support systems for your community. Crisis decision-making training is the most important part of that preparation. People who understand and are prepared for the uncertainty, confusion, and constantly changing environment of a disaster will perform better than those who are not. Train them in the concepts of crisis decision making and use the methods in the chapter on training to reinforce those concepts. Adopt the decision support systems suggested in this book to build a team and the systems they will need to respond to any disaster. An understanding of the changed decision-making environment and the creation of a structured system of decision making in an EOC will provide the best possible atmosphere for optimum performance.

Every Emergency Support Function (ESF) and emergency manager must continuously force himself or herself through an OODA loop in order to stay on top of a rapidly emerging situation. By structuring the processes in the EOC to reinforce the needed decision-making behaviors by each individual, they can assure themselves of the best possible response to a disaster. The response of a community to a disaster is not judged on how good the disaster plan was as written but how well the responders adjusted that plan to meet the needs of the community.

The most important decision that an emergency manager can take to prepare his community for a disaster is to prepare the people he or she will need during that crisis. Just placing people into the Incident Command System (ICS) or National Incident Management System (NIMS) organizational chart does not guarantee they will function well in a disaster environment. They must be prepared to face the uncertainty and fast-moving problems of a disaster. They have the skills, but they must be empowered to use those skills by understanding how to apply what they know to the problems they will face. If you prepare your people, they can overcome any obstacle that they might face. There is nothing more important than the training of those your community will depend on during a disaster. Preparing them to make decisions during a disaster will go further in preparing your community than any other type of training. A prepared team is a prepared community.

References

1. Sources of Power, How People Make Decisions, Gary Klein, MIT Press, 1999, page 17.
2. Sources of Power, How People Make Decisions, Gary Klein, MIT Press, 1999, page 32.

CHAPTER 3

Disaster Operations: The Art of Operations

"We must recognize that we were woefully incapable of storing, moving, and accessing information- especially in times of crisis. Many of the problems we have identified can be categorized as 'information gaps"... *failure to act decisively because information was sketchy at best."*

—Executive Summary of Findings, Congressional Report
The Federal Response to Katrina: Lessons Learned

Disaster operations are about bringing order to chaos. A natural or manmade event has destroyed the normal life of a community. An emergency manager's job is to as quickly as possible bring that community back to normal. To do this, you must impose a response structure onto the chaos.

There are four phases in the standard definition of emergency management: mitigation, preparedness, response, and recovery. Mitigation involves the efforts taken to reduce or eliminate the risk to a community from natural and/or man-made disasters. These efforts range from legislation to the structural strengthening of structures to withstand earthquakes. All of these efforts are aimed at the reduction of the impact disasters have on communities. Preparedness involves planning, training, organizing, equipping, and conducting exercises to improve the abilities of personnel and organizations in a community to respond to disasters. The response phase involves the mobilization and organization of the needed resources to manage the effects of a disaster. Finally, recovery is defined as the restoration of the community to its previous state through long-term programs.

As a profession we have demonstrated a great ability to develop mitigation projects, create plans for each type of disaster that may face our community, utilize our resources in preparation for a disaster, and develop programs to manage the return of our communities to normal. Yet when a disaster strikes, we seem to struggle to implement those carefully crafted plans. In fact, many of the same response problems recur in each disaster; you see them discussed in the media as the disaster unfolds or you read the after-action reports and foreseeable problems are mentioned as unexpected issues. We tend to repeat our mistakes with each new disaster without learning from previous experiences.

On top of these recurring issues there are always new and unexpected issues with each event. Disasters never seem to conform to the plans we draw up to combat their effects. Instead, they create problems and complications that even the best plans seem completely unprepared for despite their thoroughness. This reality is not because of a lack of effort or professionalism on the part of those creating those plans. Instead, its roots can be found in our emphasis on planning and mitigation over response. Disaster operations are some of the most difficult operations to manage that any organization, military or civilian, can face. Yet the operations aspects of the four phases of emergency management seem to receive the least emphasis.

The response or disaster operations phase has received less attention because it is difficult to carve out enough time to train the correct personnel. In addition, there is a pervasive feeling among many local officials that this will not happen on their watch. After all. disasters are usually a once-in-a-career event for most communities, so this is an understandable attitude.

The military, until early in the 21st century, faced the same obstacle. Military commanders could go through an entire career without ever seeing a shot fired in anger. Yet they understood, should they ever be faced with a combat command, it would make or break a career. A career that could very well been an excellent one until this one event. What many civilian officials do not understand is that they are in exactly the same position. Their careers are on the line during a disaster, and they can be made or broken by their actions over the space of a few days or weeks.

Military commanders consider operations and the implementation of their tactics an art and study it religiously. A good example occurred during the first Gulf War when General Norman Schwarzkopf gave a briefing after the war had begun. He explained that the tactics he used were the same ones a general used during the Civil War to win a battle with many similarities. He had studied the battles and tactics going to back to antiquity to learn the lessons that other generals had learned the hard way. Yet when you listen to emergency managers after a major disaster, they talk about the problems they faced as if they had never been seen before by other emergency managers.

After Hurricane Katrina local, state, and federal officials talked about the complete destruction of all forms of communications in the impacted areas and what a huge challenge it was to their response. Well, that same problem was experienced during Hurricane Hugo in the late 1980s and then again just a few years later during Hurricane Andrew. Yet professionals in emergency management spoke about the communications loss as if it were a new phenomenon created for the first time during Katrina.

This lack of historical perspective comes from not only not studying the lessons learned from previous disasters but from the lack of emphasis on the response phase of emergency management. Sure, there may be an annual exercise each year in each jurisdiction, but most of the emphasis is placed on mitigation and preparedness. Despite much good work in both these areas, an emergency manager can fail in their duties if they cannot manage the response phase of a disaster. How you implement the plans, resources, and mitigation programs you have developed will ultimately be what you are judged on by your community. These efforts will face the ultimate test during the response phase. You must be able to lead the response if you are going to serve your community, no matter how much time and effort were put into mitigation and preparedness. The response should be the ultimate test of those efforts and a reflection of a community's preparedness. Without an equal effort in the area of response the work done prior to the disaster will be of little help. After Katrina there was much discussion of how plans were not followed or were useless faced with the realities. Elaborate plans do not assure a good response; instead it depends on how the leaders and responders adjust those plans to meet the realities of the disaster.

A disaster has occurred despite your best efforts to prepare your community. Damage has been done and lives are at stake, both physically and economically. All the preparation will go for naught if you are unable to effectively lead the response. The military has a saying about operations during a battle that is very similar to a disaster-response environment: "No plan survives first contact with the enemy."

What this means is that no matter how well you plan and prepare, there will always be unanticipated problems, whether they come from the enemy or from your own units in their efforts to carry out the plan. So the military emphasizes the implementation of operations in the confusion of battle. When communications are not always working or supplies and manpower do not reach their assigned positions, they call this confusion and the fog of war. A commander must be able to adapt and adjust to this fog of war to meet changing realities in a confusing environment. It does not come easily and must be practiced repeatedly if the commander and the units under him are going to perform.

This is just as true in emergency management. No matter how much you plan and prepare, the disaster will always find your weak spot, it will always present you with unanticipated problems. It is not a thinking enemy, but it is a relentless one.

The following systems are based on the fact that a response is by its nature a confusing and difficult event to grasp as it occurs. When a hurricane or tornado strikes, the problems it produces are never quickly grasped. The problems will overlap one another, creating multiple needs for resources at the same time in different places. These demands can become a confusing mass of competing problems with conflicting priorities. In order to respond in such an environment, systems are needed that can begin to structure the response issues into a set of problems that can be prioritized so they can be managed.

WHAT ARE DISASTERS?

Disasters are low-probability, high-consequence events. Their impact can vary greatly according to the disaster and the area where it has occurred. The impact can be more economic than life-threatening. Hurricane Andrew is a good example. While "only" 44 people lost their lives, yet its impact was much greater than simply counting the lives lost.

Hurricane Andrew's Impact on South Florida

- 63,000 homes destroyed
- 1.4 million homes without power
- 250,000 people homeless
- 80,000 people in shelters
- 250 priority emergency calls awaiting public-safety responders when the winds subsided
- 3,000,000 people affected
- $3 billion in damage
- Required national resources for the response

Disaster operations are an attempt to mitigate the effect of the disasters on the lives of those involved. How quickly and efficiently the emergency manager and his team are able to respond to and manage the incidents associated with the disaster will determine that disaster's ultimate effect on their community. While a disaster does an initial amount of damage to a community, how long it takes that community to properly respond will determine the ultimate impact of that disaster.

Once a disaster occurs, it is like dropping a pebble in a pond. The effect a disaster has on a community can expand beyond its initial impact if those responsible for the response are not prepared.

So the initial actions of any emergency response to a disaster must be a rapid and focused application of available resources and the request and management of outside resources as they arrive to restore the community to normality as quickly as possible.

The first critical hours and days during the response to a disaster will determine the eventual impact of the event on a community. The first decisions made are critical because they set the direction for the entire operation. The wrong first decisions will lead to a longer disruption for average citizens and their lives and businesses. This disruption of people's lives will be the real measure of the impact a disaster has on a community.

THE PHASES OF DISASTER RESPONSE

A strict definition of disaster response does not include phases. But if you examine responses to previous disasters, patterns emerge. The types of problems and the timing of those problems begin to form recognizable and to a certain extent predictable patterns. By understanding these problem sets and the timing of their occurrence in disasters, an emergency manager can structure operations to meet a phase's needs and anticipate the needs of the next phase of the response.

Disaster response becomes a matter of understanding when and what types of issues will present themselves. By understanding and structuring your response, both the emergency manager and those in the EOC will be able to better focus their efforts and attention. Structuring the response creates a sense of accomplishment with the official finishing of one phase and movement to another. In addition, it focuses the attention of EOC on the right set of needs based on the phase. The response to a disaster has four phases.

Phases of a Disaster Response

- impact phase
- stabilization phase
- sustainment phase
- recovery phase

Impact Phase

When a community is impacted by a disaster, infrastructure is damaged, communications are disrupted, and the normal functions of the community are interrupted. The first hours or days after an event are characterized by confusion and a need to understand the size and scope of the disaster the community is facing. There is a tremendous struggle to assimilate and organize the mass of information flooding in to begin to create a clear operational picture of the extent and severity of the disaster. Until you have an understanding of the scope and severity of the disaster, you cannot begin to properly respond to the event. How many people have been killed? How many people have been injured? Just how much damage has been done? What resources are still intact? What infrastructure has been damaged?

The length of this phase will depend directly on the magnitude of the event and how quickly the community begins to respond in an organized way to the disaster. As response agencies spread through out the community, they will be reporting on the damage, problems they find, and operations they have begun. Preparation for operations includes using graphical displays to visualize the needs and operations so a Common Operating Picture (COP) can be pulled together. Out of this COP will evolve the situational awareness needed to properly respond to the disaster. The EOC will be responsible for collating and organizing the information into a coherent COP of the disaster. In an earthquake or hurricane this phase can last for 72 or more hours. In a tornado it might last a few hours or even a day. The greater and more widespread the destruction, the longer it will take to develop a coherent and accurate picture of the event.

The initial operations during the impact phase will concentrate on life safety and a basic evaluation of the seriousness of the event. These operations will include those listed in the box below.

Impact Phase Problems

- search and rescue
- care and treatment of the injured
- street clearing so life-safety operations can begin and continue
- damage assessment of critical infrastructure
- identification of resource shortfalls and request for outside resources from regional, state, or national sources
- general damage to civilian homes and businesses

These problems and their subsets will drive all operations until all have been identified and resources assigned. Search and rescue will be the first priority immediately after a disaster. There are only hours before the injured or trapped begin to die. All departments should have in place a set of expected actions for their on-duty personnel to begin these operations. Then, as a clearer picture of the disaster and its impact emerges, resources can be focused on the most serious incidents. This is a manpower-intensive operation and will require the majority if not all of the personnel that can still respond. Duties include:

- Support for the search and rescue teams and local medical facilities will dominate the impact phase. As the injured are found, they will require a large commitment of personnel to treat them and transport them to the medical facility.

- Street-clearing operations will have to coincide with the rescue efforts. Emergency personnel will have difficulty reaching the most affected areas and supporting operations on site once they do until the streets are clear enough for vehicles and equipment.

- Damage assessment is the other dominating problem. Not until the extent of the damage to the community is understood can emergency management begin prioritize the problems facing them.

- Opening of emergency shelters for displaced people is next if the disaster was a sudden event.

The community will remain in the impact phase until all major incidents have been found, resources applied, and no additional serious problems have been reported for a period of 24 hours.

This definition should be well understood by everyone and a formal declaration of the end of the impact phase should be noted and announced. The objective is to give the event a structure and with that structure a sense of accomplishment both for the responders and the public.

By defining the disaster by phases and tracking progress through those phases the emergency-management team as well as the community will have a context to understand that progress is being made even though it may not be readily apparent. Without a definition the response can seemed like a landslide of problems that never seems to end. It is critically important for the EOC team to understand where they are in the response and management of the event. It helps to structure time and prioritize resources.

Stabilization Phase

The stabilization phase produces a new set of problems to be solved. The scope of the disaster has been established. The number and types of problems have been indentified, and resources to solve these problems are either on site or have been requested from outside agencies and are on the way. Prioritization of local and outside resources can begin to be based on the common operational picture At the same time the population of the community must still be fed, clothed, and housed and their sanitation needs taken care of until a semblance of normality can be reestablished.

Operations during this portion of the response will continue to center around search and rescue, care of the injured, and identification of the dead until the final disposition of all the victims has been completed. It will also involve establishing a supply system for the distribution of food, water, ice, and temporary shelter. This system will have to handle tons of food, clothing, and ice pouring in from outside the community. It will have to be large enough and sophisticated enough to move the supplies to the people who need them the most before they have a chance to spoil or melt.

Local resources will not be able to handle these problems alone, so outside agencies and volunteers will have to be used to manage the flood of supplies, equipment, and personnel. Organization and management of the influx of volunteers become a priority in the stabilization phase. They will not be familiar with the community or its needs and will be dependent on local government to assign them to the areas where they are needed the most.

The military and other federal response agencies will also assist in the response, and they too will need guidance, all of which will require time, effort, and personnel. All of this coordination will pass through the EOC. It will be its task to coordinate the various agencies and volunteers through the ESF system. It may take more than one ESF to manage the problem, and groups of ESF personnel will form to manage a particular resource or action.

Thousands of citizens may be in shelters. These shelters and tent cities themselves will produce problems that are not normally part of their job description for the Red Cross, Salvation Army, law enforcement, EMS, fire safety, and other departments. These problems will also require clusters of ESFs to meet periodically to manage the issues.

Hurricane Charlie Shelter Lessons

During Hurricane Charlie I was working ESF #6, mass care. Given that my jurisdiction was just inland from the coast of Florida, we had thousands of people from the coast in our shelters. Issues of food, security, medical care, and other supplies were soon being reported from the shelters. To manage many of these problems, I had to call, send an email, or walk over to another ESF that had the resources to meet the needs. It became apparent that this was slowing our efforts down, and none of us had a complete picture of the shelter situation. Each of the ESFs had its own picture of the problem.

To solve this problem, we began to have shelter meetings for the ESFs needed to manage all of the shelter problems and the emergency manager. These meetings included the sheriff's office (security), the Red Cross, the Salvation Army, volunteers and donations, school boards (facilities), and public-health officials (special-needs shelters). Initially we met every two hours to discuss problems and issues in each shelter. It took several of these meetings to gain a good understanding of the situation as a whole. It sped up the management of these problems, and we reached a point where we were able to scale back the number of meetings dramatically. Then, as the shelters began to empty, we stopped meeting altogether. The coordination brought about by the meetings led to much more efficient management of the shelters during the storm.

In the stabilization phase, as you respond to all of the problems created by the disaster, there will be an unusual number of demands for public-safety agencies from the rest of the population of the jurisdiction. The populace of the community will not only be having the usual cardiac arrests, car accidents, and domestic problems, but

Hurricane Andrew Public Safety Impact

After Hurricane Andrew in Dade County fire rescue saw their number of runs tripled. The department had more fires because individuals were using candles at night for lighting. They had more medical calls as people not used to physical labor tried to perform temporary repairs to their homes and businesses. They had more car accidents because the stoplight system and stop signs were destroyed in the storm, and there were simply more people on the road. The sheer magnitude of the activities occurring within the community will strain existing resources to the limit.

because of the event they will also be performing tasks they are not used to, and these new tasks will create additional problems.

This is another example of the types of demands that will be placed on existing resources during the stabilization phase above and beyond the damage to community. All of these issues resulted from individuals trying to bring some order to their lives and to survive as best they can until help arrives. The stabilization phase and its demands will not last a few days. They could last for weeks. This phase does not end until there are enough resources on site to address all of the problems within the community. By this I mean that temporary systems have been put into place to organize, distribute, and support all operations and the needs of the community as a whole. Again, the end of this phase should be announced to the public, and the EOC staff should be made aware of this milestone. Once this happens you have now entered the sustainment phase.

Sustainment Phase

The sustainment phase begins when the emergency-management team understands the scope of the problem it is facing, has resources in place to manage all of the problems, and is making progress on solving the problems. It does not mean that the community is close to returning to a semblance of normality. It means that the issues have been identified and are being addressed. This phase is almost as challenging as the stabilization phase. All of the operations must be supported with personnel, equipment, and consumable supplies. In addition, detailed records must be kept of all of these operations if the community is to receive funds from the federal government.

Finally as in the stabilization phase the number of emergency calls and normal jobs for the community departments will not decrease. They will continue to stay at abnormally high levels for weeks or even months. It will not be until there is some semblance of normality within the community that the requests for emergency help will begin to subside. The challenge in the sustainment phase is what the military refers to as synchronization of operations. This simply means understanding the needs of the field and supporting them in a timely manner with manpower and resources. The sustainment phase is completed when all operations have been accomplished and some semblance of normality is returned to the community.

Sustainment Phase Benchmarks

- Call-volume level has returned to normal or a level normal staffing can manage.

- Enough roads are open to allow for near normal response times and access to a majority of the areas within the city.

- All search and rescue operations in affected areas have been completed.

- All hospitals in the area are now providing full services.

- All personnel in the various departments have been relieved long enough to check on families and make temporary arrangements for shelter if needed.

The progress made in the sustainment phase is the best indication that a community is beginning to return to normal. Most citizens will feel progress in this phase as their lives begin to return to some semblance of normality. These milestones will be used to determine when outside resources can be released and when normal work and shifts can begin. Again, these benchmarks will vary but the accomplishment of each one should be announced and celebrated both in the EOC and to the public.

Recovery Phase

The recovery phase can take years to complete and in some cases will completely change the community—just look at New Orleans today compared to pre-Hurricane Katrina. While emergency management is involved in the beginning of this long-term phase, it is much more a function of the economic and political leadership to reshape the community after the disaster. In some cases this task is never finished, but this is not where emergency-management efforts should be spent. Instead, they should be focused on the response and reestablishment of normal life within the community. Recovery is a political and economic function.

DISASTER OPERATIONS

Disaster operations are about creating order out of chaos. They are about taking in a flood of information, both important and unimportant, and being able to sort and prioritize it into a usable format—not all at once but through a long series of information gathering and resource application in the right order to the right problem. This process is complicated by the fact that you will sitting in a room filled with people that you are not necessarily familiar with, all depending on various forms of communication to create a picture of what is occurring outside that room. You must be able to visualize those events and the progress you are making toward the control of those events. You do this through a series of procedures that creates a picture of operations that is as simple to understand as possible. Once a clear picture is created, then everyone in the room can begin to have a Common Operating Picture of the event. From the COP you will develop situational awareness that allows you and those in the EOC to make the right decisions to begin to create order out of chaos.

The only way this can be accomplished is by structuring the time and procedures within the EOC in such a way that those occupying the various positions are forced into actions that combine to produce the needed information at the right time and in prioritized form. This is done by putting into place systems that will combine this information into an understandable picture. The following procedures are designed to do just that.

These systems are not designed for any specific type of EOC management software. Instead, the spirit of what they are trying to accomplish should be incorporated into any system the reader uses in an EOC. The point is to provide a set of overarching principles that can be used to lead any community through a disaster. These systems or any other systems will not work if people do not understand crisis decision making and how it differs from their day-to-day decision making. So always precede any system you put into place with decision-making training. It will assure the success of your systems and the people who are responsible for implementing them.

ICS/EOC Interface Disaster Operations at the Emergency Management Level

Disaster operations are at a command or operational level, as the military would call it, not the tactical level. Emergency managers do not make tactical decisions. They coordinate and support the operations of the various critical-response agencies within and outside their community. It is their job to look at the situation from a community-wide perspective, consult with all departments, and make sure that the available resources are focused on the most important problems facing them at any given time. Once the focus has been set, it will be up to the personnel in those departments to address the problems. If the emergency manager can focus the operations and therefore the resources on the proper issues at the proper time, they will have done their job.

Emergency Manager's Operational Guiding Doctrine

- Disaster operations become resource-allocation decisions based on the available resources, the known incidents, and how long it will take to put in place the needed resources and coordinate the response. The emergency manager must think in terms of time to complete operations. It will take time for a resource request to work its way through the support structure before it can be addressed and then for that resource to finally arrive where it is needed. This time delay must be factored into any request that cannot be filled immediately. If the situation on the ground is fast-moving, the emergency manager must understand that the situation will not stand still and the resources initially requested might not be enough by the time they arrive. So there must be close coordination between those responsible for the response in the field and the EOC to make sure the resources arrive in a timely manner.

- An emergency manager must understand that the subject-matter experts in everything from law enforcement to public health have more knowledge about the needs of their specific operations. So the emergency manager is the person taking the decision a step higher and looking at the response as a whole to prioritize the needs of the various departments. Their job is to look at the big picture and make sure their community is spending its critical resources in the right places and at the right time. To balance the needs of all the departments with the needs of the community and come up with the mix that best uses the available resources on the right problems is her essential role.

- Emergency managers do this through consultation with those agencies involved and elected officials. Elected officials will ultimately decide. If you have laid the groundwork as the disaster expert and a fair witness within the organization, then their role will evolve naturally from the time and effort spent prior to the event.

New Type of Organization

Normally communities are well-functioning organizations with big wheels, cogs, and specialists providing a myriad of services every day. During a disaster this organization has to change. It has to begin functioning in an entirely new way. The new organization is a hybrid of all of these parts. Under the stress of a disaster the cog deep down in the depths of the organization can bring the whole organization to a halt until his problem is solved.

Aircraft Carrier

An example is an aircraft carrier. One of the lowest jobs on the ship is that of attaching the hook to the aircraft just before it is launched. The person performing this task is part of a team that prepares the aircraft for launch. If the person who attaches the hook to the plane detects a problem with the hook or the plane and signals the plane handler, all launches are halted. The whole ship's operations are at that point focused on the launching of that single aircraft. The ship has an extensive hierarchy of enlisted soldiers and officers who are in charge of the ship. Yet when this problem occurs, that whole hierarchy collapses to that single problem until it is corrected. Until that problem is solved, no further launching will occur. One of the lowest persons on the ship has brought to a halt the operations of a ship of over 5000 personnel until that problem is solved because it is recognized as the most important problem on the ship at that point in time. All the resources necessary to fix the problem are brought to bear, and when it is solved operations can resume. This collapsing of the decision to one of the lowest persons on the ship is a perfect example of how a community's bureaucracy must behave. A new organization must evolve from the old during a disaster.

Elected and appointed officials in communities must recognize this new type of organization and be prepared to use it to respond to the disaster. In a disaster the stakes are higher for every decision made. It is not always clear which ones will be life-threatening and which ones will not be as serious. So a system must be able to differentiate between the two and respond appropriately.

The information flow of a community during a disaster must be more flexible than during normal operations. In a highly reliable system information must flow from the bottom up as well as from the top down. Those on the ground will know the status better than those in the EOC initially. They will be ones doing damage assessment and search and rescue operations. So the information they gather must flow upward as fast as possible. Only then can the EOC begin to understand the scope and seriousness of the situation. This is the opposite of the way organizations normally process information, with top down direction being the norm. So the leaders of the community and the EOC staff must understand that an atmosphere of open two-way communication must be established if no mistakes are to be made.

If this type of organization is to be created, the personnel in the EOC must understand this tenet and practice it or the right information will not be used properly. As reports from the field come in to the various ESFs, the person sitting in that chair must have an understanding of what the essential elements of information (EEI) are and which messages are relevant to those EEIs if they are to prioritize messages as they flow into the EOC.

ESSENTIAL ELEMENTS OF INFORMATION

Critical items of information regarding the enemy and the environment are needed by a military commander by a particular time to relate with other available information and intelligence in order to assist in reaching a logical decision.

EEIs are the first filter that is applied to the flood of information that inundates the EOC. ESFs use EEIs to prioritize information and understand which messages need to be passed on to the rest of staff and used for visualization. The ESFs are the key to begin to sort and prioritize the information. They understand their specific subject matter and what is important within that area, so they should determine the level of importance of each bit of information.

What information do you need to know? What systems and facilities are vital to understand the impact of a disaster on a community? How do you approach gathering the most critical information from such a wide variety of departments and infrastructures? The answer is to develop a list of EEIs for the community. They should include the critical-response departments and other critical infrastructures that impact the population and the response. The starting point should be a formal community profile.

The objective of a formal community profile is to identify all critical infrastructure in both response and civilian facilities. This list will become the starting point of any postevent damage assessment. The

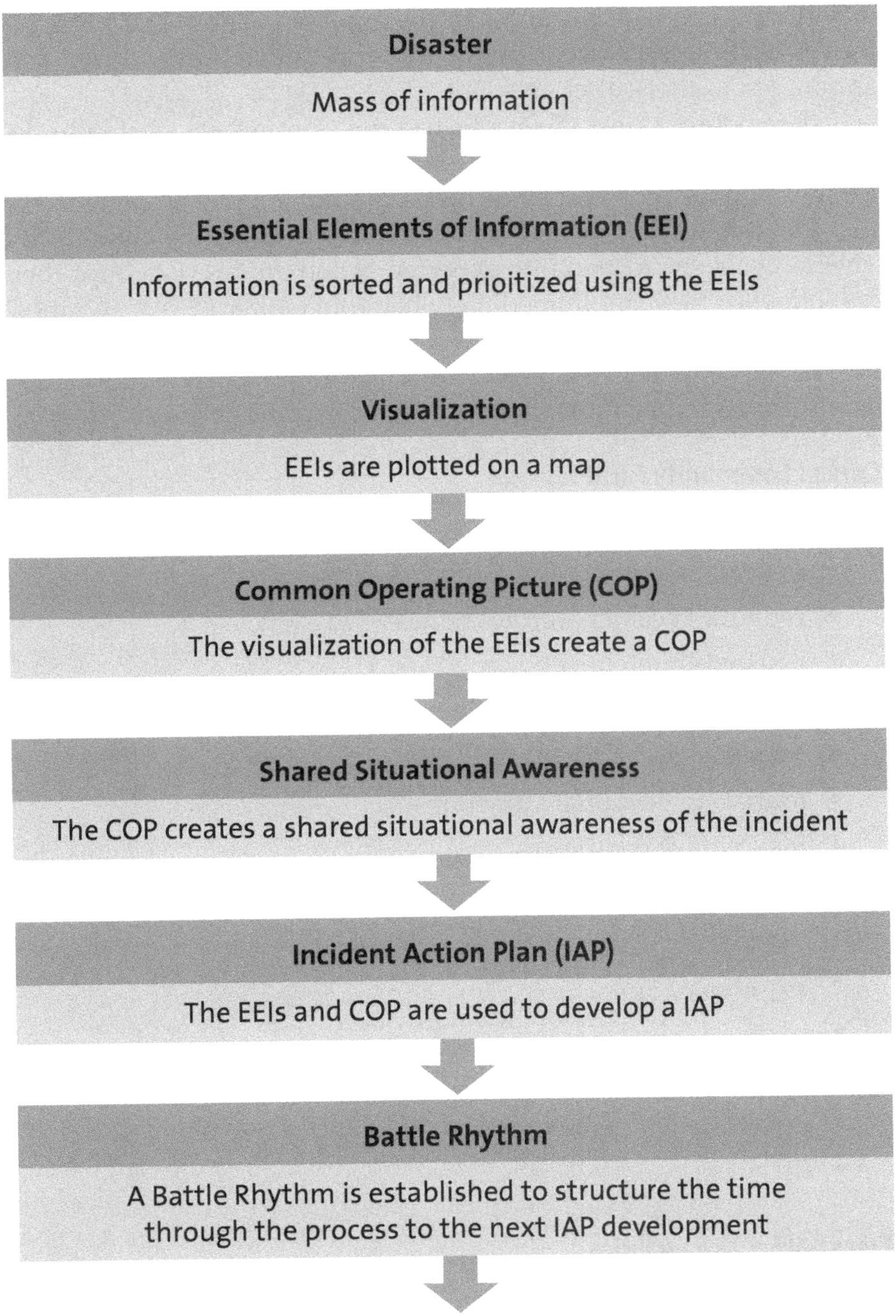

Disaster

Mass of information

Essential Elements of Information (EEI)

Information is sorted and prioitized using the EEIs

Visualization

EEIs are plotted on a map

Common Operating Picture (COP)

The visualization of the EEIs create a COP

Shared Situational Awareness

The COP creates a shared situational awareness of the incident

Incident Action Plan (IAP)

The EEIs and COP are used to develop a IAP

Battle Rhythm

A Battle Rhythm is established to structure the time
through the process to the next IAP development

Figure 3.1   Disaster operations information flow.

facilities on this list should be on the expected actions (EA) lists for the closest first responders, public-works personnel, and other public employees to check after an event.

The emergency manager will use this community profile to develop with the various departments in his jurisdiction a set of EEIs for the community. These EEIs, once determined, will begin to frame the size and scope of the disaster and its effect on the community. They will also be turned into expected action guides (EAG) for their personnel so they can immediately begin to gather EEIs without being told to do so. The following is only a partial list. Instead it should be viewed as a starting point for a community, and information should be added or subtracted to meet its specific needs.

Critical Community Facilities

- hospitals
- nursing homes
- retirement centers (group homes)
- assisted-living facilities
- shelters/special-needs shelters
- schools
- tourist/recreational attractions
- major office complexes
- shopping centers/malls
- marinas
- airports
- ports
- railway terminals or yards
- mobile- or manufactured-home parks
- RV sites

Essential Service Facilities

- police/sheriff stations and substations
- fire stations
- EMS stations

- 911 centers
- public-works yards and facilities
- sewage-treatment and pump stations
- fueling facilities
- electrical stations and substations
- telephone switching/control stations
- cell towers
- animal shelters
- communication towers
- bridges

Resource Locations

- bulk-fuel storage
- ice plants
- food storage
- construction-equipment marshaling yards

EEI Summaries

- number of deaths and injuries
- area affected
- number of people affected by the disaster
- critical-response infrastructure impacted by the disaster
- critical-support infrastructure (hospitals, power, water, etc.) and facility status
- damage to homes and commercial buildings

Response Priorities

- life safety
- critical infrastructure
- property and economic impact

Using the information gathered, begin to determine your strategic goals and short-term objectives to reach those goals. But this initial assessment is only the beginning: a continuous size-up must be consciously made by all those involved. This effort has one goal, and that is to improve the information everyone has to base their decisions on. This flow and prioritization of information begins to build a working Common Operating Picture from which decisions and actions can be based.

VISUALIZATION

As the EEIs are sorted and prioritized, they are next posted on a map so a visualization of the disaster can begin to emerge. A map is far superior to lists of issues, given the fact that to really understand the effect of a disaster on a community relationships need to be clearly visible. This map should be displayed so everyone is able to view it and the changes as they occur. Use mapping, symbols, charts, and other visual aids to create a dynamic and easily understood representation of the disaster. The larger and more complex the disaster, the more detailed visualization will help the emergency manager and the EOC team understand the spatial relationships between resources, damages, and needs. These spatial relationships are critical in understanding where resources are needed and if any of the response resources are nearby.

Anyone in the EOC should be able to sit down in front of his or her display and get a complete situation report for the current operations without asking for a shift briefing. This visualization will lead to a COP and the kind of situational awareness that breeds good decision making.

There are any number of good software packages designed to create a usable picture of your operations. Which one you decide to use will be a function of your community's size and complexity and how comfortable your EOC staff is with its use. Whatever you choose to use, it should have the capability to display the following information:

- resource and unit status
- EEIs for your community with time and actions taken
- weather data (Weather can be the cause of the disaster and it can interfere with the ongoing operations, so it is important to have a good forecast display.)
- timelines for operations

- ICS/NIMS organization chart with the current shift personnel (The personnel assigned within the organization will change with shifts and over time, so knowing who to call to address a specific problem will assure that time is not lost in trying to reach the wrong person.)

COMMON OPERATING PICTURE

As the disaster is visualized through the mapping of its effect, the staff will begin to build a COP. This picture creates a shared understanding of the disaster and its impact on the community, resources available, and resources needed.

These initial EEIs will only provide the first assessment of the damage and problems faced. Everyone in the EOC must understand that the information gathered is only a first assessment and must be constantly updated. This information will begin to form the first COP of the disaster. From this COP the response priorities will begin to become clear:

- Assessments are only snapshots in time; disasters are not static events.
- Information changes over time.
- The significance of the information will change over time.
- As the situation changes, monitoring information through the EEIs will help to clarify the most important issues.
- The time the information is received is vital to understanding its importance; without it there is no point of reference and a situation may have changed dramatically from the last assessment.

This picture will drive the initial and long-term decisions about the specific needs of that ESF and eventually the overall response. Everyone should strive to keep an accurate and timely COP in order to make the right decisions at the right time.

From the COP the first situational-awareness assessment will evolve. The following is a standard situation report that should be constructed from the COP. The situation report compiles all the EEIs and other information into a form that can be used internally and externally when reporting current conditions and needs.

Situation Report

- fatalities, injuries, missing persons
- locations of affected areas within the community
  - damaged structures
  - estimated number of people affected
- status of critical-response infrastructure and personnel
  - law enforcement
  - firefighting
  - search and rescue
  - emergency medical services
  - hospitals
  - public works
  - information systems
- evacuation orders issued (mandatory/voluntary)
- status of schools
- status of government offices
- EOC activation level
- other command posts or operations centers (firefighting, search and rescue, law enforcement, public works, etc.)
- public information
  - information line
  - press release
- shelters
  - current shelter status, names, locations, population, needs
  - anticipated sheltering needs
  - number of usable shelters and capacity
- law enforcement
  - resources deployed
  - status of personnel
  - status of facilities
  - status of equipment
  - field reports of civilian death, injuries, missing persons
  - field reports of critical infrastructure

- o roads
- o hospitals
- field reports of homes damaged or destroyed
- firefighting
  - resources deployed
  - status of personnel
  - status of facilities
  - status of equipment
  - field reports of civilian deaths, injuries, missing persons
  - field reports of critical infrastructure
    - o roads
    - o hospitals
  - field reports of homes damaged or destroyed
- emergency medical services
  - resources deployed
  - status of personnel
  - status of facilities
  - status of equipment
  - field reports of civilian death, injuries, missing persons
  - field reports of critical infrastructure
    - o roads
    - o hospitals
  - field reports of homes damaged or destroyed
- public works
  - resources deployed
  - status of personnel
  - status of facilities
  - status of equipment
  - field reports of civilian death, injuries, missing persons
  - field reports of critical infrastructure
    - o roads
    - o lift stations
    - o water treatment and waste water
    - o electrical grid

- field reports of homes damaged or destroyed
- information systems
  - resources deployed
  - status of personnel
  - status of facilities
  - status of equipment
  - damage to critical information infrastructure
    - computer systems
    - radio systems
    - telephone systems
    - 911 systems
- medical
  - status of medical facilities
    - hospitals
      - medical/surgical beds
        - physically available beds
        - staffed beds
        - unstaffed beds
        - occupied beds
        - available bed
      - critical-care units
        - burn ICU
        - pediatric
        - pediatric ICU
        - psychiatric
        - negative pressure/isolation
        - operating rooms
      - staffing
        - doctors
        - nurses
        - technicians
      - surge capacity
        - staffed beds that could be available within 24 hours
        - staffed beds that could be available within 72 hours

- ☐ electricity
- ☐ water
- ☐ generators
  - · fuel
- ☐ food supplies
- ☐ communications
- ☐ pharmacy supplies
- ☐ morgue status
- ☐ patient-transfer needs
- ☐ nursing homes

This situational-awareness report should drive the next actions and steps to be take taken and form the basis for the Incident Action Plan (IAP) from then on. By keeping this report up to date the EOC will be able to maintain constant knowledge of the issues facing it. This ongoing awareness is not something that is easily obtained or maintained over the course of the disaster. The whole process must be repeated constantly in order to keep a correct situational awareness of operations and the needs facing them.

INCIDENT ACTION PLAN

From the gathering of the EEIs to the development of a Common Operating Picture to a shared situational awareness, the emergency manager and planning officer can begin to develop the IAP. An incident action plan does not have to be a long and complex document. Instead it should be reasonably short and easily understood by everyone. The plan should contain the following sections:

- operational period and date—how long the operational period will last
- operational objectives for this operational period, lead ESF assigned to accomplish each of the objectives, resources assigned to each of the objectives
- any critical issues that need to be addressed in the operational period
- status of the operational objectives from previous IAP (accomplished or still in progress), resources assigned to each of the operational objectives from the previous IAP

- who is assigned these ongoing objectives
- organization chart with personnel assigned to the various ESFs—administration, planning, operations, and logistics
- incident name, name of incident commander (IC) of all major incidents still in progress, any shortfalls of resources identified by the IC

Once the initial IAP has been written, it can then become the basis for structuring the EOC's operations, with the schedule centered around the accomplishment of IAP stated objectives and the preparation for the next operational period. During the preparation for the next IAP the process of collecting and monitoring the EEIs, updating of the visualization that leads to an accurate COP, and finally a shared situational awareness is repeated continually. This continual process of evaluation and reevaluation will lead to accurate and timely decisions and the setting of proper objectives for the response at the right time.

BATTLE RHYTHM

One additional structure must be placed on the operational period of each IAP and that is the Battle Rhythm. The Battle Rhythm is simply the time frames for the needed information for the development of the next IAP. Structuring the time in the EOC gives everyone deadlines to determine and make recommendations for the next planning period. Without those deadlines and with the situation on the ground constantly changing, it would be difficult to draw a line and say this is the current situation. The Battle Rhythm can be driven by a number of factors—everything from the type of disaster to when the elected official will give a news conference. So the emergency manager must be flexible enough to adjust the rhythm to meet the needs of the incident. The following is an example of the Battle Rhythm of the State of Florida Emergency Operations Center for a hurricane.

State of Florida Hurricane Battle Rhythm

0700 shift change
0730 briefs (administration, logistics, operations, planning)
0800 breakfast

0900 IAP meeting, ESF #5 planning runs the meeting, governor's press conference brief

1000 National Weather Service (NWS) conference call (NWS will brief the emergency managers at the state and county level to discuss what is coming out in the next advisory)

1100   NWS advisory is released to the public

1115 conference call with all the counties in the state to discuss the actions necessary based on the newest advisory

1200 National Operations Center video teleconference including the White House Situation Room and other affected states

1300 logistics conference call with FEMA

1545 preparation for governor's briefing

1600 governor's press conference and briefing

1600 NWS conference call before the 1700 advisory

1700 NWS advisory released to the public

1745 county conference call to discuss the actions based on the new hurricane advisory

As you study the Florida Battle Rhythm, you can see that it revolves around coordination with other agencies and elected officials and is dependant on the National Weather Services advisories. The inclusion of the National Weather Service briefings in the Battle Rhythm is a unique to weather disasters. If the disaster were a pandemic, then the conference calls may be based around regular briefings from the CDC. No matter what the cause, the use of a Battle Rhythm assures that the most up-to-date information is collected for the various briefings and that the ESFs all understand the time frames under which they are working. Their time and actions are all structured together to meet the overarching needs of the response. Each disaster will require the development of its own Battle Rhythm, but once established it will assure that operations will be structured to meet operational needs and the needs of informing the public.

CONCLUSION

The previous procedures have one goal in mind and that is to structure how information is collected and distributed throughout the EOC. By structuring the information flow and the timing you will assure that the EOC will meet the needs of ongoing operations and the need for the public to know. The structure will provide the needed organization for those unused to the demands of a disaster response. By organizing the process and participant time it will provide the kind of working environment that will assist you and your staff in responding as efficiently as possible to a disaster.

CHAPTER 4

Decision Graphics: The Green Light System

E mergency management is information management under stress. Information management in this context does not mean technology but how information flows through an organization through the various technologies, written communications, word of mouth, and face-to-face contacts. This information will have varying degrees of importance. Messages, media reports, and reports from citizens flood the EOC, and the emergency-management team must categorize and prioritize each scrap of information. The team must be able to know what is important and needs immediate attention and what notifications can wait. This means that everyone at every ESF must understand the importance of the information just received to the current IAP and how to prioritize that information within the plan.

This deluge of information can lead the team away from the critical priorities and delay response efforts. Members can end up tracking too many threats and not the vital ones. If too much information is tracked, an EOC will become bogged down in recording information with little or no importance. It can overwhelm any team unless there is a specific system in place to sort and triage this information and then display it in a way so that everyone understands its importance. It is not enough to simply add a message received by an ESF to a list of "important" information. It must be put into the context of the response by that ESF, and the team must understand its relevance and how and where it should be displayed.

The military has faced this problem for hundreds of years, and through various iterations a system of symbols has evolved into a computerized battle display that allows a commander to view a dynamic picture of current operations. They call this portion of their command and control system visualization. Visualization is the graphical representation of terrain and resources and the action status of those resources. It is considered so critical that it is the first step in their decision-making process. These graphics create a Continuous Operating Picture (COP) that leads to a Situational Awareness that is focused on the most critical parts of any operation. Properly used, a commander can walk into a command post and without being briefed by anyone understand the current state of operations. Being able to visualize the dynamics of a complex and fluid situation is critical to the ability of a commander to focus on the most significant issues facing him.

The ability to visualize operations in a way that informs as much as a briefing is essential in fast-moving environments when rapid and informed decisions are needed. Verbal and written briefings can then focus on the needed decision points and bring the specifics of the decision into perspective. The ability to see the spatial relationships of the incident, progress made, resources applied, and unmet needs can clarify and prioritize decision making. Without the ability to visualize, the most crucial needs can be lost in a forest of messages, briefings, and conflicting priorities. This ability to visualize operations is lacking in the emergency-management world.

A civilian EOC is no more or less than the equivalent of a military command post. The decision makers for that community have all gathered in one place to focus their attention on the single biggest problem threatening their community. While the military uses this organizational tool every time it operates, in the civilian world this is a once-or-twice-in-a-career occurrence.

Normal day-to-day operations within a jurisdiction are the opposite in structure to those used during a disaster. Everyone resides in his or her own silo of information and decision making. Decisions are made in a set process that everyone understands and uses within her own departmental structure. Rarely are these internal priorities and decisions dependent on or prioritized against another department's projects. Yet when staffers enter the EOC, all of this must change so that they are working as a team on priorities for the city as a whole. A department's role can vary from of support to one of leadership depending on the incident.

This sudden and abrupt switch is difficult even with planning and training prior to an event; the changes in the decision-making process are too great. There need to be tools that assist everyone in this new environment. Part of the answer is the development of a system to visualize the event. This system must be as simple and intuitive as possible, yet be able to display information in a complex, rapidly changing situation in an understandable fashion. A tool that structures information for all participants is needed.

The principles used by the military have direct application to the civilian EOC. This chapter is a step towards just such a civilian system. The processes suggested are flexible enough for individual jurisdictions to adjust to meet their specific needs. The purpose is to provide tools that can be used immediately in a response and create a starting point for the development of a more sophisticated system within the emergency-management community.

THE GREEN LIGHT SYSTEM

How does someone sitting at an ESF desk in an EOC determine what information is important, then display it so everyone in the EOC understands it? How can the rest of the team at a glance understand what that information means for individual operations and how it fits within community-wide operations? Finally, how does an emergency manager roll up all of this information into an IAP that addresses the most critical needs? The Green Light System is a system that will do just that by portraying vital resource and operational information in a simple and easy-to-understand format.

The concept is a simple one. The Green Light System uses a stoplight as its metaphor for the status of units, facilities, operations, and logistical needs. It will produce a clear picture of issues and needs and the community's overall readiness to respond. When each division or department status is clear, then the jurisdiction has a snapshot of its capabilities and critical resource needs. Once they are understood, the emergency-management team can make the best use of the resources available and request the most critically needed resources and logistics.

The objective is to provide a simple set of rules that can be applied to all assets and operations of any jurisdiction no matter its size. The system can be incorporated into any ICS or NIMS to implement the right decisions.

Green signifies that the equipment, facilities, and department are fully capable of operations needed for the response up to normal operational standards.

Yellow means that there are issues that impact the effectiveness of equipment, facilities, or operations, but they are still able to operate with a reduced effectiveness.

Red means there are issues, problems, or deficiencies that are significant enough that equipment, facilities, departments, or operations are not capable of performing normal duties.

The department itself will establish a list of critical factors that affect performance prior to an incident. These criteria will reflect what a department needs to operate at its normal effectiveness. They will address personnel, equipment, and facilities. Loss or damage to those factors will be will be parsed and categorized into red, yellow, and green according to how their operational status would be affected. The designations will be used to determine their status during a disaster, so it is important for the emergency manager to be part of the planning process with each department.

The department's staff will know best which equipment, personnel, and systems are critical to the operation of the department. The emergency manager should be involved in their development by assisting the department to understand how to apply the system to their resources and processes. Understand that they are the subject-matter experts in their field and know its intricacies better than anyone; the emergency manager is there simply to facilitate in the development. To develop these criteria, all of the participants must determine the following:

- Identify and prioritize the basic critical performance standards to be tracked for each major division or subdivision of their department.

- Use those standards to evaluate their departmental operations and facilities after an event to designate the department's color.

- Ensure that all department personnel understand these criteria.

- Establish a set of Expected Actions that explain when and how this information will be collected and passed on through management structures.

A fire department is a clear example because it is a mix of facilities, personnel, and equipment that are distinctly identified by geographic area and capabilities. To develop a set of Red, Yellow, or Green designations for each station, there are three factors that would come into consideration: facilities, meaning the station itself; equipment, meaning the trucks; and personnel, the crews on the trucks. Each would be evaluated separately and given a Red, Yellow, or Green designation. These designations would then be rolled up to a Red, Yellow, or Green overall designation for the station (see Figure 4.1).

If the station had significant damage to the building itself but the equipment and crew were unharmed, the facility portion of that station would be coded Red and the equipment and personnel would be Green. Given that the station has a Red rating, the department pre-event evaluation qualifies this station for a yellow designation. It is capable of response, but without a facility the response will eventually be affected and needs to be addressed at some point. So while the station has a Yellow designation, the department might concentrate on other stations with more critical needs that affect response.

Fire departments are divided into subdivisions called battalions. Each station assigned to a battalion has the same designation. The station designations are rolled into an overall Red, Yellow, or Green rating for the battalion as a whole. Let's say that the department determined that if over half the stations reported a Red or Yellow designation, the battalion's designation would be yellow. The battalion chief would report his overall designation and the designations for each station.

All of the reports from the various battalions would be rolled up to an overall designation for the department as a whole. Let's say that the established department criterion was that if more than one battalion had a Red or Yellow designation, the department's overall des-

Each senior station officer will conduct a Green Light System assessment of the station as soon as conditions allow. The information will be communicated as soon as possible by normal means or, if those are not working, by the use of personnel from the nearest station with communications.

1. **Personnel:** the physical condition of all personnel
   a. Green = no injuries
   b. Yellow = minor injuries
   c. Red = serious injuries
      All injuries, minor or serious, are to be detailed and any actions taken noted.

2. **Equipment:** the ability of the units to respond
   a. Green = all in service
   b. Yellow = in service but in need of repairs
   c. Red = out of service
      All needed repairs will be noted.

3. **Facilities:** physical condition of the facilities
   a. Green = minimal or no damage
   b. Yellow = serious damage, repairs to be given priority
   c. Red = uninhabitable, personnel to be located to another location until repairs can be made.

4. **Communications**
   a. Green = all station communications including phones, radios, and inter- and intranet working
   b. Yellow = one or some of the normal communication capabilities not working
   c. Red = no communication possible.

5. **Station Access**
   a. Green = streets near station clear
   b. Yellow = minimum blockage, still able to respond
   c. Red = blockage to require heavy equipment before units can respond

6. **Station Overall Score** based on the above assessments (Any yellows make it a yellow and any reds make it a red.)
   a. Green
   b. Yellow
   c. Red

7. **Stations Neighborhood** (A quick windshield damage assessment for the neighborhood will be made.)
   a. Green = most streets clear and minor damage to structures
   b. Yellow = most streets blocked with major damage to some structures
   c. Red = many blocked streets, majority of the structures have significant damage or are destroyed

FIGURE 4.1   The Green Light System.

ignation would be Yellow. This means that, while units were available for response, the effectiveness of the department was affected. By combining all of the designations from the station level, to the battalion level and finally to the department-wide level, a rapid and clear picture of the department's capabilities emerges. This designation would identify where the largest problem was so it could be addressed by shifting available resources or by requesting additional resources. For example, if most of the Red designations were due to damage to facilities, the department could still operate, but long-term operations would be affected and the repair or replacement of facilities would have to be addressed at some point.

This Yellow designation would then be added to the designation of the other departments within the jurisdiction to determine the overall capabilities of the critical infrastructure response agencies. The number of Red, Yellow, and Green departments would be rolled up to give the jurisdiction as a whole a designation. Let say there had been enough damage that the community as a whole had a Yellow designation. This designation would be displayed in the EOC and on computer screens so that everyone would know the strengths and weaknesses of the various agencies and their needs.

This system creates a Situational Awareness of the community and its immediate needs and capabilities. From these designations priorities can begin to be set for initial operations. For example, while the fire department has a number of stations that are designated Red, their units and personnel are still capable of response. But if the public-works department reports a Red designation because of major damage to the water-supply system, the population would have no portable water and the fire department would not be able to fight fires despite availability of personnel and equipment.

This would become one of the most critical issues in the jurisdiction because it affects the ability of a critical department and the population in a way that could lead to public health and safety issues. Let's say the public-works department determines it will take 48 hours to repair and to restore the water supply. Then the first priority becomes the needs of that department. Does it have the manpower and equipment needed to restore the water supply? If not, then which types of equipment and personnel need to be requested from outside the jurisdiction? In addition, the loss of water for the citizens must also be addressed, so a request for the delivery of drinking water will have to be generated.

This is a simplified example of a much larger and more complex set of problems that arise after an event such as an earthquake, but it is instructive. It gives a sense of how the system can be used to quickly identify and then prioritize the needs of the community. As supplies, equipment, personnel, and resources flood in from the outside, they can be used to address the most critical issues. A simple Excel spreadsheet or whiteboard with a marker can be used to track all of these issues. Because simple color-coding is used, anyone who walks into the EOC can at a glance see the status and progress of operations.

From this chart anyone glancing at the ratings can see immediately where the major deficiencies exist. This visualization of capabilities and needs generates an understanding that is the basis for decisions and priorities. Progress is obvious, and the focus of

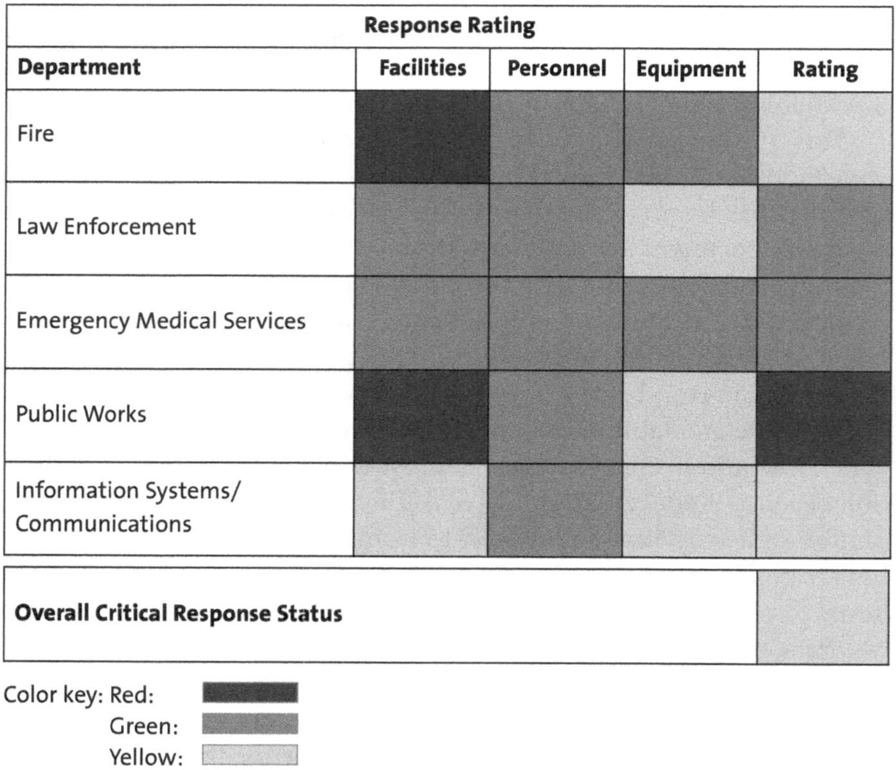

Response Rating				
Department	**Facilities**	**Personnel**	**Equipment**	**Rating**
Fire				
Law Enforcement				
Emergency Medical Services				
Public Works				
Information Systems/ Communications				
Overall Critical Response Status				

Color key: Red:
Green:
Yellow:

FIGURE 4.2 The Green Light System in action after a disaster.

the operations can shift as needed. Thus, an easily understood visualization of a complex and changing event creates a situational awareness that is critical to disaster response.

OPERATIONAL GRAPHICS

The basic tenets of all disaster response call for the initial size-up of the situation, followed by the development of an action plan, and finally the implementation of that plan. If emergency managers are to adhere to these tenets, they must be provided with operational information in a format that assists them in rapidly adapting to the changing operational factors as they occur. The operational environment demands the ability to make rapid and frequent changes in operations as an incident unfolds. Information has to be displayed in a fashion that provides not just the location of the incident but the resources applied and progress made. The spatial relationship between damage, critical infrastructure, and available resources in the recognizable context of a community map is critical to understand a complex operation and vital in developing situational awareness. Again, the military has developed a large library of symbols for every conceivable operation in order to be able to develop just such a continuous situational awareness. The following is an adaptation of a few of those basic system tenets to disaster operations.

Figure 4.3 shows two examples of the types of critical infrastructure whose status a community would want to track during operations, fire stations and hospitals.

Fire Station 24 is a yellow in the Green Light System because of damage to its facilities. The arrow points to its exact location. The same is true of the hospital graphic. Hospitals are as much a part of any disaster response as any public-safety facility, and there is an essential need to track their status. In this case the hospital, while full, has no critical needs at this point in the response. A community would also want to track the status of temporary facilities such as shelters.

This shelter was opened on June 6, 2010, at Edgewater High School with a capacity of 1000 and a current a population of 975. The green fill would show that there are no unmet needs at the shelter. The circle symbol could be used for any and all temporary facilities or other types of response operations such as points of distribution.

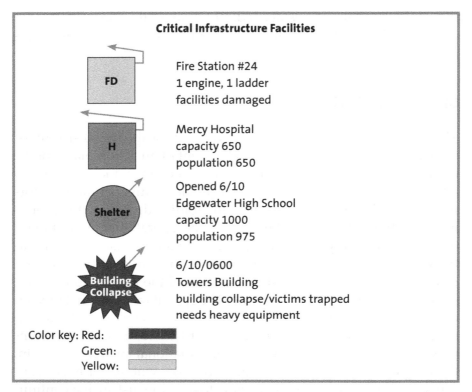

FIGURE 4.3 Decision graphic symbols. Facility and incident symbols, the squares are permanent facilities, the circles are temporary facilities and the star is an ongoing incident.

An operational symbol would denote each major field operation that was currently in progress and, using the Green Light System, would show its status. In the example the incident was a building collapse with victims trapped and a critical need for heavy equipment.

VISUALIZATION

These symbols, placed on a map, become a situational template for the entire disaster, and the resources and operations needed to respond to that disaster. The symbols don't just represent resources or facilities but actions and the status of those actions according to the overall plan. This provides a continuous size-up of the critical information that forms the basis for a Common Operating Picture (COP) of the incident and allows for the development of team situational awareness.

Remember the old military saying that no plan survives the first contact with the enemy? No civilian disaster plan will survive the first rain bands of a hurricane. In order to properly respond to a fast-moving situation, you must have a way to create a dynamic and accurate visualization of the event and the resources and operations that are currently in progress. This visualization allows the emergency-management team to react and adapt during a response to redirect resources to meet changing conditions.

Air-traffic controllers have complex electronic representations of the current situation in the air and, using these symbols, are able to keep a very fluid situation under control because they are able to visualize the information and take action on that information. During a response to a disaster those in an EOC must strive to continually improve the information they base their decisions on, and a visual reference is the quickest and best way to do that.

The Green Light System will allow them to anticipate needs and begin the process of meeting those needs before they are requested. If they learn to develop a system of visualization, as a situation increases in complexity and size they will be able to better understand the most critical needs and focus their resources on those needs.

Remember, too many charts, lists, and spreadsheets are worse than too few. Too much information without context and importance will only confuse. With the Green Light System only the most mission-critical information will be displayed in a way that allows the participants to quickly understand the information and its priority.

The system is flexible enough so that a jurisdiction can adapt it to meet their needs. It can be as complex in its evaluation and designation of a color code as the jurisdiction deems necessary, or it can be as simple as another jurisdiction thinks is necessary. The objective is to create an easy-to-understand visualization of the resources, operations, and the status of both.

CHAPTER 5

The Emergency
Operations Center

The Emergency Operations Center (EOC) is where the entire decision-making infrastructure for a community collapses into a single room or cluster of rooms to focus all of the jurisdiction's efforts on solving the most critical problems created by a disaster. This means that all of the normal offices and bureaucratic organizational structures that everyone is used to disappear and are recreated in these rooms. Everyone from elected and appointed officials to field operations managers coalesces into a new environment in order to have all of the needed leadership and subject-matter expertise in one place at one time so the right decisions can be made and then implemented.

EOCs can take many forms from jury-rigged conference rooms to dedicated standalone faculties. Either can work well for the job; it all depends on how the facility is equipped to meet the needs of those who are brought together there. In other chapters I have discussed the training and the new type of organization that are needed to manage disasters; in this chapter I will address the equipment and facilities needed to support those decision-making systems.

No matter how well trained or prepared those reporting to the EOC are, unless they have the tools needed to carry out their jobs, the response will suffer. A community does not have to have a dedicated and ultramodern facility to accomplish the task. While this is the ideal, it is hardly feasible for most communities. Instead, some sort of compromise must be established that still meets the need of the participants. It takes some imagination and cooperation from the right departments, but it can be accomplished.

As I have said before, emergency management is information management under stress. The EOC is where all of the information is gathered, sorted, prioritized, presented, and acted upon. An EOC is an information-management and command-and-control tool for the leadership of a community. The better the information flow, organization, and presentation, the better the decisions that can be made by the leadership. So think of an EOC as an information and decision-making hub. It is completely dependent on the communication and information systems that connect it to the rest of the community. Without these systems it is cut off from the disaster and the decisions that need to be made. So the single most important systems in the EOC are its communication and information-management systems.

Classrooms as an EOC

The first preplanned EOC my community ever had was a set of training classrooms in the city's police headquarters and jail. The facility naturally had heavy security and a backup generator, so it met a couple of the needed criteria right away. The police department was more than happy to lend us the classroom with one stipulation. Whatever we did could not interfere with their use of the classrooms on a daily basis. They were used extensively for in-service training of officers and important team meetings. We agreed, but that meant that none of the equipment we would need during an activation could be stored in the room. We would have to store it somewhere and then, if we had time before the event, reconfigure the room into an EOC. Given that my jurisdiction was in Florida and our most likely event was a hurricane, this worked out fine for us.

Once we knew where it would be, we needed to work with our information-systems department to determine what would be needed to transform the classroom into a working EOC. We knew what we needed in general, but the department expertise in the specifics was critical. We were given no money to accomplish this—we were going to have to secure the funding from another source—so it was vital to understand what our existing information systems could accomplish without additional funding, then identify what we would need to complete the transformation.

We determined that we were going to need computers and a phone for each ESF, video projectors, and cable connections and TVs for monitoring local and national news. The list was much longer, but those were the basics. Information-systems personnel could wire a set of phones with dedicated numbers in the classrooms without outside funding. That gave each ESF its own phone number. The phones were stored in the basement of police headquarters so they were close to the EOC.

Next, with the help of information systems, we developed the technical specifications for the computers and projectors. Then we applied for and received a grant to purchase the equipment. We purchased a laptop for each ESF. At the time we had no EOC software, so information management assigned a laptop to an ESF as if it were a person and gave it an address on the city's intranet. That way it did not matter who was sitting at the ESF desk; all messages were simply sent to the appropriate function and not the person. We would use the city's existing email software as our EOC software—not ideal but it worked. We did not need a dedicated server because police headquarters was only a few blocks from city hall, where the city's main servers for its network were housed. There were multiple redundant network connections, so even if we lost one there were secondary backups, allowing us to continue to use the laptops. The laptops were stored with the phones on a pallet that could be taken to the classrooms. We permanently mounted the video projector and TVs in the classrooms because the police department could use them in their training and were happy to have the additions.

So with a little outside money and a lot of bureaucratic maneuvering we had ourselves a decent EOC. Working with information systems, we determined that they would need at least 12 hours to reconfigure the room for use as an EOC. This became one of our benchmarks for ramping up for a hurricane. When to tell information systems to get the EOC ready was a critical decision, because it did cost money (overtime generally) and the police did lose their classrooms. Both of these decisions could not be taken lightly. We had to weigh the money and inconvenience against the certainty of a hurricane strike—something that is rarely clear-cut. This arrangement was adequate for our needs for several years and, given its low cost, was a good solution for us at the time. In my travels as a consultant I saw this same arrangement in rural and suburban jurisdictions around the country. They too felt it met their needs, given the number of disasters or near disasters that threatened their communities.

A last observation about this configuration both in my own jurisdiction and in the others I visited: If the elected officials ever participated in a training or a real response and were therefore involved with the setup and running of operations in this configuration, they walked away with the same decision, that they needed something more permanent. Almost to a person they were supportive of a more permanent and dedicated site for the EOC. In my opinion, although none ever shared their reasoning with me, they realized just how much they would depend on the EOC as their tool for leading during a crisis.

PHYSICAL CONFIGURATION OF AN EOC

There are a number of factors to consider in determining the physical configuration of an EOC. An EOC has to be sized and configured to meet the needs of the jurisdiction it is to serve and the number of personnel needed:

- There should be a minimum of 50 to 85 square feet per EOC staff member.

- It is very important to have conference rooms in close proximity to the EOC so groups of ESFs can confer out of the noise and disruptions of the EOC floor.

- There should also be a separate room for the elected officials and other policy group members. It needs to have the same information feeds as the operations room so they can be kept abreast of the situation.

The center must be accessible by the handicapped. It should comply with the rules and regulations as specified in the Americans with Disabilities Act.

You will need a desk or a shared table space for each ESF, as well as a phone and computer hookup. In addition, you will need televisions with cable or a satellite disk so various channels can be monitored. There should be video projectors capable of projecting the television or computer screens in the EOC. All computers should have access to the Internet and, if your jurisdiction has one, its intranet.

The EOC must have all of the jurisdiction's communications capabilities including radio communications, computer systems, and communications systems with outside jurisdictions. Your EOC will be no better or worse than the communications systems that support it. An EOC is a information-processing center to enable the right decisions to be made. Without the proper communications the EOC will turn into a room full of decision makers with no way to understand what decisions need to be made or to carry out any decisions that are made. The computer systems should include the jurisdiction's GIS capabilities. These GIS systems should include the ability to display or print GIS layers to include:

- major road networks
- evacuation zones for coastal communities including any established during the event
- shelters
- adult congregate living facilities
- community resident homes
- daycare centers
- county jails
- electrical service areas
- telephone service areas
- cell-tower locations
- sewer service areas
- subregional waste-water treatment plants
- lift-station locations
- parks and park areas
- libraries
- jurisdiction-owned properties
- schools
- political boundaries
- jurisdictional elected-official districts
- population per census tract
- dwellings per census tract
- jurisdictional zip codes
- future land-use maps
- jurisdictional sections grid
- planning districts

Protection should be an integral part of planning, building, and equipping the EOC. Protection means planning for security, stability, and accessibility. The building should be designed for survivability and operability. There are several ways to achieve survivability, including hardening facilities, locating facilities outside known risk areas, developing redundant capabilities at an alternate location, developing a mobile capability at an alternate location, or developing a mobile capability that can be moved away from the threat.

EOCs should be physically arranged to permit close, continuous coordination and immediate, positive action by all interested departments or agencies. Typically, there will be several functional areas housed in the EOC that will need to coordinate their operations, such as information gathering (planning), operational control (operations), logistical support of operations and the civilian population (logistics), and the capturing of needed administrative details associated with the disaster (administration).

FIGURE 5.1   Emergency Operations Center functional layout.

When designing the EOC's functional layout, keep the following points in mind:

- The emergency manager should be in a position where they can keep abreast of the current situation and manage operations. They could be located in the main operations room with connecting communications and appropriate displays. Others may prefer to remain in the central location but isolated from other groups.
- ESF staff whose functions interface continually, represent outside agencies, or are in direct support of one another should be collocated. For example, the public-works ESF and the energy ESF might be collocated.
- EOC staff sections should be located adjacent to displays pertaining to their activities. This allows for ease of posting and ready reference.
- Agencies that operate through their own communications must be able to use those communications. In some cases the strengthening of the structure can interfere with radio communications in and out of the building. It may be necessary to place them in a location where they will be able to use their radios.
- Noise levels are a problem, so try to position offices or functional groups with adequate space between them so as to lessen interference.

Having worked in a number of these facilities over the years, I can tell you they are one of the loudest and busiest environments you can imagine. Add to that noise the difficulty of dealing with problems that are affecting you community, your friends, and your family, and you have created one of the most stressful environments you can imagine. There are simply too many people using too many different forms of communication and talking to one another to ever control the noise adequately. The single best way to give groups that need quiet is to have offices where they can meet in a separate environment. If you are constructing a standalone center, either have meeting rooms built into the design or use private offices.

Organizing the EOC

There are many variations in EOC structures; each situation is unique. The type and size of the disaster or emergency will drive the number of people and the size of the organization needed to manage the emergency. There are no fixed rules in NIMS or ICS that you must use all of the positions or ESFs. Instead, think of NIMS and ICS as building blocks for the construction of the type and size of organization you need. Only use the roles and responsibilities you need to manage the event that you and the community are facing. I cannot emphasize this enough. Too many people think that if you use either system, then you must fill all of the roles. This is simply not true; use the roles that make common sense and fit your and your community's needs. Mix and match between the two systems. I am a firm believer in using the four major divisions in ICS—Administration, Logistics, Operations, and Planning—to group my ESFs and give them a coordinating officer.

Consider levels of activation for your EOC. The level of activation will depend on the type and size of the event. In Florida there are three official levels of activation: Level 3 is normal day-to-day monitoring; Level 2 is a partial activation where only certain ESFs report; Level 1 is full activation with all ESFs and personnel reporting for duty. I changed these slightly for my jurisdiction and used the EOC levels as the levels for the entire community. Level 3 was a monitoring level, since hurricanes give a long lead time I would issue a level 3 activation and begin to send out email updates with the latest hurricane information. This was not to alarm prematurely but simply to begin to get everyone's attention and give them a heads-up that they may have to take some steps in the not too distant future. Many times the forecast would change, and I could cancel the alert. Other times we would move to Level 2, which would mean that certain ESFs would report to the EOC and begin monitoring the storm. Level 3 was a full activation. I never had the occasion to use Level 2 to activate only certain ESFs because of a specific event, but I always intended to use it that way. Because everyone was used to Level 2 as a partial activation, I knew they would be comfortable with such a request. If you do institute levels of activation, make sure they match your state's levels. It will add legitimacy to your declaration of a certain level. A typical organizational chart of an EOC for a major disaster is shown in Figure 5.2.

If you manage a county with a number of municipalities in your jurisdiction that will have to be coordinated during a major event, representatives from those municipalities should have space in your

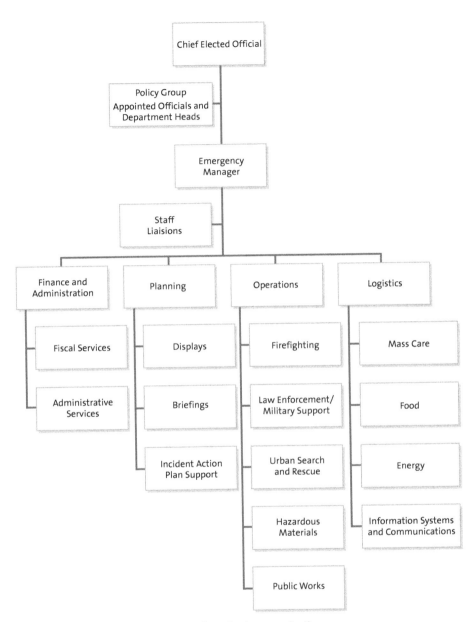

FIGURE 5.2   Local Emergency Operations Center organization.

EOC. By having designated representatives in your EOC you will have a continuous operating picture of their problems that will be much more accurate than if you had to work through communications. The following graphic is a good illustration of such an event. As I write this section of the book, the massive tornado outbreak of April 2011 has just ended. In county after county throughout the South communities are facing devastation that has rarely been seen. The coordination of the efforts in each county is daunting, no matter how well prepared an EOC is. The complexity of the operations will only be overcome by organization and cooperation at all levels of government.

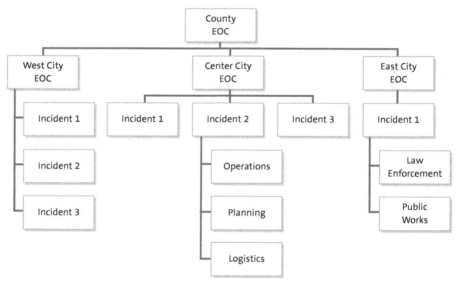

FIGURE 5.3   County wide disaster ICS/EOC interface.

The Policy Group

You will always have to provide space and personnel to keep elected officials separate but informed no matter what the size of the event. Ideally you can use a separate room directly off the operations floor, giving them the privacy they need and yet have the ability to see the information that is being displayed on the operations floor. Keeping them separate will also reinforce the fact that they are at a higher level and need to let the people on the operations floor do their jobs. Many personnel are not comfortable working in front of elected officials. It will only add stress to an already stressful environment. At the same time the elected officials want to be seen to be on top of the situation. By locating them near but separate from the operations floor you will meet both of those needs.

The Media Room or Area

As you design your EOC, you must have an area or room designated for the media and press. This can be a separate room dedicated to their needs, which would be ideal, or it can be a separate area. Since you will be holding regular press briefings, this area will give them a place to gather and set up their equipment. Ideally, they could have a window on the operations room so they can see the level of effort going on there. I first saw this at the State of Florida Emergency Operations Center. The governor would hold a briefing and behind him you could see the operations floor with people moving and working. It provided a great visual to reinforce the statements by the governor. When my jurisdiction built an official EOC, I made sure that the design had the same type of press room. During hurricane management it provided exactly the visuals I had hoped it would for the press conferences.

Communications/Message Center

The establishment of a communications/message center with a published number available to the public is one of the keys to managing public information and perception of the response. Provide a published phone number that is clearly identified, not a 911 number but instead a number for information or to report nonemergency problems. It provides the public with the ability to talk to a human being instead of being relegated to the Internet or public announcements. While not everyone will need this type of contact, there will be some who will relish this ability to gain information directly from a real person. The message-center personnel will have to be kept abreast of the latest information on the various distribution points and how and where people will be able to seek additional help. The message center can become a vital information-sharing as well as gathering point in the disaster.

Security

Security for your EOC is a real concern—not because it is going to be attacked by terrorists but simply to control the flow of people in and out of the facility. Whether you have to use converted rooms in an existing facility or are able to build a separate EOC from the beginning, think about how you are going to provide security. By security I mean the ability to monitor and control who has access and when. Those reporting to the EOC to work at an ESF ideally would be issued badges, either from a list of authorized personnel or beforehand after a training session. If it is a major event, there will be more people reporting than those on the original list, and someone will have to be in charge of keeping up with the growing number of people and checking credentials. The ideal organization to handle this is the local law-enforcement agency with jurisdiction over the EOC. Its presence alone will lend an authority and intimidate any press or members of the public trying to bluff their way into the facility. This will not always be possible given the type of event, since the agency may not be able to spare the officers to staff the post. Always have a backup plan for someone to staff the security desk and control access to your facility.

Staffing the EOC

Whenever possible assign personnel to roles that are similar to those they perform in their normal nondisaster jobs. Do not try to place people who might have received your EOC training in ESFs that are responsible for different subject matter than they manage daily simply because they are trained in general. If an untrained person has to be assigned to an ESF, try to assign an ESF-trained person as a contact to help the new staff member ease into the new environment.

The EOC should be able to accommodate minimum personal comfort that includes sleeping and eating capabilities. The EOC will be open and running during a disaster 24/7 for days or even weeks and open for more limited time periods for weeks. Meals will have to be provided for those staffing the center. Have each person who receives a meal sign a meal log for possible reimbursement documentation.

I cannot emphasize enough how important it is to provide decent food to those who are working at the EOC. They have left their families to sit in a room and manage the problems of the jurisdiction. If you want the staff members at their best, they will need to be provided with nutritious food. Many will spend days without ever leaving the building, sleeping where they can and working their positions. The right food can make a big difference in not only their morale but their energy level.

Do not fall for the vending-machine option. Instead try to provide nutritious fruits for snacks and well-balanced meals for the personnel. It will provide them with the kind of foods that will help sustain them in a time of long hours and high stress. In addition, provide healthy drinks—water, Gatorade, juices, and other types of drinks that provide energy for a long siege. Do not rely on lots or coffee and caffeinated drinks; for all of the boost they give, there is always a resultant crash as the caffeine wears off.

To provide healthy food, arrangements will have to be made prior to any event. A vendor can be hired to provide the food or a volunteer from your jurisdiction who is used to providing for a large number of people can provide the food. A budget will have to be set aside for this service and plans will have to be in place, because it will be one of the last things you will want to be worried about during an event.

The Three Hurricane Season

In 2004 my jurisdiction was struck by three different hurricanes in a matter of weeks, with very little time between the strikes. I was at the time working an ESF; it was my first time working a station instead of running the room, and it proved to be a huge learning experience.

After the first storm struck, the EOC was provided with some of the best food you could have asked for given the circumstances. Volunteer county employees who had no roles in the EOC provided the service. The county bought the food, and the volunteers prepared it. It was frankly the best morale builder we could have had. The first of the three storms, Hurricane Charlie, was the worst and most destructive. None of those in the EOC were capable of cooking anything nearly as good at home, and to have a few good meals really made a difference in morale and productivity.

The next storm struck when we had barely cleared the remnants of Charlie. Power had just been turned back on at my house. This storm was not as severe as Charlie, but nonetheless we found ourselves back in the EOC. There was a marked difference in the food and how it was served, with a resulting decline in morale and productivity. Reporting to the EOC seemed even harder, not just because we were facing another storm but because it felt as if we were not as appreciated the second time.

When the third storm struck, we found ourselves served with hastily thrown-together sandwiches. The food became a joking matter among the staff. This may sound petty against the backdrop of the suffering outside the room, but I learned a vital lesson reinforced by experience. You have to provide for the people in the EOC as well as those out in the field. Their personal needs are important if they are going to perform through the most difficult of circumstances. For many of us it was the only decent meals we had during the storms. If you are going to ask people to leave their families and work to help others during an event, they must feel as if they are appreciated. Having good, nutritious food is a simple yet effective way of showing that appreciation. If the bean counters begin to question the money spent, remind them it will be paid back in performance and more efficient operations.

The other critical requirement to keep your EOC personnel working at their best is the sleeping arrangements. Many will be unable to leave the facility for several days until operations have slowed. They must have somewhere to rest. An EOC is a very loud and hectic environment with radios blaring, phones ringing, nonstop television coverage, and all the other sounds created by a large number of people working on different problems. When someone is off shift but cannot leave yet, they need someplace to rest.

Ideally you would have a dorm in your EOC complex. This is rarely feasible given space restrictions and money needed for such a space. A simple and effective solution is to use one of the many large, open cubicle-filled offices somewhere else in the building as a designated dorm. The simple solution is to keep the lights out in the room at all times, since sleeping time during 24-hour operations will be around the clock. Ideally a cot could be placed in each cubicle so workers can use their pillow and sleeping bag and have some privacy. A simple requirement of no talking, loud music, or TV in the room will give you a working dorm. I spent several nights in just such a dorm, and it worked well. The ability to get some rest between shifts or when events have slowed down can do wonders for the efficiency of the personnel. Include plans for a dorm in any plans you make for your EOC.

CONCLUSION

An EOC can be anything from a converted set of conference rooms or classrooms to a dedicated, sophisticated facility. The key to making it the facility your community will need during a disaster is the planning, organization, and training done prior to an event. Without that effort it will not matter how sophisticated or jury-rigged the facility is; it will not be what your community needs. It comes down to two factors. One is how well prepared the people who walk in the door to face the problems are, and the other is how well prepared you are to support and provide them with the equipment and decision-making aids they will need to do their jobs. So do the homework necessary to have the best EOC your community can provide.

The EOC is a difficult and stressful environment no matter how well prepared your personnel are to face the challenges. Do not forget this in the midst of operations; just because they are not out combing through the rubble does not mean that they do not need to have their needs addressed. Remember that they have left their homes and families to be there and may not know how their property or their families are faring.

Appendix to Chapter 5

FEMA EOC CHECKLIST

The following pages contain a checklist created by FEMA in an effort to provide guidance to state and local governments as they design a new facility or assess an existing EOC. It is a comprehensive list and not all jurisdictions have the resources to construct such a facility but it is a valuable document for planning and assessing any EOC. The checklist is a guide and is intended to be an all-inclusive.

The checklist first asks questions about the physical features of a facility housing an EOC/EOC Alternate, and then addresses the characteristics of Survivability, Security, Sustainability, Interoperability, and Flexibility. The checklist may be used for state or local EOCs. For this reason, some questions may warrant different responses depending on the type (state or local) or functional nature (primary or alternate) of the EOC.

FACILITY FEATURES

Facilities—examines the physical features of EOC facilities: siting, structure, available space. EOC spaces to consider are an operations area, conference rooms, communications center, secure communications room, and multi-use space. Multi-use space is space that is not dedicated to EOC operations, but can quickly be made available to support EOC requirements for additional space during major disaster or surge situations.

95

Primary EOC

- Is there an EOC?

- Is the EOC located in an urban, suburban, or rural area?

- Is the EOC in the proximity of a government center (i.e., city hall, county courthouse, State capitol, etc.)?

- Do government executives/key officials have rapid access to the EOC?

- Are additional government personnel readily available to augment the EOC should the emergency escalate beyond the capability of the on-duty EOC team?

- Is the EOC in a centrally located site allowing rapid response to all parts of the jurisdiction?

- Is the EOC in an area that avoids congestion (i.e., transportation chokepoints such as inadequate thoroughfares, bridges, etc.) or debris from collapsing buildings?

- Is the EOC located in a facility that has structural integrity? Is the EOC located in an area where it can quickly be secured?

- Is the EOC located in a known high-risk area; e.g., floods, earthquakes, nuclear power plant, Hazardous Material (HAZMAT) sites, etc? If yes, explain. Are there any plans to mitigate risk?

- Is the EOC located near an adequate road network for ease of access?

- Is the EOC located in a building (basement, ground floor, upper floor) or below grade in a "shelter"?

- Is the building/shelter housing the EOC close to or set back from a tree line?

- Does the building/shelter have adequate parking? Is the parking available in a parking lot or garage (above or below ground)?

- Does the building/shelter have space to accommodate a helicopter landing pad? Is the surrounding area sufficiently clear of obstructions to allow a helicopter to approach and land?

- Is the EOC in a Government owned or leased facility?

- Does the EOC occupy its own building/shelter or does it share a building/shelter with another organization; e.g., State or local police headquarters, emergency medical services facility, National Guard armory, commercial building?

- Is the EOC space dedicated (set aside and configured for EOC use only) or multiuse (not dedicated)? (Multi-use space is usually an office, administrative, or conference area that is used for day-to-day functions and can be made available to support emergency response and management operations. Typically, the day-to-day staff are displaced to another location.)
- Is the EOC one large room or is it a complex; i.e., several rooms that collectively comprise the EOC?
- Does the EOC have space, whether in one large room or complex of rooms, for an operations area (to perform emergency response and management functions), conference/media room (for meetings and press briefings), communications room (for centralized facsimiles, radios, and video teleconferencing [VTC]), and secure communications (secure voice, facsimile, and VTC)?
- Does the EOC have a dedicated Operations Room? Is the space adequate to support the emergency response and EOC staff?
- Does the EOC have a dedicated conference/media room(s)? Is the conference room size adequate to support meetings and media briefings? Can the conference room be physically separated/isolated from the operations area so that media briefings do not interfere with on-going operations?
- Does the EOC have a dedicated communications room/center? Is the size of the communications room/center adequate to support EOC communications requirements?
- Does the EOC have a secure communications room? Is the space adequate to support cleared EOC staff and secure communications requirements?
- Does the EOC have designated multi-use space? Is the size of this space adequate to support expanded operations? Is the space readily available?
- Can the EOC support augmenting staff from Other Federal or State Agencies in a major disaster or surge situation?
- If not, can it be reconfigured or are there plans to provide the necessary space?

Alternate EOC

- Is there and Alternate EOC? Is the Alternate EOC located in an urban, suburban, or rural area?
- Is the Alternate EOC in the proximity of a government center (i.e., city hall, county courthouse, State capitol, etc.)?
- Do government executives/key officials have rapid access to the Alternate EOC?
- Are additional government personnel readily available to augment the Alternate EOC should the emergency escalate beyond the capability of the on-duty EOC team?
- Is the Alternate EOC in a centrally located site allowing rapid response to all parts of the jurisdiction?
- Is the Alternate EOC in an area that avoids congestion (i.e., transportation chokepoints such as inadequate thoroughfares, bridges, etc.) or debris from collapsing buildings?
- Is the Alternate EOC located in a facility that has structural integrity? Is the Alternate EOC located in an area where it can quickly be secured?
- Is the Alternate EOC located in a known high-risk area; e.g., floods, earthquakes, nuclear power plant, Hazardous Material (HAZMAT) sites, etc? If yes, explain. Are there any plans to mitigate risk?
- Is the Alternate EOC located near an adequate road network for ease of access?
- Is the Alternate EOC located in a building (basement, ground floor, upper floor) or below grade in a "shelter"?
- Is the building/shelter housing the Alternate EOC close to or set back from a tree line?
- Does the building/shelter have adequate parking? Is the parking available in a parking lot or garage (above or below ground)?
- Does the building/shelter have space to accommodate a helicopter landing pad? Is the surrounding area sufficiently clear of obstructions to allow a helicopter to approach and land?
- Is the Alternate EOC in a Government owned or leased facility?

- Does the Alternate EOC occupy its own building/shelter or does it share a building/shelter with another organization; e.g., State or local police headquarters, emergency medical services facility, National Guard armory, commercial building?

- Is the Alternate EOC space dedicated (set aside and configured for Alternate EOC use only) or multiuse (not dedicated)? (Multi-use space is usually an office, administrative, or conference area that is used for day-to-day functions and can be made available to support emergency response and management operations. Typically, the day-to-day staff are displaced to another location.)

- Is the Alternate EOC one large room or is it a complex; i.e., several rooms that collectively comprise the Alternate EOC?

- Does the Alternate EOC have space, whether in one large room or complex of rooms, for an operations area (to perform emergency response and management functions), conference/media room (for meetings and press briefings), communications room (for centralized facsimiles, radios, and video teleconferencing [VTC]), and secure communications (secure voice, facsimile, and VTC)?

- Does the Alternate EOC have a dedicated Operations Room? Is the space adequate to support the emergency response and EOC staff?

- Does the Alternate EOC have a dedicated conference/media room(s)? Is the conference room size adequate to support meetings and media briefings? Can the conference room be physically separated/isolated from the operations area so that media briefings do not interfere with on-going operations?

- Does the Alternate EOC have a dedicated communications room/center? Is the size of the communications room/center adequate to support EOC communications requirements?

- Does the Alternate EOC have a secure communications room? Is the space adequate to support cleared EOC staff and secure communications requirements?

- Does the Alternate EOC have designated multi-use space? Is the size of this space adequate to support expanded operations? Is the space readily available?

- Can the Alternate EOC support augmenting staff from Other Federal or State Agencies in a major disaster or surge situation?

- If not, can it be reconfigured or are there plans to provide the necessary space?

SURVIVABILITY

Survivability—sustain the effects of a realized potential risk and continue operations from the EOC or a fully-capable alternate location; (e.g., have an alternate EOC that can be activated and used if the primary is destroyed, damaged, or not accessible).

Primary EOC

- Is the EOC located in a known high-risk area; e.g., floods, earthquakes, nuclear power plant, Hazardous Material (HAZMAT) sites, etc?

- Can the EOC survive the effects of relevant risks; e.g., natural and manmade hazards? Does the EOC have special structural capabilities that improve its survivability?

- Does the EOC have a collective protection system for Chemical, Biological, Radiological, or Nuclear (CBRN) agents?

- Does the EOC have protection from blast effects? Is the EOC above the ground floor, on the ground floor, or below grade?

Alternate EOC

- Is there an Alternate EOC location identified to assure continuity of operations (COOP)?

- Is the Alternate EOC located in a known high-risk area; e.g., floods, earthquakes, nuclear power plant, HAZMAT sites, etc?

- Can the Alternate EOC survive the effects of relevant risks; e.g., natural and manmade hazards?

- Does the Alternate EOC have special structural capabilities that improve its survivability?

- Does the Alternate EOC have a collective protection system for Chemical, Biological, Radiological, or Nuclear (CBRN) agents?

- Does the Alternate EOC have protection from blast effects? Is the Alternate EOC above the ground floor, on the ground floor, or below grade?

SECURITY

Security—guard against potential risks and protect operations from the unauthorized disclosure of sensitive information; (e.g., have sufficient security and structural integrity to protect the facility, its occupants, and communications equipment and systems from relevant threats and hazards).

Facility

- Is the EOC/Alternate EOC located in an urban, suburban, or rural location?

- Are physical security measures (barriers, security cameras, etc) presently used in the EOC/Alternate EOC and are these existing security features adequate?

- What security features, such as access controls, barriers, secure areas, and surveillance devices, are required?

- How is access to the EOC/Alternate EOC controlled? Is a badge or card-swipe system in use? Is it adequate to control access to the facility? Is it adequate to control access within the facility?

- Does appropriate staff have 24-hours access to the facility?

- Are there any access control systems (card access, elevators, lock-out stairwells) that, if non-operational, could preclude access to the facility? If yes, what alternate plans are in place to ensure access?

- Can security capabilities be increased commensurate with higher threat levels (e.g., additional barriers, increased surveillance, additional guards)?

- Can areas where classified and/or unclassified but sensitive information is discussed be isolated from unauthorized/uncleared individuals?

- Does the EOC/Alternate EOC have an existing secure communications area/room? Does it meet FEMA-provided security requirements? Is the size (square footage) of the room adequate?
- How is access to an existing secure communications area controlled? Are existing controls adequate?

Communications/Networks

- Do Local Area Networks (LAN) used in support of emergency operations have adequate protection against cyber attack (e.g., unauthorized access, denial of service, or malicious code)? If not, what capabilities are needed?
- Do State Wide Area Networks (WAN) used in support of emergency operations have adequate protection against cyber attack (e.g., unauthorized access, denial of service, or malicious code)? If not, what capabilities are needed?
- Do you have a secure voice capability? If so, is it adequate to support you emergency operations needs?
- Do non-secure telephones have a privacy feature?
- Do you have a secure facsimile capability? If so, is it adequate to support your emergency operations needs?
- Are radio communications protected; i.e., encrypted or have privacy features?

Personnel

- Are personnel with security clearances required?
- Are there at least five (5) personnel with security clearances?
- Are cleared personnel trained to:
  - Use secure communications equipment?
  - Control and protect classified material?
  - Manage and control communications security (COMSEC)?
- Are individuals with a security clearance identified (e.g., unique marking on ID badge, recognition)?

SUSTAINABILITY

Sustainability—support operations for extended durations; (e.g., be able to sustain operations 24/7 during all emergency situations without interruption; to the extent practical, be located in a place that is not a high-risk area for known hazards, such as flood zone, other natural hazard, nuclear power plant, hazardous material sites, etc.).

Facility

- Can the EOC/Alternate EOC support operations 24 hour a day/7 days a week for an extended period of time? Are operational and administrative supplies adequate to sustain operations; e.g., food, water, fuel for backup generators, paper products, office supplies, etc?
- Does the EOC/Alternate EOC have backup power? (Backup power typically refers to generator power.)
- Does the EOC/Alternate EOC have an uninterruptible power supply (UPS)? (UPS units typically use batteries to provide power for a limited duration; e.g., 10–20 minutes depending on the load.) If yes, what systems/functions does the UPS support? Is the duration of the UPS adequate to support these systems/functions until the backup power to comes on line?
- Are Heating, Ventilation, and Air Conditioning (HVAC) systems centrally (building-wide) or locally managed?
- Are HVAC systems available and controllable 24-hours a day, seven days a week (24x7)?
- Does the EOC/Alternate EOC have access to support areas; e.g., file rooms, server sites, and the like?
- Are there any special constraints that must be met to sustain operations? Special access needs?
- Does the Alternate EOC have the same capabilities as the primary location? If not, what are the differences?

Communications/Networks

- Is the number of telephones, secure or non-secure, adequate for the EOC/Alternate EOC to conduct emergency response and management operations?

- Are telephones connected to an in-house Private Branch Exchange (PBX)?

- Are telephones connected directly to a local commercial carrier; i.e., draw dial tone from the local switch rather then from the PBX? (These telephones are just like those found in a home or office. The advantage is that if the EOC/Alternate EOC loses power to the PBX, telephones connected directly to the dial central office will continue to function.)

- Is the number of facsimiles, secure and non-secure, adequate to conduct emergency response operations?

- Does the EOC/Alternate EOC have dedicated transmit and receive facsimiles? Does the EOC/Alternate EOC have a secure facsimile capability?

- Is the number of printers adequate for the EOC/Alternate EOC to conduct emergency response operations?

INTEROPERABILITY

Interoperability—share common principles of operations and exchange routine and time-sensitive information with local jurisdictions, State-level EOCs, and FEMA's network of operations centers; (e.g. be able to communicate with key State agencies, local government EOCs, emergency response teams at or near an incident site, near-by State EOCs, and Federal authorities to include the FEMA Regional Operations Center (ROC) as well as the FEMA Operations Center).

Communications

- Does the EOC/Alternate have a requirement to monitor the communications of key emergency services; e.g., police, fire, emergency medical services (EMS), HAZMAT, and public works? Is there a requirement to monitor the communications of other services? If yes, does the capability exist and is it adequate?

- Does the EOC/Alternate have a requirement to establish an emergency communications network that includes the key emergency services and local EOCs/jurisdictions? If yes, does the capability exist and is it adequate?

- If a requirement exists, can the EOC/Alternate EOC communicate with the following entities:
    1. Local EOCs throughout the State?
    2. FEMA ROC and/or FEMA Regional Staff?
    3. Federal Disaster Field Office (DFO)?
    4. EOC/Alternate EOC of other States?
    5. Operations centers of State-level emergency services organizations?
    6. Incident Commander or incident site command post?
    7. Operations centers of regional and local airport, highway, port, and waterway authorities; hospitals and ambulance service providers; nuclear power plants; dams; private sector utilities (power, telephone, sewerage, and water) and chemical companies?
- Are the EOC/Alternate EOC communications means adequate to satisfy communications requirements? (Consider radios, telephones, cell phones, available frequency spectrum, and other issues.)

Procedures

- Do the State and local government EOCs/Alternate EOCs have common operations, reporting, and communications procedures that will be used during the response to and management of an All Hazards event?
- If the EOC/Alternate EOC has a requirement to exchange information with local EOCs/jurisdictions and key emergency services; e.g., police, fire, EMS, HAZMAT, and public works, are there procedures/checklists in place to facilitate the exchange?
- If required, are scheduled reports assembled and disseminated?

Training

- Do the State and local government EOCs/Alternate EOCs conduct routine, recurring, or periodic joint communications training to exercise the communications capabilities that will be used during the response to and management of an All Hazards event?

- If conducted, are the results of joint communications training maintained in a "lessons learned" document and used to improve communications operations? Are the results also used to identify communications deficiencies and develop solutions that correct the deficiencies and improve communications capabilities?

- Do the State and local government EOCs/Alternate EOCs conduct routine, recurring, or periodic joint training exercises to practice, test, and refine their common operations, reporting, and communications procedures?

- If conducted, are the results of joint training maintained in a "lessons learned" document and used to improve common procedures?

- Are actual experiences used to validate existing or create new common procedures?

FLEXIBILITY

Flexibility—scale operations and adapt operational pace to the All Hazards event (e.g., have sufficient space, equipment, furniture, administrative supplies, and the like available to satisfy mission requirements).

Facility

Primary EOC

- Is space dedicated for an EOC? If not, does the EOC occupy space within another organization's facility; e.g., State or local police headquarters, emergency medical services facility, National Guard armory, commercial building?

- Whether dedicated or shared, is the square footage available for the EOC adequate to conduct emergency response operations?

- Is the EOC operational only when emergency response and management operations are being conducted? Or, is the EOC operational 24x7 (staff and capabilities are present and active) whether or not emergency response operations are being conducted?

- Are there activation, layout, and setup procedures for the EOC?
- Can EOC activation and operations be tailored to the scale of emergency response activities? (For example, a small-scale event might require the activation of fewer staff and capabilities, and the conduct of limited emergency response operations; a large-scale event, the activation of all staff and capabilities, and the conduct of extensive emergency response operations.)
- Have the conditions that would cause the EOC to be relocated been identified? Are there procedures for relocating from the EOC?
- Are EOC activation and relocation exercises held periodically? Is the level of participation by member agencies sufficient to ensure an efficient and timely activation during actual events? Do participants include key personnel assigned to the EOC?
- Is there a dedicated conference/media room in the general vicinity of the EOC? Is the square footage adequate?
- Is there multi-use space available in the general vicinity of the EOC?
- Is the square footage adequate? (Multi-use space is usually an office, administrative, or conference area that is used for day-to-day functions and can be made available to support emergency response and management operations. Typically, the day-to-day staff are displaced to another location.)

Alternate EOC

- Is there an Alternate EOC identified and established to ensure COOP for emergency response operations?
- Is space dedicated for an Alternate EOC? If not, does the Alternate EOC occupy space within another organization's facility; e.g., State or local police headquarters, emergency medical services facility, National Guard armory, commercial building?
- Whether dedicated or shared, is the square footage available for the Alternate EOC adequate to conduct emergency response operations?

- Are there activation, layout, and setup procedures for the Alternate EOC?

- Can Alternate EOC activation and operations be tailored to the scale of emergency response activities?

- Have conditions been identified that would cause the Alternate EOC to be activated rather than the primary EOC?

- Does the Alternate EOC have the same capabilities as the primary EOC? If not, what are the differences?

- Are Alternate EOC activation exercises held periodically? Is the level of participation by member agencies sufficient to ensure an efficient and timely activation during actual events? Do participants include key personnel assigned to the Alternate EOC?

- Is there a dedicated conference/media room in the general vicinity of the Alternate EOC? Is the square footage adequate?

- Is there multi-use space available in the general vicinity of the Alternate EOC? Is the square footage adequate?

Communications/Networks

- Is the number of computers available in the EOC/Alternate EOC and any multi-use space adequate to support emergency response operations?

- Is the number of servers adequate to support emergency response operations?

- Is the number of telephones, both secure and non-secure, available in the EOC/Alternate EOC and any multi-use space adequate to support emergency response operations?

- Do the EOC/Alternate EOC and any multi-use space have telephones that are connected to a local dial central office? (These telephones are just like those found in a home or office. The advantage is that if the EOC/Alternate EOC loses power to the PBX, telephones connected directly to the dial central office will continue to function.)

- Do any telephones have a:
  - Recording capability?

- Caller ID capability?
- Voice conferencing capability?

- Is the number of printers available in the EOC/Alternate EOC and any multi-use space adequate to support emergency response operations?

- Is the number of facsimiles available in the EOC/Alternate EOC and any multi-use space adequate to support emergency response operations?

- Do the EOC/Alternate EOC and any multi-use space have the capability to display video? If yes, do they also have the capability to distribute audio associated with the video display?

- Do the EOC/Alternate EOC and any multi-use space have a video teleconferencing (VTC) capability?

- Do the EOC/Alternate EOC and any multi-use space have the capability to receive public (intercom) announcements?

- Can the telecommunications capability be configured to support the scale of emergency response and management activities?

CHAPTER 6

The Press, Friend and Foe

A disaster creates a unique and difficult public and political environment, a volatile mix of public expectation and extensive coverage of every decision that may have large and sometimes complex consequences that are not just local in their effects. It is literally a minefield where a misstep can have not just political consequences but economic and even physical ones.

Political decisions will have operational consequences. In New York after 9/11, as rescue operations continued on the wreckage of the World Trade Center towers, the mayor's advisors recommended a shift from rescue to recovery operations. The timing of this decision can certainly be argued from both sides, but the decision nonetheless created a political firestorm.

Firefighters and police officers were shown on television across the country protesting the change in the direction of the operations. By changing to recovery there would be fewer personnel working on the wreckage to recover remains, and this angered the firefighters and police officers who felt it was tantamount to giving up all hope for friends and relatives still missing in the wreckage. The media covered their protest with the usual second-guessing by a long line of "experts." The mayor quickly reversed his decision, and rescue operations were resumed. It had been an operational decision based on a number of factors, but the decision to reverse the initial decision was a political one based on the public outcry. An operational decision was based on public perception and political problems that were simply not needed at that point in the response.

Another example happened during Hurricane Hugo in South Carolina. After the storm, ice was being delivered by truck to various neighborhoods in Charleston. In one neighborhood when the truck showed up the residents swarmed it, desperate after days without water or ice. Unable to control the crowds, the police department had to leave the truck and deliver the ice to another neighborhood.

As it turned out, the ice was taken from a poor neighborhood and delivered to an affluent one. The local paper discovered the story and reported that relief supplies were being delivered to the more affluent neighborhoods instead of equally throughout the city. This created a local political firestorm. The better neighborhoods were being given preferential treatment over the poorer ones. A disparity in the delivery of desperately needed supplies to the public colored the response for some time and had to be dealt with repeatedly. A simple operational decision, not done deliberately, well away from the spotlight can suddenly emerge to create a serious problem. This is a prime example of actions in the field during a disaster that have unintended political and public-perception consequences.

THE REALITY OF THE PRESS

Like it or not, want it or not, the press is the most direct and effective way to communicate to the public during a disaster. While there are other avenues now with social media, nothing is as personal and effective as being seen or heard by the local population on local media. Visuals of local officials talking to the citizens they represent are powerful and not easily replaced; people want to see and hear their leaders during a crisis.

An example of the power of being perceived to be a champion of your constituents comes again from Hurricane Hugo. I had been sent to interview the local officials to learn as much as I could about the lessons that were learned during the hurricane by the public-safety agencies. As I was checking into my hotel, the bellhop who happened to be helping me with my bags asked why I was visiting. When I told him it was to learn from his officials, his face brightened and he began to regale me with tales of how great a mayor the city had because he had stood up to state and federal officials to make sure his city received the help they needed.

Now remember that this occurred close to three years after the storm had struck, yet this young man was just as excited and proud as if the storm had only just taken place. The man who was mayor at that time is still the mayor as of this writing; his actions during Hugo created a long legacy. The constituents want to see and hear their leaders during a disaster, and the press is the best and most personal way to accomplish that goal.

UNDERSTAND THE MEDIA'S JOB

I have listened to elected officials rail against the media in private as if they simply refused to accept the role they play in our democracy. The press by definition is supposed to be the unbiased watchdog for the public. The skill and integrity with which reporters accomplish this role can certainly be argued; nonetheless, it is their role. They are not there to be a cheering squad for your actions. If you simply understand this and plan for it, you can to a certain extent manipulate the kind of coverage you receive by viewing events from their perspective and being prepared and proactive in your response.

Reporters and announcers also have another role that needs to be clearly stated: a duty to report the facts you need to reach the public, such as evacuation notifications or shelter openings. These facts need to be broadcast in a timely and accurate fashion, and you have a right to expect as much. If they make a mistake, you can expect them to correct it as soon as possible.

During one of the hurricanes that struck Florida in 2004 the local media incorrectly reported which schools were opened as shelters, and this was causing quite a bit of confusion for those of us running the shelters and for the public. This is a small example but nonetheless an important one. Be able to call the media outlet and have the report corrected as soon as possible. You need to develop a working relationship prior to an event. Use the media or it will use you. Call to check in even when there is no big news to make sure reporters and news announcers feel as if you understand their job and are trying to assist them.

WHAT THE PUBLIC WANTS

The public will judge the effectiveness of your response to the disaster by the speed with which you are able to deliver valuable information that helps to cope with the effects of the disaster. Citizens need to know that the people they have elected have put together a response that is managing the disaster as quickly and efficiently as possible and giving them information they can use to cope with it.

They need to be able to trust the information they receive and get it in time to be able to use it. If they receive information too late, they will begin to distrust those who have given it to them. Information needs to get to the public in time for them to use it and to act as you need them to do. They need a straightforward and clear message from those in authority. This message needs to be simple and actionable:

- They want to know that you are on top of the situation. By appearing as early as possible the public perceives you as competent and prepared to deal with the situation.

- They want information as soon as possible. They want information that can help them cope with the situation and to make their own decisions about steps they can take to make their family safer or more comfortable.

- They want a clear and consistent message from authorities. There can be no competing among jurisdictions. Should multiple local jurisdictions hold separate news conferences releasing differing information, it will only serve to lower the public's confidence in their leadership. If the public perceives a struggle or disconnect among the people they elected to lead their communities, it will lose confidence in local government's ability to manage the situation.

- They want to know immediately when progress is made.

- They want a consistent message.

MANAGING THE BEAST

The reason you are speaking to the press is to reach the public; craft your releases to reflect the fact that you accept the public as your partner. If you can communicate what people need to hear and what you need them to do, then you make them a partner in the response—not just an unwilling mob but a partner. Be sure to address the specific concerns of the public as directly as possible.

Lead with an expression of sympathy for those most affected by the disaster. By leading with your understanding that many in the community have been dramatically affected you will show that you have their interest uppermost in your mind. The public needs to know the whole response is directed at making people's lives return to normal as soon as possible and that you understand what they have already gone through.

Be frank, open, and honest. If you are asked a question that you do not know the answer to, simply state that you don't have that answer at hand but you will investigate and get back to the press with the answer. This may happen frequently, especially early in the disaster. The press will be asking questions that you do not have an answer to because it is too early in the response to have such an understanding of the situation. A prime example is a public information officer at a major fire. Time and again you will hear the press asking what caused the fire. Behind the spokesperson you can still see the fire roaring out of control, yet they ask the question long before an investigation can even begin, much less have an answer. Just answer that it is too early to know and that you will have that answer later.

Meet the needs of the press. Reporters have deadlines for stories. They have to have something to turn in, or they will not have a job for very long. If you do not give them something, they will find someone who will. That someone more often than not turns out to be the one citizen with a gripe about how they are not being taken care of or an unofficial source with an axe to grind about the response. Feed the press or they will find somewhere else to eat, and you can almost guarantee that you will not like what they report.

Concern for people must come first. Make sure you address the public's distress and loss in any and all of your interviews. People must feel as if their interests are uppermost in your mind. While everything you are doing out of the view of the cameras and microphones is based on their needs, they do not know this. You have to state it again and again for that message to get across.

Don't deny the obvious by trying to minimize the seriousness of the disaster or tragedy. Always express the seriousness of the situation and the fact that the whole of the community response and administrative apparatus is hard at work to respond and restore the community to normal as quickly as possible. Repeat this message every time you get the opportunity. Remember that during any disaster not everyone in your community is listening every time you speak; it can take some time for everyone to hear your mantra.

Never pick a fight with the media. They report every day, and you won't have the opportunity to get in front of the media every day. If reporters are adversarial, manage it with facts and correct them with simple answers filled with the best information available.

There are no secrets. Assume that anything you say will be news. Just because you said something off the record does not mean that it will not be printed or broadcast. The simple rule is that if you don't want it out, do not tell a reporter.

Don't assume anything. Do not assume that the reporter you are talking to is well versed in your profession and understands the intricacies of a response. Make sure she understands what you are saying, or she might report your statement through the filter of a lack of understanding. Their job is reporting, not emergency response.

Keep it simple. Not matter how complex the situation, simplify and summarize your major points more than once. Write important data and facts down in handouts; do not depend on the reporters to take accurate notes. Do not use technical terms no matter how easily understood you might think they are to anyone listening. And no acronyms.

Treat reporters professionally. Treat them with respect and hopefully they will treat you the same way. Always answer a call immediately, and make sure they have a number that allows them to reach you with important or controversial questions. Make yourself as accessible as possible.

Don't lie. No matter how bad a situation might be, do not lie about it. Don't share opinions or views with the press; stick to the facts. Not knowing all the facts, no matter how "bad" they are, is worse for those hanging on your every word than understanding what they are facing. The fear of panic by those in power is a false one. Time and again the public has responded in a reasoned and cooperative fashion. In New York after 9/11, in spite of what appeared to be a catastrophic event, perhaps only the beginning of the attacks, the public began to calmly walk out of the city as directed. There was no panicked crush of people clamoring to cross the bridges; instead you saw people helping one another and assisting those who needed to evacuate. The fear of public panic is an overstated and to a large extent unproven one, that flies in the face of documented incident after incident of people helping people during a disaster.

Don't tell people not to worry. They know things are bad; they just don't know how bad or how long the situation is going to last. The public does not have all the information that you do to put the situation in context. There is plenty to worry about and will be for some time. The best strategy is to acknowledge their concerns and fears and assure them that everyone on the response team is working to address the problems facing the community.

Never promise anything that you are not positive you can deliver. No matter what you want to happen, make absolutely sure that your team is going to be able to deliver the promised results. Whether it is street clearing, ice or water deliveries, or the restoration of power, know with certainty before you say that you are going to be able to deliver. If you promise something and you are not able to deliver, that will break any trust the public has in you and the response. They will remember the broken promise long after the community has been returned to normal.

Before any interview ask what the interview is about, establish what you can and cannot discuss at this time, and stick to it. Choose your words carefully, because they will be reported and used in a story. If a bad story gets into the media, it is too late to correct it. Address their questions—you might as well get your side of the story into the mix. If possible, use facts from official or authoritative sources to counter bad stories. Try to anticipate the interview questions and have ready answers with facts to back them up. Release only information you have verified before the interview. If they do ask you something you are not prepared to answer, then tell them you will have to get back to them with the answer. Make sure you do get back to them.

Escort the press everywhere. Do not allow reporters to wander around the disaster site unescorted. This can lead to misinterpretations as they view operations without understanding the entire situation. Simply walking up to a disaster scene can give a false impression, since you are only viewing a small portion of the operation. To really understand what is happening, you must understand the situation as a whole.

Make sure you have a trained and designated a public information officer who can be your first line of contact. Since the press is his primary job, he will be invaluable in tracking and managing its representatives as time goes on and operations become more complex. Work with the press officer to establish a schedule to contact the press with new or updated information.

Use prescripted notifications and news releases. Prior to any event one of the many official actions you can get off your plate prior to the event are notifications and press releases that you know you will need. You will need to work with your jurisdiction's attorneys to make sure the language meets local and state laws. With their help you can have these releases ready for signing long before they are needed. It will save time and discussion at the beginning of the disaster when you have many issues competing for your time and attention. A number of these standard releases are included here.

SAMPLE NOTIFICATION OF OUTSIDE AGENCIES

Notify (FBI, CDC, ATF, Coast Guard, EPA, FAA, FBI, FEMA, National Guard, State Police, State EOC)

This is the City of Centerville be advised we have just experienced an explosion at the Federal Building that is a possible terrorist event. We are currently responding with local assets but will be requesting state and Federal assistance as soon as we can determine our specific needs.

We are requesting that you stand by until we have more detailed information.

SAMPLE PRESS RELEASE

State of Emergency

This is Bill Smith Emergency Manager of Center County at the Emergency Operations Center. At 0800 hours today the County Chairman Jones declared a State of Emergency. This State of Emergency was declared in order for the City to be able to qualify for the outside help it needs to manage this emergency. By doing this the Chairman Jones will be able to request the Governor and the Federal Government for assistance in the days and weeks ahead. At this time it is unknown how long this Declaration will need to be in place but the Chairman Jones would like to assure every citizen of Center County that this Declaration will only be in place until this emergency is under control.

Note: underlined text is for example only. Blank copies of these examples and more types of press releases can be found in Chapter 11 Resources.

SAMPLE PRESS RELEASE
Curfew

Whereas, the City of <u>Centerville</u> has experienced a <u>tornado</u> resulting in the wide spread damage, death and injuries to our community.

Whereas the services to City residences, power, water, and other utilities have been disrupted; and

Whereas it is in the public interest and for the safety of the community, that a reasonable restriction be placed on the use of streets until such time as the consequences of the <u>tornado</u> have been stabilized; and

Whereas in order to protect, preserve and promote the general health and welfare and safety of the community and it citizens it is necessary that a curfew be established to restrict the use of the street of the County/City during this emergency.

Now therefore, I <u>Mayor Robert Johnson</u> and Chief executive officer of <u>Centerville</u> in furtherance of public health, safety and welfare do hereby declare a state of emergency to exist and do further declare and require, in the interest of safety to persons and property that the streets of the City be hereby closed to the general public for travel both vehicular and pedestrian, for the hours of <u>6:00 pm to 6:00 am</u>.

Note: underlined text is for example only. Blank copies of these examples and more types of press releases can be found in Chapter 11 Resources.

SAMPLE PRESS RELEASE

Isolation

Whereas, the City of <u>Centerville</u> has experienced an outbreak of <u>Swine Flu</u> resulting in the death and illness of a number of it's citizens.

Whereas the health and well being of those not infected could be jeopardized by public contact.

Whereas it is in the public interest and for the safety of the community, that a reasonable restriction be placed on public contact until such time as the epidemic has been controlled and public contact is again without infectious risk; and

Whereas in order to protect, preserve and promote the general health and welfare and safety of the community and it citizens it is necessary that area of isolation be established to restrict travel into and out of the designated area (s) during this emergency.

Now therefore, I <u>Mayor Robert Johnson</u> of the City of <u>Centerville</u> in furtherance of public health, safety and welfare do hereby declare a state of emergency to exist and do further declare and require, in the interest of safety to persons in <u>Centerville</u> and those within the State that all roads into and out of an area bounded by <u>Smith and Princeton, Harvard and Yale, Edgewater, and North Trail</u> be closed to all modes of transportation both vehicular, pedestrian, rail or air are hereby prohibited until further notice.

Note: underlined text is for example only. Blank copies of these examples and more types of press releases can be found in Chapter 11 Resources.

SAMPLE PRESS RELEASE

Public Gatherings

This is <u>Joan Smith the Public Information Officer</u> of Center County at the Emergency Operations Center. At <u>8:00 am</u> today the <u>County Chairwoman Louise Johnson</u> in consultation with the State and CDC have banned all public gatherings and are closing all businesses. Given the outbreak of <u>Swine Flu</u> and its' continued spread through the citizens of <u>Center County</u>, the <u>Chairwoman Johnson</u> has taken this step to try and stop the spread of this terrible disease. The Chairwoman and the County Council do not take this step lightly and understand the impact it will have on the community but it is an absolutely necessary step to stop the spread of this disease.

Anyone found to violate this ban will be arrested and placed in quarantine until it can be determined if they have been exposed to <u>Swine Flu</u>. The <u>Chairwoman Johnson</u> would urge everyone to heed this ban. It is the only way this terrible epidemic can be stopped. This is only a temporary measure and will be lifted as soon as possible. The <u>Chairwoman Johnson</u> would urge every citizen to heed this ban.

Note: underlined text is for example only. Blank copies of these examples and more types of press releases can be found in Chapter 11 Resources.

SAMPLE PRESS RELEASE
Quarantine

This is Public Information Officer Robert Smith of the City of Johnsonville at the Emergency Operations Center. At 8:00 am today the Mayor Patricia Johnson has ordered the quarantine of the City of Johnsonville. The epidemic of Bird Flu that has occurred here cannot be allowed to spread to other cities and counties in the State. In an effort to stem the tide of Flu cases the Mayor Johnson in close consultation with the Governor and the Center for Disease Control have taken this step.

No one will be allowed to enter or leave the City by any means of transportation. The roads in and out of the City will be blocked. No bus traffic will be allowed in City or out of the City. The airport is closed to all traffic immediately. This quarantine will remain in effect until the epidemic is stopped. The Mayor Johnson would urge every citizen to remain calm and to listen carefully to the media for updates over the next days.

Note: underlined text is for example only. Blank copies of these examples and more types of press releases can be found in Chapter 11 Resources.

SAMPLE PRESS RELEASE

Hurricane
Prestorm Instructions

Our community is under a Hurricane Warning for Hurricane <u>Marion</u> is a Category <u>4</u> hurricane with winds up to <u>140</u> miles per hour and a storm surge of <u>15 feet</u>.

If you live in the following evacuation zones <u>Pleasant Beach, West Beach, South Beach</u> you are ordered to evacuate. Consult your local newspaper, our web page, or the local media for the evacuation routes and traffic status of those routes.

The following areas <u>Zuma, the City of Pleasant Beach Shores</u> are under a voluntary evacuation order and anyone living in those areas are urged to evacuate. Hurricane <u>Marion</u> is a dangerous storm.

Consult your hurricane guide in the local newspaper or on our Hurricane <u>Marion</u> web site. Sign up for hurricane updates from the Department of Emergency Management on our Twitter site <u>Twitter @ beachcountyema</u>.

The <u>Beach County</u> office of emergency management has the following recommendations.

1. Have at least a seven-day supply of nonperishable food.
2. Have at least a seven-day supply of water, a minimum of two gallons a day per person.
3. Have a portable radio with batteries.
4. Have a flashlight with extra batteries.
5. Gather all medications and keep them with you at all times even if you move to a shelter.
6. Have a first-aid kit with you.
7. If you decide not to evacuate, move to an interior section of your house, preferably an interior bathroom.
8. Make sure you have a full tank of gas in your car.

Please stay tuned to the emergency broadcast system on radio channel 98.9 for future updates.

Note: underlined text is for example only. Blank copies of these examples and more types of press releases can be found in Chapter 11 Resources.

SAMPLE PRESS RELEASE

Post Hurricane Landfall

Hurricane <u>Marion</u> made landfall in this area a short time ago. Fire, law-enforcement, and EMS crews are fully staffed and working. In order to ensure the public safety, fire and EMS officials ask that you follow the following instructions:

1. Stay tuned to any radio or TV station that is still broadcasting.

2. Stay indoors until your receive an all-clear from police, fire, or community emergency management.

3. Do not drink water from the tap without boiling it for the next 72 hours or until you are told that it is safe to drink by authorities.

4. Do not touch fallen or hanging wires of any kind under any circumstances, whether on the ground, hanging free, or attached to an object.

5. Do not call to report individual interruptions in electric or phone service.

6. Do not call 911 for information on the storm; instead call the hurricane hot line at <u>612-555-1234</u> for information. Only call 911 for life-threatening emergencies.

Please stay calm; local, state, and federal response teams are on the way.

Note: underlined text is for example only. Blank copies of these examples and more types of press releases can be found in Chapter 11 Resources.

ADDITIONAL PRESS RELEASE

Hurricane Language That May Be Considered if Your Jurisdiction Takes a Direct Hit From a Storm

If you or someone in your family or neighborhood is in need of emergency medical assistance, it will be available at all shelters. If you need assistance removing victims from debris or reaching injured persons, go to the nearest major intersection. Police and fire-department units are making their way to these locations as quickly as possible.

Be aware that after a storm there are many unusual hazards such as chemicals leaking from storage containers, downed power lines, broken water mains, or open sewage drainage. Stay away from these hazards and report them to any police, firefighters, or other city/county workers you see.

Use caution in filling portable generators and using small tools such as power saws. Be sure to allow the motor to cool before refilling with gasoline. The hot motor casing could ignite gasoline if not allowed to cool.

If you are relocating to an emergency shelter now because of damage to your home, be sure to take medications, toiletries, nonperishable food, pillows, blankets, and other items to make yourself comfortable. Bring enough of these supplies to be comfortable for up to 72 hours.

Public-safety official vehicles and other city/county vehicles will be in the streets doing damage assessment, clearing roads, and making other repairs; if you need assistance, wave a towel or other article of clothing to signal them.

If you need emergency police, fire, or medical assistance, call 911 or 612-555-1678 should the 911 lines be down or busy.

Note: underlined text is for example only. Blank copies of these examples and more types of press releases can be found in Chapter 11 Resources.

CHAPTER 7

The National Incident Management System and the Incident Command System

T he National Incident Management System (NIMS) and the Incident Command System (ICS) are two of the most misunderstood and misinterpreted systems ever produced. I once had an emergency manager tell me that he did not believe in them, as if they were some sort of religious belief. Others question whether their tenets apply to private industry, since private industry uses its own organizational systems to accomplish its specific goals.

The origin of NIMS can be traced back to August 1991 and a report produced by the Office of the Inspector General that identified many of the logistical and response problems associated with the federal management of Hurricane Andrew. The glaring problems could be traced back to a lack of an overarching response plan for all of the various agencies that would need to respond to a catastrophe of that magnitude. This led to the creation in April 1992 of the Federal

Response Plan, which organizes the Emergency Support Functions within the federal government with lead and support agencies for each ESF.

This served as the guide to federal disaster operations until Homeland Security Presidential Directive 5 in 2003 established NIMS as the national standard for all federal, state, and local agencies. It was described as:

> "a consistent nationwide approach for federal, state, tribal, and local governments to work effectively and efficiently together to prepare for, prevent, respond to, and recover from domestic incidents, regardless of cause, size, or complexity."

NIMS is a core set of doctrine, concepts, principles, terminology, and organizational processes that can be applied to all hazards. It strives to provide a national framework that all levels of government, local, state, and federal, can use to respond to all types of disasters. It is not an operational incident-management plan, nor is it a resource-allocation plan, or a terrorism/WMD-specific plan. Nor is it designed to address international events; instead, its aim is to organize domestic responses to all types of major incidents.

Major Components of the National Incident Management System

- **Command and Management**—establishes a consistent organizational structure for all response agencies to use
  - **Incident Command System**—establishes a national tactical incident-management system
  - **Multiagency Coordination System**—a process that allows all levels of government and all disciplines to work together more efficiently and effectively (Multiagency coordination occurs across the different disciplines involved in incident management, across jurisdictional lines, or across levels of government. Multiagency coordination can and does occur on a regular basis whenever personnel from different agencies interact in such activities as preparedness, response, recovery, and mitigation.)
  - **Public Information Systems**—establish protocols and procedures for the coordination and dissemination across agency and governmental lines of authority of timely and accurate public information

---

(continued)

- **Preparedness**
  - planning
  - training and exercises
  - personnel management
  - equipment acquisition
  - mutual aid
  - publications management
- **Resource Management**
  - standardization—establishes consistent typing, inventorying, ordering, and tracking of resources to better manage the flow of equipment and supplies during a disaster
  - mobilization
  - deactivation
  - skills validation

The objective was to provide a common set of doctrines, principles, terminology, and organizational structures that would make responses to major disasters more efficient and more effective. It is not an operational plan or a resource plan; it is the structure to implement those operational plans at the local, state, and national levels. It recognizes that the response begins with and must be responsive to the local level—that is, the people with their feet on the ground trying to directly manage the incident. Its purpose is to provide common command and control structures and procedures to better integrate the needs of those local responders as they move through the system to the federal level.

Area Command is an organization that oversees the management of multiple incidents handled individually by separate incident-command organizations or of a very large or evolving incident engaging multiple incident-management teams. Area Command should not be confused with the functions performed by Multiagency Coordination Systems (MACS), as area command oversees management coordination of the incident(s), while a MACS element (such as a communications/dispatch center, EOC, or MAC group) coordinates support.

The initial concept for ICS goes back to the 1970s and the wildland fire community. As fires became larger and more complex to manage because of the rapid population expansion into what had been open wild lands, a more sophisticated command and control structure was needed. The military also had an influence on the ICS structure, since it is built around a single person in charge with specific people assigned to Administration, Logistics, Planning, and Operations—all roles in any military operation. In designing the ICS structure it was clear that a military system could not be replicated at every level, so a modular organizational structure was developed.

This structure served as a guide for a commander to the size of organization he or she needed to meet the needs of the specific incident. The system has been perfected over the years, and today an organizational structure can be built that can manage the largest wildfires, where thousands of firefighters, hundreds of pieces of equipment, and even aircraft can be brought together quickly and efficiently within days. This concept slowly spread across the country until it was adopted to meet the needs of not only wildfires but all types of fires and hazardous incidents.

NIMS and ICS are no more and no less than modular organizational structures specifically designed for responses to disasters and other types of emergencies. They allow a jurisdiction to build the size and type of organization it needs to manage an unusual event. This organization will be made up of the men and women within that community who have specific skill sets that meet the needs of the various jobs in the NIMS or ICS structures. Using NIMS and ICS does organize your response, but it is not a response plan.

Both are command and control structures that have proven to work in developing the size of organizations to manage all types of emergencies. An organization chart does not respond to the incident. It is who is assigned to each job within that organization, how well they are trained, and how well they understand how to use the structure to implement their decisions. NIMS and ICS simply provide the ability to build the right decision-making structure; they do not guarantee that decisions will be implemented properly; that is determined by the information-processing structures used within NIMS and ICS. So my focus will be on staffing and how to use these organization structures to carry out a response.

NIMS uses ESFs to organize the various capabilities. During a disaster the number and types of problems become so large that individuals must be assigned to specific areas to be able to address the problems appropriately. More simply put, the job is so large that a few people cannot manage all of the issues properly, and the specific tasks must be addressed individually. It can take more than one person to staff any one of the ESFs, and it can take more than one ESF to manage a single problem.

During the 2004 hurricanes that struck Florida I was staffing the ESF #6 desk, mass care. We had so many shelters open that it became necessary to have a shelter meeting that included the Red Cross, the Salvation Army, law-enforcement representatives, the ESF in charge of volunteers and donations, and the public-health representative whose nurses were staffing the special-needs shelters. It is not uncommon for an EOC to have more than a hundred different people working in the room at one time. I am going to make recommendations for who might be best placed in these roles; these recommendations are based on a local, county, or municipality jurisdiction. Obviously at the state or federal level the number and types of people who would be assigned would be a very different matter.

While the following recommendations are examples of who should staff the various desks, they by no means constitute a complete list. Some jurisdictions will have more people to assign, while others may have to combine several ESFs because of their smaller size. The overarching theme here is to build the organization to fit your needs and capabilities, not the organizational chart. The ESFs are a guide to the types of roles and responsibilities that will need to be addressed, but it is not set in stone that every role must be staffed or that it cannot be combined with another when conditions dictate.

EMERGENCY SUPPORT FUNCTIONS

The ESF approach helps you to focus on the basic mechanisms and structures by which you will mobilize resources and conduct activities to augment your response efforts. Under this structure, each ESF is headed by a primary agency, which is selected based on its day-to-day operational capabilities and the resources in a specific area. Other departments may be designated as support for one or more functional areas. The purpose of the ESF model is to allow the jurisdiction to build the size and functionality of the team it needs to manage the disaster no matter its size or type.

The following list of ESFs includes the functions most commonly used by the federal government; many states and jurisdictions have modified the number and responsibilities to meet their needs. I will mention those that have been added to the federal list as examples of the ways NIMS can be adapted to meet the needs of the community. Again, NIMS is a template that can be used to build the organization that best meets a community's needs. This ability to change the organization within the overall structure is one of its strengths.

ESF #1 Transportation

This function coordinates transportation support to federal, state, and local departments; volunteer organizations; and federal agencies requiring transportation to perform disaster assistance missions.

EOC activities include:

- identification of events that need transportation assets and coordination with the on-scene commanders
- overall coordination of transportation assistance to other Emergency Support Functions and volunteer agencies requiring transportation to perform emergency-response missions
- prioritization and/or allocation of all transportation assets
- processing of all transportation requests
- operational coordination of ground, air, and rail service where appropriate
- assistance with the transportation requirements of special-needs populations
- assistance with evacuation of persons in immediate threat or danger
- monitoring, coordination, and control of vehicular traffic flow

Specific activities include:

- assistance in the evacuation of persons who need assistance
- coordination of traffic flow with law enforcement in support of those who self-evacuate and organization of transportation for emergency resources
- transportation of personnel and supplies in support of emergency operations being conducted by the other ESFs
- transportation of relief supplies as they begin to arrive from outside the area

Who should be assigned to ESF #1:

- jurisdiction fleet management
- bus service
- transportation department of local school board

Common incidents include:

- downed trees blocking streets or highway lanes
- roads washed out
- overturned boats
- downed aircraft or aircraft damaged at airport

Common requests include:

- civil air patrol personnel
- civil air patrol aircraft
- tolls lifted
- maps
- transport of all kinds
- official road information
- barricades
- street sweepers
- street and traffic signs
- overweight permits
- bridge inspectors
- structural and civil engineers

ESF #2 Communications

This function coordinates communications support for the incident with other departments and agencies, including volunteer organizations.

ESF #2 is critical for any EOC, but at the local level it is even more important. During my tenure as emergency manager I worked more closely with my jurisdiction's information-systems department than with anyone else. For years we had no standing EOC and had to convert classrooms when needed. It was the information-systems department I contacted first so they could install the computers, build the computer network, and install the phones, projectors, and other communications equipment we would need to make a bare room into a working EOC. Because these people deal with a jurisdiction's most critical records daily, they deal with disaster contingencies on a regular basis; in fact, they may deal with as many information emergencies as public-safety departments deal with day to day. The information-systems department within your jurisdiction will have one of the most sophisticated disaster plans of any department. They are an invaluable resource because their job requires them to think and plan for emergency contingencies all the time.

Your jurisdiction's information-technology and radio-support departments will not only have to deal with issues outside the EOC but inside as well. There need to be radio and communication technicians assigned to the EOC for as long as it is open. Problems will crop up with computers, phones, and radios in the EOC. Without those capabilities the EOC will simply be a room filled with people who can only talk to one another. After the event they will be faced with the restoration and repair of the local communication infrastructure, including phones, cell phones, radios, internets and intranets, and connections with local radio and TV stations. Coordination with outside agencies both public and private at the local, state, and federal levels will also fall to them.

EOC activities include:

- identification of events needing communication equipment and support and coordination with the on-scene commander about their use
- emergency notification of key personnel as needed during operations
- identification of communication facilities and resources available for use
- coordination, acquisition, and deployment of additional resources, equipment, and personnel to establish point-to-point communications as required

Responsibilities of ESF #2 include:

- establishing essential communications as needed or required before, during, or after the event
- deploying damage assessment teams

- if shelters are opened, verifying that they have communications
- keeping in contact with telephone and cell-phone providers to update the jurisdiction's needs
- temporary repairs to communications systems within the jurisdiction as the need arises

Who should be assigned to ESF#2:

- information systems
- 911 communications
- radio-system technicians
- RACEs

Common incidents include:

- land-line and cell outages
- downed radio and cell-phone towers

Common requests include:

- cellular phones
- pagers
- phones and lines
- amateur radio
- handheld radios
- 800 lines
- conference-call bridges
- fax machines
- antennas
- radio towers
- repair of landlines
- EAS activation
- dispatchers
- temporary cell-phone sites

ESF #3 Public Works

ESF #3 provides support for an incident through engineering services, technical evaluation, inspection, damage assessment, and debris clearance and disposal.

EOC activities include:

- identification of the status and availability of equipment and facilities needed to assist in the response to the incident
- identification of events needing public-works resources and coordination of their response with on-scene commander
- coordination of emergency clearing of debris
- coordination of emergency demolition or stabilization of damaged or contaminated private houses, building, or structures to facilitate search and rescue and/or protection of public health and safety
- coordination of emergency environmental waivers and legal clearances for disposal of contaminated materials or debris clearance and disposal

Responsibilities include:

- emergency clearance of debris for reconnaissance of damaged areas and access needed for lifesaving, health, and safety purposes during the immediate response phase
- temporary clearing, repair, and/or reconstruction of emergency access routes
- streets
- roads
- bridges
- facilities necessary for passage of rescue personnel
- emergency restoration of critical public services
- adequate supply of potable water
- temporary restoration of water-supply systems
- provision of water for firefighting
- restoration of waste-water capabilities

- engineering services and construction advice and management
- building damage assessment and emergency demolition or stabilization of damaged infrastructure and buildings

Who should be assigned to ESF #3:

- building department
- facilities management
- property appraiser
- public utilities
- solid waste

Common incidents include:

- sewage lift stations without power
- raw sewage leak/cleanup
- water testing

Common requests include:

- forklifts
- debris removal from roads and highways
- dump trucks and drivers
- rear loaders
- front-end loaders
- traffic-signal heads
- bulldozers
- wood chippers
- sandbags
- floodlights
- concrete barriers
- electricians
- laborers

ESF #4 Firefighting

This function provides resources for the detection and suppression of urban, rural, and wild-land fires resulting from the incident and directs and assists in rescue operations as necessary. It provides firefighting services to any fires resulting from or after the incident. The fire service in your community will play a myriad of roles during a disaster given the various services it provides each day and the types of specialized equipment and training firefighters have. Many jurisdictions, my own included, rolled several ESFs under the fire service given its training and equipment.

EOC activities include:

- identification of the status and availability of all firefighting equipment, facilities, and personnel
- identification of events needing firefighting resources and coordination of the response with on-scene commander
- identification and dispatch of resources to manage or support incident operations as necessary once specified by the incident commander
- requisition of additional firefighting resources through mutual aid agreements
- initiation of mutual aid as necessary
- identification of staging areas for firefighting forces, supplies, and resources

Who should be assigned:

- jurisdictional fire-service agency

Common incidents include:

- structure fires
- hazardous-materials fires
- hazardous-materials spills
- people trapped

Common requests include:

- fire crews
- fire equipment

- water tanker (nonpotable water for firefighting)
- urban search and rescue teams
- firefighters
- engines
- rescues
- public-address system

ESF #5 Information and Planning

This function is responsible for the collection, organization, prioritization, and dissemination of all information as it relates to the incident, including the following essential elements of information:

- severity and boundaries of the incident area
- status of functional-area activation
- status of critical facilities
- weather data affecting operations
- security information
- major issues and activities of the functional areas
- resource shortfalls as identified by functional areas
- status of transportation system
- reported access points to the incident site
- status of communication systems
- casualty information
- disaster declaration
- contamination zones
- quarantine zones
- healthcare-facilities status
- donation information
- special needs information

ESF #5 plays a critical role in organizing, displaying, and disseminating information within the EOC. It is responsible for collating, processing and prioritizating information as it is received through the various ESFs.

EOC activities include:

- collation of information for the development of the IAP with the other necessary functional areas
- display and updating of information for the EOC
- development of periodic situation reports in support of the IAP
- maintaining displays of information by updating any charts, maps, and status boards either physical or through computer programs
- serving as the center for gathering information on the progress of ongoing operations for the development of the IAP
- tracking the progress of the IAP
- leading all briefings with updates to information on operational progress and logistical needs to assist in determining the next IAP

ESF #5 does not set the goals; it supports their development with information and tracks their progress. Its job is to provide the emergency-management team with information and to track operations in progress to prepare the information needed to determine the next set of goals.

Who should be assigned:

- emergency-management staff
- public-safety officers
- individuals familiar with NIMS, ICS, and disaster response and the needs of the EOC

ESF #6 Mass Care

ESF #6 coordinates activities involved in the emergency provision of temporary shelters, emergency mass feeding, bulk distribution of coordinated relief supplies for victims of disaster, and disaster welfare assistance.

EOC activities include:

- coordinating the tasking of all sheltering activities during the event

- coordinating the establishment and operation of mass feeding facilities
- coordinating relief efforts provided by volunteer organizations
- coordinating the opening of public shelters and special-needs shelters to meet the needs of the disaster
- coordinating the sheltering, feeding, and emergency assistance to those sheltered
- coordinate medical assistance at shelters
- coordinating security at the shelters
- keeping records of the shelter population
- determining the food, water, and other essential services at the shelters

ESF #6 cannot provide all of the services to the shelters; it will need to coordinate with a number of other ESFs in order to properly manage issues as they arise.

Who should be assigned:

- Red Cross
- Salvation Army

Common incidents include:

- open shelters
- shelter population
- no hotel rooms for evacuees
- overcrowded shelters

Common requests include:

- security at the shelters
- medical assistance for shelter victims
- shelter workers
- cots
- blankets
- location of individuals in shelters

- meals for shelters
- pillows
- canteen trucks at shelters
- comfort station not at shelter
  - showers
  - food canteen
  - ice
  - portable toilets
  - tents
- personal and shelter cleaning kits
- special-needs shelters
  - trained personnel
- diapers
- ready to eat military meals

ESF #7 Resource Support/Logistics

This function is responsible for providing logistical management and resource support to all agencies and departments involved in the response, including supplies, facilities, equipment, fuel, office supplies, contracting services, and all other resources that may be required. ESF #7 provides logistical support to the disaster operations.

EOC activities include:

- establishing, staffing, and coordinating supply-distribution centers to include medical as well as other types of supply to support the incident
- identifying and procuring processes, materials, and supplies needed by the various departments to perform their missions
- coordinating with the state and outside sources to acquire resources not available within the local area
- contracting services from vendors, relief supplies, EOC supplies, and any other needs that may present themselves
- recording all expenditures, leasing of equipment, and any other type of logistical expenditure during the disaster
- assuring that proper procurement procedures are followed and

detailed records maintained by all ESFs in accordance with FEMA rules, regulations, and policies in order for the community to receive the proper amount of reimbursement

Who should be assigned:

- purchasing department
- budget department
- human-resources department
- property and real-estate department

Common incidents and requests include:

- contractors offering their services
- equipment not readily available or in short supply
- chainsaws
- generators of all sizes

ESF #8 Health and Medical

ESF #8 coordinates with the medical facilities in the community to provide medical care and health services throughout the event. ESF #8's purpose is to provide a wide range of services and advice on public health issues during an incident.

EOC activities include:

- assessment of health/medical needs
- organization of health/medical-care personnel
- identification and coordination of health/medical equipment and supplies
- supporting patient evacuation from critical healthcare facilities within evacuation zones
- maintaining status of available hospital beds
- maintaining status of available critical medical equipment
- maintain status of available supplies of critical medications
- assessing public health and medical needs for the community before and after the event

- tracking the current status of all hospitals
- provide medical-care professionals
- coordinating victim identification and emergency mortuary services
- providing medical staff for special-needs shelters
- coordinating and validating the credentials of all medical volunteers who respond to the event
- coordinating disaster medical-assistance teams and disaster mortuary operational response teams if necessary
- conducting disease-control/epidemiology activities
- assuring food and drug safety
- conducting vector control and monitoring
- advising on potability of water and waste-water and solid-waste disposal
- providing emergency health advisories and related data for public information

Who should be assigned:

- local public-health agency
- medical examiner
- representatives from local hospitals
- emergency medical-service providers

Common incidents include:

- mass casualties
- medical-supply shortages
- medical personnel shortages
- contaminated water
- disease outbreak

Common requests include:

- ambulances
- advanced life support

- basic life support
- paramedics
- portable toilets
- food-safety inspections
- special-needs transportation
- portable oxygen units
- cervical immobilizers
- tetanus shots
- nursing personnel
- medevac helicopter
- insulin
- crisis counseling
- ampoules and syringes
- insect sting kits

ESF #9 Search and Rescue

ESF #9 provides search and rescue capabilities in support of the response to the event.

EOC activities include:

- identifying and locating existing equipment and personnel for search and rescue missions
- identifying and coordinating with mutual aid search and rescue as needed
- locating, rescuing, extricating, and treating victims who may be trapped or injured
- coordinating, allocating, and prioritizing additional public and private resources including personnel, materials, and services in support of the operations
- providing any search and rescue service that might arise from the event
- requesting and coordinating the arrival and support of USAR teams
- coordinating local search and rescue response

Who should be assigned:

- fire department
- law enforcement
- emergency medical services

Generally there is no separate agency to provide only search and rescue services; many jurisdictions give this ESF to one or all of the above agencies as additional duties. In many places these duties are taken on by several departments and can be shared by all.

Common incidents and requests include:

- people trapped
- search of heavily damaged areas for victims

ESF #10 Hazardous Materials

ESF #10 provides advice, response capabilities, and mitigation efforts for actual and potential discharge or release of hazardous materials including bioterrorism resulting from natural, man-made, or technological disasters

EOC activities include:

- receiving, collating, and prioritizing reports of spills, releases, and deliberate events
- alerting and coordinating with response jurisdictional agencies
- alerting and coordinating with mutual aid hazardous-materials teams as necessary
- contacting cleanup contractors
- providing expert advice and response to any and all hazardous-materials incidents or concerns

The number of hazardous-materials incidents can be overwhelming after an incident. There were dozens of incidents waiting for response after Hurricane Andrew, everything from backyard propane tanks leaking to major damage at major hazardous-materials sites. Depending on the type of event, this can be a very important ESF in the early hours after a natural disaster as the sheer number of calls stretches resources thin. You should have a pre-event priority list established so those calls can be handled in the proper order with the most serious managed first.

Who should be assigned:

- firefighters

At the local level this type of response is usually handled by a fire department or in some cases another agency. This ESF can be assigned along with the firefighting ESF or the appropriate ESF for the department or agency that handles these types of emergencies.

Common incidents include:

- natural-gas leaks at homes
- propane-tank leaks at homes and businesses
- damaged hazardous-materials target hazards
- unknown container substance leaking
- diesel spill
- gasoline spill

Common requests include:

- authorize hazardous-materials disposal sites
- authorize burning of hazardous-materials debris
- hazardous-materials cleanup team

ESF #11 Food and Water

This function determines the food and water needs during an event and coordinates the location, transportation, and distribution of these needed supplies through supply centers. (Many states and local jurisdiction differ in their ESF structure from that of the FEMA. Under FEMA this ESF is termed agriculture and natural resources. Given the amount of problems associated with these issues, many states and local communities adapt this ESF to one that better meets their needs. I am most familiar with those that use food and water. ESFs #11 through #16 are often changed to meet the needs of the community.) The strength of NIMS is that it is not a mandated organizational chart but adaptable to meet your needs.)

EOC activities include:

- identifying the scope of the need for food and water—i.e., number of victims

- identifying and inventorying warehouses that can accept food and water supplies
- determining distribution centers
- coordinating with transportation for the movement of supplies to distribution centers
- identifying and securing food supplies based on the scope of the disaster
- determining the need for distribution of household goods to the population
- determining the points of distribution for food, water, and ice
- establishing communication with the distribution sites
- supporting ESF #6 mass care food and water needs at shelters

This can be a huge effort depending on the type of event. If it is a widespread event such as a hurricane or earthquake that affects tens of thousands of people or more, then the complexity of the operation can be enormous. ESF #11 will work closely with a number of other ESFs to accomplish its responsibilities. Like resource management, this function can quickly grow into a large and complex operation.

Who should be assigned:

- community affairs or outreach department
- facilities management
- Red Cross
- Salvation Army

Common incidents include:

- shelters needing additional food supplies
- ice for populations without power
- water for populations without water supplies
- food

Common requests include:

- obtain food supplies
- arrange points of distribution for the various needs

- arrange transportation of supplies to points of distribution
- coordinate food-stamp assistance with state and local agencies
- ensure that nursing homes have sufficient food, water, and ice
- ensure that hospitals have sufficient food, water, and ice
- potable water
- water tankers
- refrigerated trailers
- freezer trailers
- semi-truck loads of ice
- dry storage trailers
- food
- ice
- associated food products
- dry ice
- baby formula
- ready-to-eat meals
- mobile kitchens

ESF #12 Energy

This function coordinates the restoration of energy systems and the provision of emergency power as necessary and available.

EOC activities include:

- assessing energy-system damage, energy supply, demand, and requirements to restore and provide additional sources of energy as needed
- assisting emergency agencies in obtaining emergency/temporary energy for emergency operations
- assessing and coordinating fuel supplies for responding agencies
- damage assessment of the energy infrastructure
- prioritization of repairs needed
- coordination and oversight of those repairs

- coordination of needed outside resources to complete repairs
- providing emergency power as needed in support of rescue and postevent response efforts

Hurricanes provide the biggest challenge, with entire electrical-distribution grids needing replacement after some storms. Some site-specific incidents such as terrorist events can require special construction of new electrical feeds for long-term operations. The restoration of power after an event may be the single most effective means of returning a community to the semblance of normality. In addition, studies have shown that power loss is the single largest contributor to business disruption and therefore the size of the economic impact on that community. The sooner business can return to operation, the sooner many of the ESF functions can be discontinued, as they are provided as they normally are in the community by local businesses.

Initial actions include:

- contact gas and electric providers serving the community to obtain damage assessments and assistance needed
- establish priorities and develop strategies for the initial response
- assign local disaster-assessment teams to determine local needs for utility restoration
- inform PIO of any precautions local citizens should take

Common incidents include:

- provide emergency power to support emergency response operations
- power outages
- power restoration
- lift stations
- special-needs-shelter support

Common requests include:

- technical assessment and knowledge for response and recovery

- energy information—outages and restoration
- power restoration
- refueling trucks for crews doing restoration
- coordination of mutual aid power-restoration crews
- LP gas
- generator vendors

ESF #13 Law Enforcement and Military Support

ESF #13 establishes command and control of all law-enforcement personnel, equipment, and activities in the event of a disaster or emergency. (In FEMA's plan this is known as public safety and security. Many local communities and states use this as military support or a combination of law enforcement and military support. Law enforcement is an ideal fit for both security and the military support contact coordinating the use of military resources, both Department of Defense and National Guard, to support the emergency response and recovery operations of the local jurisdiction.)

EOC activities include:

- coordinating military operations in support of emergency-response efforts
  - transportation
  - communication
  - mass care
  - resource support
  - medical facilities
  - public health
  - search and rescue
  - food and water
  - energy
  - security
- planning and coordinating employment of state and federal law-enforcement resources
- establishing and staffing traffic-control points

- maintaining law and order
- providing security when and where it is needed
- assisting in the dissemination of evacuation information and directing traffic during the evacuation

Who should be assigned:

- local law-enforcement agency
- state National Guard representative if available

Common incidents include:

- coordinating evacuations through dissemination of information and enforcement of mandatory evacuations
- road checkpoints
- price gouging law enforcement
- traffic control
- security at shelters
- security in badly damaged business areas
- enforcement of curfews
- enforcement of access to disaster areas
- logistical support from the military

Common requests include:

- rapid impact-assessment teams
- helicopters
- liaison officers
- cots
- generators
- trucks
- guards
- vehicle maintenance
- ready-to-eat meals
- high-wheeled vehicles

- maps
- blankets
- showers
- front-end loaders
- tents

ESF #14 Public Information

Known as long-term recovery in the FEMA plan, this function provides continuous information to the public through any and all means available including press conferences, Internet sites, and social networking. Providing reliable and continuous information to the public after an event is vital to any response. It is the only way a community can assure its population of what is being done to meet their needs and the status of those efforts. Without this information the public's perception of the response, even a good one, can be skewed. People must feel as if everything possible is being done to meet everyone's needs. I cannot emphasize enough how important it is for the public to stay informed. Disasters are as much a political and media event as they are physical destruction. Without an aggressive public information operation even a quick and effective response can be viewed as a failure, and perception is reality in public opinion. The wrong perception can not only affect the careers of those involved in the response but also increase the long-term impact of the disaster on the community's economic well-being.

EOC activities include:

- establishing a central point to gather information concerning an emergency
- establishing a central point to disseminate information to the public concerning an emergency or disaster
- establishing a central point for the media to gather information concerning an emergency or disaster and disseminate it to the public
- establishing a format for disseminating information to the public during a emergency or disaster
- establishing a schedule for press briefings and news releases

- establishing a public information line and the message to be recorded on it
- coordinating with the senior elected offical and the emergency manager to determine what information should be released to the media
- writing and distributing news releases
- answering all media calls regarding emergency/disaster situations
- escorting reporters in the EOC and enforcing EOC media guidelines
- keeping senior elected official's press liaison informed of all matters pertaining to the event
- monitoring media sources to ensure that correction information is received and correcting misinformation
- planning and coordinating news conferences
- identifying the need for a joint information center and coordinating with the elected official and the emergency manager about who should be part of it

ESF #15 Volunteers and Donations

In large disasters the area will be flooded with goods and volunteers anxious to help. The number and type of volunteers will take a considerable amount of coordination with the centers receiving them and with the ESFs who might need their assistance. Those involved with this function deal with the following:

- determining and validating volunteers and relief supplies through ESF assessments and requests
- communicating equipment, materials, and supplies needed to the appropriate volunteer agency or private organization offering assistance
- coordinating with ESF #6 (mass care) and ESF #8 (health and medical services)
- coordinating volunteer needs with the appropriate state and federal agencies
- determining the appropriate volunteer agency or private source to fill requests received

- recording the pertinent detailed information about all who have donated to the response
- coordinating with volunteer staging areas to fill needs as appropriate

ESF #16 Animal Protection

The care and rescuing of abandoned pets and animals has become increasing important issue after disasters. Thousands of animals left on their own if not rescued, will grow from a nuisance to a public safety and health issue. After Hurricane Andrew volunteers searching the abandoned and destroyed houses were issued large sticks to ward off the growing packs of hungry dogs. If they are not rescued their decomposing bodies will pose an increasing risk to public health. Today there are a number of excellent volunteer organizations that respond to help manage this specific problem after a disaster. ESF #16 will coordinate the local and outside agencies response to the large complex problem. This function fulfills the following:

- managing all issues dealing with animals after the event
- coordinate with incoming volunteer animal-rescue teams

Who should be assigned:

- local animal-control department
- ASPCA

Common incidents include:

- livestock problems
- dead livestock and pets
- damaged animal shelters
- abandoned pets

Common requests include:

- animal food
- long-term feeding of animals
- temporary animal shelters
- find lost pets

INCIDENT COMMAND SYSTEM

The Incident Command System (ICS) is a management system designed to control and direct resources committed to an incident. It operates under the overall direction of one person, who is called the incident commander (IC). The IC exercises command by virtue of explicit legal, agency, or delegated authority. In some instances, federal, state, or local regulations may require or suggest the use of ICS. The use of ICS provides the following advantages to its users:

- common terminology—allows anyone from any part of the country to effectively communicate within the ICS system; common terms for similar functions, actions, and personnel prevent confusion

- modular format—top-down structure consisting of five functional areas, command, operations, planning, logistics, and administration/finance, allows the user to build an organization with capabilities needed to manage the incident they are facing
  - command: to direct, control, or order resources, including people and equipment, to the best possible advantage during the event
  - operations: coordinated by the operations section chief, who reports to the IC; responsible for tactical concerns at the incident
  - planning: coordinated by the planning section chief, who reports to the IC; responsible for the collection, valuation, dissemination, and use of information about the incident as well as the status of resources of staff, equipment, and supplies used or needed for the scene
  - logistics: coordinated by the logistics section chief, who reports to the IC; responsible for providing facilities, services, staffing, equipment, and materials for the incident
  - administration and finance: coordinated by the administration and finance section chief, who reports to the IC; responsible for tracking all incident costs and evaluating the financial considerations of the incident

- integrated communications plan—coordinates the use of available communications means and establishes frequency assignments for the various functions

- effective span of control—one of the single most important aspects, controlling the number of people reporting to a single person guarantees that the proper level of command and control is being applied to all facets of an incident (any given supervisor should have no less than three and no more than seven personnel reporting to them, with five being the ideal number.)
- command post—all operations directed from a command post

ICS/EOC INTERFACE

The two command structures are designed to manage two different levels of the incident. ICS is designed to manage the tactical, feet-on-the-ground operations of an event, while the EOC is structured to manage the operational needs of the incident. The EOC is the connection between the IC on the ground and the resources, organizations, and agencies from the county, region, state, and federal assets that may assist in managing the incident.

While an IC is responsible for the operations at a single incident, the EOC may be working with several ICs across the county or state. The EOC must balance the needs of all these incidents as well as other issues that it alone will have to address. Thus, the interface between these commanders and the EOC is an important one. As they need additional staff or resources, it will be up to the EOC to make sure they receive them in a timely manner. Sorting through these requests is the reason the EOC uses the ESF organizational structure. By using ESFs each of the subject areas has a team of people to manage their needs. If an IC needs an urban search and rescue team, the agency responsible for ESF #9 will work through the myriad of details needed to put a team on site as soon as possible. This is true of every request from the field. The appropriate ESF will be tasked with securing and monitoring the progress of putting the needed asset or team in place.

This interaction between the EOC and the IC and their Staff is not always an easy one. Communication from the field to the EOC can be confusing unless a system is established before the incident. Field personnel could directly contact the appropriate ESF and request the needed supplies, or the request could go through the IC, who contacts the emergency manager, who then tasks the ESF. Either way can work, but everyone must understand which of those models will be used before the incident. Certain operational departments may feel most comfortable working through their representative ESF—i.e., firefighting, law enforcement, or public works. Working with personnel who understand their specific operational language and needs may be a better and more efficient way to interface between the two different levels of command. This interface is not an easy one and will need practice before an event occurs. Ideally the EOC and the various operational departments would exercise together to see which communication protocol would be the best to use during an incident. No matter which is chosen, it will take time and effort on both sides to make this interface runs smoothly during an incident.

CONCLUSIONS

NIMS and ICS are modular and easily adaptable command structures that can be built to suit the needs of the jurisdiction and the incident. Both grew out of lessons learned from major disasters, where confusion and lack of coordination contributed to a slow and disorganized response. They will work if everyone understands how they work and why they work. It will assure that both local and outside agencies that respond to assist in the operations will understand the command structure and how to interface with it during operations. Using NIMS and ICS does not assure you a smooth operating response. It provides a structure with the needed commonalities for a very diverse group of agencies to work together. It will be up to the men and women in those various jobs to make the command structure work, but using NIMS and ICS will make their jobs easier and more efficient.

CHAPTER 8

Technology and Social Media

Emergency management is information management under stress. Without the right information technology an emergency manager cannot do his job. By definition emergency management collects, collates, prioritizes, and then acts on information. This information can come from dozens of sources and media. Any technology chosen by an emergency manager has to address one or more of those needs, or it is not going to be useful. The emergency manager can only lead if he or she is informed in a timely and accurate manner and then has the wherewithal to take action on that information.

The types of technologies needed are information-management and communications technologies. In today's wired society an EOC must be able to manage the flood of information that will be generated by a disaster in the community. It is difficult even with the right technologies in place. It is almost impossible without those technologies. The issue is to choose the right technologies that fits the needs of the EOC and can be supported by the information-management department of your community.

Before your purchase any technology for your EOC, coordinate that purchase with your information-systems department. Its staff will be responsible for integrating any technology you purchase into the existing networks. They must be able to support it before, during, and after an event. Without their support the technology simply will not be used to its potential. So before anything is done develop a partnership or a permanent contact who can help you evaluate any software or hardware purchase from the information-management perspective. The combination of the emergency manager's knowledge and the information technologist's understanding of the technical details will assure you of acquiring the right software or hardware.

COMMUNICATIONS

An EOC must be able to communicate with the field responders and other EOCs during an event. This communication can be by radio, cell phone, land-line telephone, or any combination of the three. If your EOC has been hardened to withstand hurricanes or earthquakes, make sure you test your radios and cell phones inside the building long before an event. In my own experience we found that our radios and cell phones would not always communicate outside of our new hurricane-hardened EOC. We had to add equipment to assist with cell phones and radio communication. This was not an insignificant challenge, and it took some time, effort, and money to solve. So make sure that you test before you assume that radios and cell phones can call out of the EOC. Never assume, test. That means test all of the various radio systems in your jurisdiction. Public-safety agencies use different frequencies than public works or other departments, and they all must test their systems to see if they will work.

Once you know that they can be used, you will need to do something about the noise of ten radios in the same room on different frequencies and used by different departments. If the departments in your community do not have earpieces for their radios, then either ask them to purchase them or purchase them yourself. An EOC is a very loud environment to begin with, without the additional noise of a number of radios with their speakers blaring adding to the din. A simple earpiece for each radio will lower the noise level significantly and allow the user to hear over the din in the EOC.

TELEVISION FEEDS

It is critical that you have television feeds into the EOC with multiple sets displaying the various local and national channels. Some may question this need, but you must be able to track what media representatives are saying, if for no other reason than to make sure they report the announcements you have drafted properly. During a hurricane our local stations gave out the wrong list of shelters that had been opened, and we would not have known about it had we not been monitoring what they were saying.

The EOC should have enough screens so that each of the local stations has its own screen, with one or two additional screens to monitor the national news networks. Only one of these feeds should have the sound on so those in the EOC can monitor the shows. You should be able to change the audio feed from one to another when it appears that it is reporting on something that is important enough to monitor.

The public will listen to these stations, and you need to know what they are saying and when they are saying it. In spite of the changes in how people gather information, whether it be the Internet or Twitter, a certain demographic is going rely on the tried and true old media. Monitoring of the media is your Public Information Officer's (PIO) job. They and any other personnel assigned to them must be on top of what is being said so they can craft press releases that will correct mistakes or reinforce points that are missed in the coverage.

EOC SOFTWARE

The next important piece of technology that you will need to properly run your operations is a good EOC software package. There are literally hundreds available now, and each has its own strengths and weaknesses. It will be up to you and your information-management representative to investigate and find the one that fits your needs, your budget, and your infrastructure. It is not an easy task.

Before you look at any of the packages, develop a list of the needs that you have identified as critical to your operations. This list will evolve into a set of requirements that a software package must have if you are going to purchase it. These requirements will go a long way toward sorting through the myriad of packages and capabilities. You can develop these requirements by bringing together your staff and personnel representing the departments that will be assigned to the EOC during an event. Work with them to develop your set of requirements. From this effort a clearly defined minimum set of capabilities can be developed and used as a filter to help to narrow the search.

It is critical that the software meets your needs; it will be your tool to organize and display information and communicate within the EOC. So it has to do what you need to accomplish this task. Some of the requirements that should be considered when choosing the right EOC software include:

- information visualization—the ability to place incoming information on a map so EOC staff can begin to visualize the disaster in a way that assists them in understanding the overall picture (you will find a number of different approaches to this capability; it will be a matter of preference and ease of use that will drive the choice)

- collaborative technologies—a means of working collaboratively among the staff in the EOC within the software (messaging, common displays, and other types of collaborative capabilities will help frame the working groups in your EOC)

- plans—plans developed prior to the event must be easily accessible to the user without leaving the software
    - expected actions—ability to add a locally developed expected actions list for each of the ESFs and field personnel to be checked off as they are accomplished and the information is gathered

- operations tracking and status board display—ability to track the progress of those operations and update information as the operation proceeds

- log—ability to log and archive messages, maps, and other critical information for future reference and record keeping

- organization chart with the latest staffing in the place

- contact lists of internal and external vendors, personnel, and agencies

- resource directory with local critical-response resources and lists of vendors with the types of resources they can provide

- references—ability to enter or have installed standard references such as the *Emergency Response Guidebook* from the

Department of Transportation and any other reference materials you might want to have available in the software

- ability to use the Internet from inside the software
- ability to support the type of organizational structure you have chosen for your EOC—ESF, IC, etc.
- availability of ICS and NIMS forms within the software (these forms are critical to obtaining the resources needed at the right time and in the right place)
- NIMS-compliant resource typing for proper record keeping (using the NIMS resource types will facilitate any requests for assistance since what is needed is in proper NIMS language)
- technical support—help and troubleshooting information inside the software so your information-systems department can support it before, during and after a disaster (IT staff input and expertise with specific types of software will be important in making any decision. They should be part of the final selection since they will be responsible for keeping the software in working order.)

These are just a few of the requirements you might want to include in your capabilities list before you begin your search, but they are certainly not exhaustive. A specific jurisdictional list may be much longer or much shorter, depending on local technological capabilities and budget constraints. Going through the process of identifying your needs before you begin your search will shorten the time and effort that is needed to make the best selection for your needs.

A balancing act must take place between your list of needs and capabilities and the ease of use of the software. Unless the software is simple and intuitive, it will take constant use to assure that your personnel are familiar enough to use it when a disaster strikes. This is difficult to accomplish given the limited time most emergency managers have to teach their EOC personnel. There is a very difficult balance between training and access to the personnel you need to be comfortable with the software. The more capabilities the software contains, the more complex the software and the more it has to be used before real familiarity can be acquired.

If you chose a software package that requires constant use to take advantage of its full capabilities but you cannot schedule enough training sessions to keep everyone current, you will have to develop some sort of workaround. There are a couple of solutions, but they are staff-intensive to put into place. You either need roving personnel in the EOC, who can assist individual users in the first hours or days of the response, or you need to assign someone familiar with the program to each person requiring assistance to make sure the software is properly used. I have used this type of system in training situations where it worked well, and the persons assigned to the position because of their expertise were able to concentrate on the response and not on how to use the software.

This issue of familiarity with the software will always be present. There are no simple solutions because the software capabilities are essential while familiarity with the software will vary directly with how much time you have to train and exercise the users. Another step you can take is to assign one person either on your staff or as a liaison who can take advantage of every aspect of the software and provide the needed capabilities for many of the tasks. This person should be assigned to the planning section of your EOC to assure that at a minimum someone can produce the types of products, reports, and displays needed.

One person cannot provide a completely accurate picture, but it is better than not having anyone but yourself to do the work required. As I said in the beginning of this discussion, this is a difficult balancing act and will require constant attention to find a solution that will work for you and your organization.

SOCIAL MEDIA

A recent study by Arbitron and Edison Research found that nearly half of all Americans over the age of 12 had a presence on at least one of the social-networking sites. Japan's 2011 earthquake may have offered the necessary proof that social media can save lives if used properly and thus opened the door to full acceptance of the value of social media to emergency management.

Japan's national meteorological agency combined the science of earthquakes with social media to field an early-warning system for the public. Earthquakes produce different types of seismic waves when they occur. There are P waves and S waves. P waves travel much faster than S waves. P waves do not cause the shaking damage;

instead, they travel through the earth ahead of the S waves. It is the S waves that produce the shaking and the damage to buildings and infrastructure. P waves precede the S waves by several seconds to several minutes, depending on how close you are to the epicenter of the quake.

The Japanese meteorological agency used this fact to develop a warning system for the public. Seismometers detect the P waves created by an earthquake. They quickly analyze the strength of those waves; if they cross the threshold of a lower 5 magnitude quake, they automatically send out an alert.

Text messages went to millions of individual cell phones; bullet trains were stopped in their tracks; factories and petrochemical plants were notified to shut down their operations; and television stations interrupted programs to notify the public that an earthquake was imminent. The entire process took only 8.6 seconds yet went out nationwide. It saved countless lives. The power that today's technology places in the hands of emergency managers was only dreamed of ten years ago, and it continues to grow each year as new technologies emerge.

Even if emergency-management offices do not use social media, the public will flock to Twitter and Facebook for instant information from the impact area. During the Japanese earthquake Twitter was filled with tweets from people in Japan. People were downloading videos of the quake and its damage over an hour before any of the major news networks had the same footage. When the US Airways airliner went down in the Hudson in New York, the first picture that flashed around the world did not come from a news organization—it came from someone on Twitter. During the earthquake in Haiti Twitter became the main source of information for the majority of people who were closely following the events. Twitter beat the Geological Surveys Earthquake Hazard Program by several minutes in reporting the earthquake in Mexico in 2007.

People are starved for information about disaster events, and if they have loved ones at risk then that concern only increases. So if they cannot obtain the information they need from traditional news outlets they, will turn to "less reliable" but much faster social media. The ability to directly contact a loved one or to read a message on Facebook can go a long way in calming them once they find out their loved ones are all right. This relieves the local emergency-management establishment of some of the traditional pressure to find ways to let families outside the affected area know that their loved ones are safe.

But social media are not just for notifying the public of dangers. As Craig Fugate, the head of FEMA, recently said, "We have got to stop looking at the public as a liability and start looking at them as a resource. Social media allows for a two-way conversation in the impact zone, so that we can link people with information, resources, and ideas." The public can become a source of information for emergency responders. Social media does exactly that by allowing emergency-management agencies to directly contact people individually.

Crowd Sourcing

Ushahidi (Swahili for testimony or witness) is an open-source (free) application first used in Kenya to map reports of political violence during the 2007 elections. Users collected reports of violence sent in by email and text messaging and placed them on a Google map. Later the application was used to track anti-immigrant violence in South Africa. When the earthquake in Haiti occurred, a joint effort among Uhahidi, the Fletcher School of Law and Diplomacy at Tufts University, UN OCHA/Columbia, and the International Network of Crisis Mappers implemented this application. They created an interactive map that showed the location of requests for assistance. By aggregating these disparate messages on a map, it became clear where most of the damage had occurred and where most help was needed. Even people trapped in the rubble were tweeting for help. This allowed resources to be used in the areas where they were most needed. The Marine Corps and the Coast Guard used the maps to assist them in their relief efforts.

Since Haiti crowd sourcing has been used in a number of different disasters and social disruptions. It was used in the Chilean earthquake to map damage and injuries. It was used in Libya to map acts of violence against demonstrators. During the Japanese earthquake it was used to report on shelters, food stores, open gas stations, road closures, building damage assessments and cell-phone charging centers. It was even used in Washington, D.C., during a snow emergency to map closed streets. So the use of the public as a source of information has been proven to be a resource of real and actionable intelligence that can increase the efficiency of the response.

While there is much to celebrate, the use of social media still has many problems to work through. One of the biggest is validating the messages and culling out misinformed and outright bogus reports. Yet the overall experience in using social media to assist in the response and not just as a means to communicate with the public has to be viewed as positive and successful.

One of the simplest ways to use crowd sourcing is to enlist public employees who are off-duty when the event occurs. Simply have a standing order that all off-duty public employees report damages and injuries as soon as they can through their personal cell phones. These personnel will be widely scattered and can give you an early picture of your jurisdiction and where the worst damage and injuries are located.

Couple these reports with another set of trusted agents, your locally trained community emergency-response teams, and the picture becomes even clearer. CERT teams are trained by neighborhood, so they provide an even more organized and thorough picture. If you couple these two sources with the public, you can quickly begin to draw together the beginnings of a Common Operating Picture (COP) of the event.

In the meantime there are a number of groups, including the originators of Ushahidi, working to develop software that validates, structures, and prioritizes the data that flows in after a disaster. As we move forward, more tools will emerge that will assist local emergency managers in sorting and prioritizing this mass of information to assist them in their response.

Facebook

A Facebook page that the public can go to for timely and accurate information is another way to reach out to the community. None of the social-media tools take the place of the local press. People still want to see and hear from their local officials during a crisis. But Facebook pages and other types of media can go a long way in giving them even more information that is specific to their needs. After Hurricanes Andrew and Hugo the local papers were filled with long lists of where people could obtain food, ice, water, and other assistance. It could take days to get this information out, but by using Facebook and other technologies this can be accomplished almost in real time.

Facebook allows the official word to be published for everyone to see. It is a balance to the vast flow of "unofficial" information that is being published by individuals. It allows the local jurisdiction to become part of the social-media conversation. People are starved for information that can help them, and the local emergency-management agency needs to be the source of that information. Facebook is ideal for listing where needed supplies and assistance can be obtained almost as soon as they are established, as well as answering directly other questions from the public. It allows for a two-way conversation to happen at precisely the time people need the information.

If you are going to use Facebook, you need to establish a Facebook page prior to the event. While this may seem premature, if you have a presence it will be noticed. You will attract some followers—your CERT team members, for example. Once you establish your page, publish messages often. Safety tips, weather alerts, and any and all types of information that an emergency-management office might want the public to know. The Los Angeles Fire Department posts alerts about fires and road closures due to accidents and has more than 10,000 followers. Minneapolis uses its Facebook page to provide information on closed streets and winter parking restrictions. The Washington State Department of Transportation uses Facebook to post traffic alerts, ferry schedules, and other transportation information.

You could publish links to weather web sites that provide good local weather reports and other sources of emergency educational information. Provide reports and links to information concerning other disasters when they occur. Become the go-to place for disaster information both before and after the event. I once created a web page for my jurisdiction made up of nothing but links to weather and hurricane information sites. It became one of the most popular sites in the city. In today's environment if you don't publish information people will quickly stop visiting your page. Publish or get lost in the mass of information. Do not get discouraged if there are few "friends" once you do establish your page; if an event occurs, people will find you and your following will grow exponentially.

When an event does occur, repeatedly refresh your Facebook page with specific types of information and questions that may not be answered in the press releases. List locations for supplies and where volunteers can report to help with the cleanup. Make sure all of the information is relevant and useful to the reader. Do not use the page to give general "we are doing the best we can" messages; instead post needed, actionable information.

Answers to questions posted by individuals can go a long way toward making the public feel as if the response is more personal and aimed not just in general ways but toward their needs specifically. Facebook is not the be-all, end-all answer, but it is an important part of any response if used properly, because it allows a two-way conversation between the local jurisdiction and the individuals in the community. As someone who after a hurricane was starved for information and unable to find what I needed, I can attest to the fact that a page with the needed information available on the Internet would have relieved me of a lot of uncertainty. A presence on the Internet can go along way to helping you reach more citizens during a time of crisis.

Twitter

In a study immediately after the Japanese earthquake it was found that Twitter was the only working communication technology. Most users were tweeting that they were safe to those who were following them, but there was a downside. A number of false rumors were tweeted and then retweeted until they spread much further than they should have. The fact that there was no "official" tweet with an official hashtag identifying the source only reinforces the need for emergency management's presence in the Twitter world.

Twitter is a 140-character messaging service that has exploded because of its ease of use and immediacy. It provides a quick and direct link to the public for any emergency-management agency. By establishing a Twitter account and providing up-to-the-minute emergency and disaster information, your "tweets"—messages—are broadcast to your list of followers, who want to monitor any messages that you may send out. Messages about blocked streets, major fires, tornado warnings, and other day-to-day emergencies can be sent out to your followers.

Get "verified" by Twitter so people will know that your information is to be trusted and is not from someone imitating you. In your tweet you can ask people to retweet the message to people they know. If the information is an important announcement about a local emergency, it can go viral as one after another of the people who received the original tweet retweet it. You can also include in your tweet a link to your web page for more information than the 140 characters can contain. This allows for important information to be accessed by smartphones as well as portable computers. Twitter worked in Japan when cell-phone and Internet service was down—very similar to 9/11 when cell-phone circuits were overloaded and texting was the only option working.

This ability to directly contact people is a giant step in emergency management. Until Twitter you had rely on the local media to get the message out through the emergency broadcast system, and those messages were reserved for only the most severe and life-threatening situations. With Twitter you can become almost a daily source of information that will make your followers' lives easier and safer. You will be able to reach them with information no matter where they are—all they need is a smartphone or a computer. So should a severe thunderstorm or tornado suddenly blow up and become a threat to your community, you now have another more immediate way of reaching your constituents in addition to a siren or EBS. Twitter is another avenue to raise your community's awareness and emergency management's visibility within that community.

CONCLUSION

Even if you choose not to get involved with social media, it will be part of the response to any disaster in your community. Google and YouTube both open person-finder sites to assist people in locating loved ones during disasters. The public will use it to check on their loved ones in the disaster area from outside as well as on Twitter and Facebook, as witnessed in the Japanese earthquake most recently. This will assist your own efforts to help reunite loved ones. Remaining on the outside of these services keeps you from taking full advantage of the technologies at your disposal. Outside agencies, volunteer groups, and individuals will be using various media to gather information and assist victims within your community. This outside assistance only reinforces the need to be involved and have your own outlets that people can use, and you will also receive information from these groups.

Use multiple channels and be consistent across all channels—if you post information through Twitter, then that same info should be posted on your Facebook page. Pull information using crowd-sourcing programs to assist in your response. Push information out to the public using Twitter and Facebook.

Social media should be your tool of choice during an emergency; coupled with a consistent media strategy, you will be able reach the citizens in your community with the information they need when they need it.

Technology is the single most powerful tool an emergency manager has in his arsenal. When the entire decision-making apparatus of a jurisdiction collapses into an EOC, it must have the needed information to make the right decisions. Technology provides the means to gather that information, to sort and prioritize it, and to finally to communicate the decisions made. Technology can also make that decision making easier by displaying the information in a format that will enhance the ability of everyone in the EOC to share a COP, which leads to a shared situational awareness and the proper decisions. The technology must be chosen carefully to meet the needs, budget, and technological sophistication of the jurisdiction. With the myriad of different software, hardware, and unique technologies available, every jurisdiction, big and small, will be able to put together a package that meets its needs. It will take time, effort, and the right group of people, but it can be done—in fact, it must be done if that jurisdiction is going to be prepared for a disaster.

CHAPTER 9

Building the Team:
The Core Liaison Group

At all levels emergency managers must work through officials who "own" the resources in a jurisdiction or department. Unless the jurisdiction is a major metropolitan center, an emergency manager will at best have a very small immediate staff to assist him. Unlike a fire chief or police chief, who has personnel and equipment that are under his control, an emergency manger has none of those resources and yet will be responsible for the performance and coordination of his own and other departmental assets during an event.

This fact of life is not going to change. Budgets for emergency-management departments are not going to dramatically increase, enabling them to create a staff or have a set of resources assigned to them for response. Even at the state level most emergency-management personnel have a "day" job, with their response responsibilities as a second hat to be worn in the event that a disaster occurs. There is a solution to the problem, one that does not cost anything and yet is very effective in providing the needed staff to lead the coordination of the various departments during a response. It is the Core Liaison Group.

THE CORE LIAISON GROUP

The Core Liaison Group is a simple concept that will provide the emergency manager with a trained team of interdisciplinary personnel who will become the "command staff" during an event. An emergency manager cannot have the level of expertise or the departmental understanding of capabilities for all the disciplines that will be needed during a response. They needs subject-matter experts to assist them. Emergency managers will also need other individuals trained in disaster response and coordination who can step in to assist in the overall command. That is the job of the liaisons.

The Core Liaison Group is made up of representatives from the departments within the community that are most critical during a disaster. No matter what the event, these departments will play a critical role. Even if they are only peripherally involved in the response, the skills that the members of these departments develop during daily operations will make them valuable in any type of incident.

The Core Liaison Group will vary from a minimum of four to as many as seven individuals, depending on jurisdiction size, availability of personnel, and the emergency manager's perceived needs. These individuals will be assigned as liaisons from their respective disciplines within a jurisdiction. They will have regular duties with their departments but also train and help develop the community's disaster plans and procedures before an event. During a disaster they will temporarily step out of their departments to become the community's emergency-management team and assist with coordinating the disaster response.

This is the tricky part, because they will still technically belong to their old departments but will be trusted agents of that department representing it within emergency management; they will be walking a very difficult bureaucratic line. This relationship will have to be well understood if the concept is to work. It may even require a memorandum of understanding between emergency management and each department, but whatever it takes it is worth the effort.

Team members will represent that department during the response, working with emergency management to assure that their departments' skills, equipment, and needs are best used and represented. This role could easily mean that they will be working and coordinating with personnel who would normally be their superiors. Yet during a disaster the liaison must now be viewed as a bureaucratic equal. This is not an easy role for anyone; both the emergency manager and the liaison will have to work to legitimize this niche function. It will not be easy to accomplish, but each liaison will have to carve this role out.

Ideally these liaisons would be assigned to the office of emergency management for a tour of duty of, say, two years. This is long enough to become well trained and part of the emergency-management team but not long enough to adversely affect their careers within their departments. But in to today's environment this type of assignment would be almost impossible except in the largest of communities. Departments do not have the personnel to be able to permanently assign people to another department. Instead the situation would be similar to any number of multidepartmental committees that make up so many coordinating task forces for issues that cross departmental lines. The liaison team would meet regularly to plan and train together for disasters as well as be sent to conferences and training for disaster responses.

The Core Liaison Group should be comprised of personnel from the critical-response departments within your community. By critical-response departments I mean departments that, no matter what type of disaster your community would face, these departments would play a role. These roles will vary with the size of the jurisdiction and the services provided by the community. The following recommendations for the Core Liaison Group are just that, recommendations, and any emergency manager can add, subtract, or combine the roles to fit their needs. There are simply too many different organizational structures within communities to say that these are the only departments that should be involved. The community itself should make those determinations, but here is what a basic Core Liaison Group might look like:

The Core Liaison Group

- law enforcement
- fire department
- emergency medical services
- public works
- information-systems/technology management
- public information
- public health
- medical

This group comprises the "operational" arm of any community. Each of these disciplines has vital day-to-day operational responsibilities that keep the lights on and traffic flowing, protect the public, and process information. These are the exactly the same critical-response capabilities that will be needed during a disaster.

Law Enforcement

This department is included for obvious reasons. The restoration of order and security after an event is critical. Before or during a disaster, if evacuations are necessary, the bulk of the responsibility for their planning and coordination will fall to law enforcement. If the disaster is the result of a terrorist attack, the law-enforcement liaison will be responsible for the coordination of the investigation with local and outside agencies for emergency management.

If the jurisdiction has more than one law-enforcement agency within its boundaries, some adjustments will have to be made in terms of representation. Ideally one individual would have the cachet to represent all of the agencies within a county. If not, then some thought needs to be given to who and how many should be involved. Should the emergency manager's jurisdiction include an elected sheriff, a representative from that agency would be prudent.

Elected officials, whether they are law-enforcement officers or politicians, will perceive that their political futures depend on the disaster response. So the emergency manager wants to make sure that an elected emergency-response official representative feels as if they are being properly represented and has a say in the planning and response. Law Enforcement is the first of the critical-response infrastructure departments needed.

Fire Department

The fire department is another of the critical infrastructure departments, with responsibilities for fire suppression, search, and rescue. Given the destruction caused by so many types of disaster, firefighters become the first responders to the event. Their credo of saving lives and property is by definition the response priority for the first hours and days of a disaster. Fire departments have in most communities evolved from just firefighting to more of a general emergency-services organization. They handle not only fires but at least some of the following services: hazardous-materials incidents, below-ground rescues, swift water and other types of water rescue, high-angle rescues, collapse rescues, and even aircraft crash response. All of these specialized types of responses require not only special training but also specialized equipment that can be used in any number of different ways during a disaster.

Fire stations are strategically located throughout a community based on growth, traffic patterns, and special target hazards such as hospitals, oil refineries, and other types of facilities that create unique hazards or provide important services for your community. These stations can serve as temporary staging areas, distribution points, vaccination or medicine-distribution centers, and other types of temporary disaster points of service for the community. In addition to the other roles already mentioned, in many communities the fire department also provides emergency medical services to the community, still another critical-response capability.

Finally, fire-department personnel are trained to perform a wide variety of services in addition to those listed. This ingrained versatility in their daily activities make them an ideal resource for any number of disaster-related jobs.

Emergency Medical Services

EMS responders are the front-line care providers for the medical community of any jurisdiction. They are the eyes, ears, and hands at the hospitals and public health provisions on the street. EMS units are on the street every day providing medical care to citizens and interacting with local medical facilities. During a disaster their skill set is particularly important because of their familiarity with operating outside a hospital's controlled environment. EMS's ability to transport patients in and out of the disaster area is critical to being able to provide proper emergency care for the community during a disaster. In a disaster this skill becomes even more important, as some medical facilities are damaged or lost completely. Coordinating with physicians in damaged medical facilities, their skills have been used to extend the medical profession's reach into the community to help provide medical care after major disasters.

Public Works

The public-works department provides the fundamental services of any community. They keep water flowing, electricity on, streets clear, and all of the other basic infrastructure of a community. The longer basic services are disrupted by a disaster, the larger the economic impact on that community. In addition, when basic services are disrupted, the likelihood of public health issues increases dramatically by the day; repairing and replacing these basic services are vital for a community to begin to return to normal.

Not only do public-works employees provide these services, but they have heavy equipment and staff who know how to use it and who can provide all manner of support and cleanup that will be needed after a disaster. Not only are they important to the restoration of daily services, but they can help other departments return to normal with their specialized equipment and trained staff.

The individual who represents public works ideally would be able to speak to all of the basic services, water, sewage, and electricity. In many communities this is not always possible. Many times there is a separate power , or water company that provides service to a larger area. Ideally you would have someone from that service in your group as well, but the company may balk at that, given the number of communities it serves. It is the age-old problem—if you say yes to one jurisdiction, then you would have to say yes to all of them, and that can be a burden. So if your public-works representative does not represent those specific areas of expertise, then they should have contacts with all of the critical services and be able to call on them as needed.

Information Services/Technology Management

Repeating the point made earlier, emergency management is information management under stress. Planning for and keeping information flowing into the EOC are critical; without this flow you have a room full of people who can only stare at one another. The information infrastructure within the EOC and with the outside world is your lifeline. Restoring the critical-response communication infrastructure of your community is an additional critical task for information systems. The IS department may be able to accomplish this task on its own or may have to coordinate with outside vendors to do so. Communications vendors understand the critical nature of their service after a disaster and have teams and equipment ready to respond to affected areas. It will be up to information systems to coordinate with these teams.

Data and voice communications in your jurisdiction must be robust and redundant if they are to survive the event and manage the use overload after the event. Having someone who is not only familiar with the infrastructure but who can respond to outside needs during an event is as critical as any law-enforcement officer, firefighter, or EMT. Without that function the emergency-management team cannot do its job. Ideally you would have a representative from the department that manages the information for your community to assist with the planning and acquisition of the proper equipment for the community and a person or team of technicians assigned to respond to the EOC during an event. This combination would assure that you had the right resources assigned to all of the needed systems.

Public Health

Public health is an agency that is often left out of emergency management planning unless there is a direct threat from a disease or biological terrorist event. Yet its expertise can be used in a number of different ways and should be included in any response planning. In the author's own experience this department was critical during hurricane responses because it was responsible for special-needs shelters. Public-health nurses ran those shelters, and without them we could not have provided the skilled personnel to open the shelters.

Public health can also identify problems that responders might miss because of their own professional focus. Special health problems created by the disaster are often avoidable if they are addressed early enough in the response, and public-health professionals can identify these problems long before they become critical. A perfect example would be air-quality testing during the World Trade Center response. Public-health representatives need to be in on any planning for disaster, either man-made or natural.

Public Information

The Public Information member of the liaison team will take the role of Public Information Officer (PIO) during a disaster. Management of information given to the press and the public is critical during a response. The press used to be the only way the emergency-management team could speak directly to the public. Now any PIO would coordinate not only with the press but through social-media messages and web sites, as discussed in Chapter 8. While a single person may be the lead on the liaison team, she will need several other individuals to assist her in monitoring the various types of media and making sure that the correct messages are delivered.

The PIO's job is to manage requests from the press, monitor reports by the press, and help elected officials and emergency managers craft press releases. If the public needs information, it is up to the PIO to work with the appropriate emergency-management team members to craft that message and determine the best method or methods to disseminate the information to the specific audiences.

It very important that the public be kept abreast of the efforts being made by the emergency-management team members to return the community to normal. Not because it is good for their careers or reputations but because it will increase the speed of the response. If the public is aware that its needs are being addressed and how and where help is available, that knowledge will translate into a smoother transition for everyone. An informed public is an asset to the recovery.

Medical

A medical representative is a critical participant in any liaison group. Hospitals in the community are not only critical to a response but also critical as infrastructure that must be supported during and after the response. They receive and are responsible for the care of the sick and injured. Coordination with the various medical facilities before, during, and after a response is vital.

An ideal candidate for the liaison job is the EMS medical director, who is usually an emergency physician. This physician works on a day-to-day basis with emergency responders yet has standing in the medical community. The medical community is a very insular one, and the person on a liaison team must be able to bridge the gap between emergency management and the medical community. The EMS director is just such a candidate with connections in all the needed agencies. Another possible candidate is an emergency physician from the local trauma center or emergency room. Emergency physicians have been in the forefront of disaster planning and response for years. They must plan and drill for disasters as part of their hospital's accreditation. So they already understand many of the concepts of disaster management and would be a valuable asset to any liaison team.

Either of these types of doctors would have the right kind of experience and medical community contacts. Be aware that any physician wearing this many hats will be a difficult person to pin down for planning or training sessions, but he or she will be invaluable during an event. Inclusion even on a limited basis will provide huge benefits in a response.

HOW TO CHOOSE YOUR TEAM

The people chosen to be on a core liaison team have to be carefully selected. Very senior people within an organization are not good candidates for the team. Their day-to-day responsibilities within the organization and their leadership during a response will likely make them unavailable both before or during a disaster. The ideal candidate would be a mid-level manager with enough experience to understand the intricacies of their department's operational workings and senior enough that the head of their department will listen when they need to coordinate plans or be kept abreast of issues.

It would be best if the person chosen for each function had an interest in emergency management for their department and for the community. There are individuals who will find the subject matter a new challenge and look forward to learning new skills. What you do not want is a careerist, someone who thinks that becoming a liaison is going to further their career. In most cases this is not going to happen. Emergency management on someone's internal department resume will not help him or her climb up the promotional ladder. In fact, in some departments it will appear to be a dead end. Yet if a disaster strikes anyone in one of these positions will have the opportunity to make a difference for their department and community. Political and departmental officials will see them in a leadership role. It can be a stepping-stone to promotion within their department or even outside positions because of the experience. To the right person the liaison's position can be a real opportunity for the future.

So as you look to fill the spots on your liaison team, interview each candidate closely. If you find that one department is not sending the right types of candidates and you cannot get it to change, the best decision is to simply leave that function off of the team. It is better to have the right members on your team than to have a reluctant member. Make do with good candidates and, if a disaster occurs, the department without a representative will be noticed and you may find a much more receptive head once the elected officials have noted the lack of cooperation.

TRAINING TO BUILD THE FIVE CORE COMPETENCIES

You cannot simply assign people to the team, then expect them to perform under the stress of a disaster; you must build the team. Team building with people from different backgrounds, professional cultures, and skill sets is a challenge. At the same time, because they all are subject-matter experts whose various skills are needed, they all come to the table with capabilities that have to be respected by other members of the team.

Adults learn best by doing not by being told what to do or being lectured to by an instructor. Design short exercises that allow the members to work together as a team. Each exercise should emphasize coordination and interaction among the team members so they get a chance to work together as a team. As they work together through different types of problems, they will begin to build a dynamic that will lead to teamwork. Vary the subject matter so different team members will need to take the lead during the exercise. Over time they will come to understand each others' expertise and naturally begin to work as a team. These exercises do not have to be large and elaborate; instead they should be designed to bring into focus a single type of problem and all of the associated issues that have to be addressed to properly solve that problem. See Chapter 10 for a more detailed discussion of training and some exercises that can be used to train your team.

Day-to-Day Operations Before a Disaster

Another way to prepare your community and team for a disaster is to have each member of the Critical Liaison Group keep a Common Operating Picture (COP) of their department at all times. Members should be aware of any and all major projects currently underway that could affect their departments' ability to respond to a disaster. Examples could be major public-works projects that disrupt traffic or the loss of a piece of equipment or personnel that would impact the department's ability. The objective is to develop a COP of your community at any given moment so that, if a disaster strikes, you have a baseline to work from as you begin your response. Without that baseline you would have to develop one before you could begin your response.

The Big Hole

I was delivering training to another community in hurricane preparedness. Before I began the exercise, I talked in general terms about how even the best-written plans were always affected by the day-to-day operations of a community, which could make those plans useless. I looked around the room and asked, "Are there any projects currently underway that would affect your response if a hurricane warning was issued for your community?"

I really expected the usual types of small problems that would have to be addressed before the storm hit; instead I saw one man's face fall with a sudden realization. I looked at him and said, "You look like you like you just realized you had a big problem."

He was the head of public works, and his department had just begun a major upgrade of the storm-water system for a large part of the city. They had pulled apart a major part of the underground system and were just starting to replace it. It would take more time to temporarily repair the system so that it could work at some level during the storm than they had before the hypothetical storm struck. Because the storm-water system was torn up, he explained, there would be serious flooding if a hurricane were to strike, and its impact would be worse because of the job they were doing. No matter how good a plan is as written, the real world will sometimes throw that plan out the window.

It is just this type of awareness that the team should strive to have at all times—a knowledge of projects, public events, and other major operations or breakdowns that would affect the response of the community. A community is a living, breathing organism that changes each day, and if a community is to be prepared, emergency management must be aware of changes that could affect a response. While these are not part of the Essential Elements of Information (EEI) of a disaster, they are important in understanding a community's capabilities at any given time. Asking the liaisons to maintain this type of awareness not only fosters the development of teamwork but makes the concept of a COP a true picture of a community at any given moment and not just an operational concept.

Should a disaster strike, it would be the Critical Liaison Group members' job to take the lead in gathering the EEI about their respective departments. Without being told to do so, the liaisons would begin to gather information about their specific areas of expertise whether they are in the EOC or not. By beginning to gather information they are beginning to answer the first vital question, what have we got.

Daily Essential Elements of Information

- law enforcement
  - resources deployed
  - status of personnel
  - status of facilities
  - status of equipment
  - field reports of civilian deaths, injuries, missing persons
  - field reports of critical infrastructure
    - roads
    - hospitals
  - field reports of homes damaged or destroyed
- firefighting
  - resources deployed
  - status of personnel
  - status of facilities
  - status of equipment
  - field reports of civilian deaths, injuries, missing persons
  - field reports of critical infrastructure
    - roads
    - hospitals
  - field reports of homes damaged or destroyed
- emergency medical services
  - resources deployed
  - status of personnel
  - status of facilities
  - status of equipment
  - field reports of civilian deaths, injuries, missing persons
  - field reports of critical infrastructure
    - roads
    - hospitals
  - field reports of homes damaged or destroyed

- public works
  - resources deployed
  - status of personnel
  - status of facilities
  - status of equipment
  - field reports of civilian death, injuries, missing persons
  - field reports of critical infrastructure
    - roads
    - lift stations
    - water treatment and waste water
    - electrical grid
  - field reports of homes damaged or destroyed
- information systems
  - resources deployed
  - status of personnel
  - status of facilities
  - status of equipment
  - damage to critical information infrastructure
    - computer systems
    - radio systems
    - telephone systems
    - 911 systems
- medical
  - status of medical facilities
    - hospitals
      - medical beds/surgical beds
        - physically available beds
        - staffed beds
        - unstaffed beds
        - occupied beds
        - available beds
      - critical-care units
        - burn ICU
        - pediatric

- pediatric ICU
- psychiatric
- negative pressure/isolation
- operating rooms
  ☐ staffing
    - doctors
    - nurses
    - technicians
  ☐ surge capacity
    - staffed beds that could be available within 24 hours
    - staffed beds that could be available within 72 hours
  ☐ electricity
  ☐ water
  ☐ generators
    - fuel
  ☐ food supplies
  ☐ communications
  ☐ pharmacy supplies
  ☐ morgue status
  ☐ patient transfer needs
  ☐ nursing homes
- public health
  – special threats or ongoing issues
- public information
  – scheduled events or meetings

The Team

By organizing and training together this liaison team would prove to be invaluable during a response. Local subject-matter experts who know their departments and yet have the overall perspective of the community in mind, available at a moment's notice, would be an invaluable asset during a response.

The liaisons would already have a working knowledge of the COP of their department before the event; if a disaster did occur, they would be able to gauge the impact on their departments almost immediately. Working under a set of expected actions (EA), the liaisons would quickly begin to size up the disaster. This will multiply the effect of emergency management on a community. A team of critical subject-matter and emergency-management experts would dramatically decrease the time it takes to organize a response. Working with and through their various departments the liaisons could begin to organize the community's response long before other communities were just beginning to organize.

Once they have reported to the EOC, the liaisons would assist the emergency manager in organizing and running the overall response. They could be split up into the needed leadership roles within the ESF structure by assuming administration, logistics, planning, and operations positions. As ESFs reported, the liaisons could organize and assist them in beginning the response.

One of the issues that will arise and that must be addressed prior to the event is the very real pull that the event will have on the liaisons. They will want to respond to the scene or scenes of the event with their departments. I speak from experience: I had to be ordered at one point to stay behind and open the EOC when I had finagled my way onto a task force that was headed to fight the Florida wildfires.

Those interested in emergency management and disaster response will have to fight old instincts to respond to an event. This impulse will have to be addressed before the event with frank conversations and agreements by the liaisons. Yet even that might not be enough, and the emergency manager may have to work with the heads of the liaisons' departments to reinforce their agreement to report to the EOC. The opposite side of the same problem is the department head who suddenly realizes just how valuable someone with disaster skills would be and tries to prevent him from reporting. The emergency manager has to have the backing of the community's leaders in order to inform the department heads that the liaisons' responsibilities are not with the departments but at the community-wide level at the EOC. They will still be coordinating with their departments, but they have larger responsibilities representing their department at the highest levels of the community.

Should the disaster be a specialized type of event such as a pandemic, then the liaison with the most expert knowledge in that area could become the lead subject-matter expert for the response. In this case that would be the public-health representative. The medical liaison would also be very important in such a response, and the other liaisons and emergency manager could take their directions from those with the most knowledge.

This organizational fluidity is needed as the type of disaster changes. It would not change who was in charge, only who would be the leader within the team because of specialized knowledge. This ability to retain an organizational structure while still moving the best qualified into a leadership role is the best way to assure the best response possible. Not all disasters are the same; the problem sets can require very specialized knowledge if the best decisions are to be made. That is why the liaisons come from such different disciplines within a jurisdiction. They will be able to understand the effects of a specific type of event on their area of expertise as well as lead should that discipline be the area most affected.

The Critical Liaison Team Effect

The team as described is a vital step toward a higher state of readiness for any community. If you combine it with the technology and day-to-day integration of emergency management into the fabric of a community, you begin to build the type of capabilities than will make a true difference during a disaster. The most critical parts of any response are the men and women who handle that community's daily operations, for they must shift from normal operations to those needed during a disaster. The liaison team will make that shift a much more rapid and effective one. People make the difference; they overcome a lack of equipment and technology or other obstacles to a response. Organizing a Core Liaison Group is a way to spread preparedness much further across departmental lines and deeper down into other departments within a community. This change in culture by members of their own departmental culture will have a greater effect than any policy or plan could ever have. The development of the Core Liaison Group becomes one of the most effective preparedness actions any community could take.

CHAPTER 10

Training the Team

When you bring together your entire emergency-management team to respond to a disaster, you are combining very different cultures under very difficult circumstances. Normally during day-to-day operations each is functioning in its own silo, with its own policies and procedures. The clash of these different cultures can cause problems both personally and operationally.

One of the primary aims of training for response is to familiarize the various people and cultures with one another and to develop a way to work together. If you do not practice working together, you cannot expect these personalities, cultures, and organizational norms to work efficiently together under the pressure of a disaster response.

You are not just fighting the various professional cultures when you bring them in for training. You are fighting a culture of not training. Most of the people who will be assigned to the EOC during a response come from professions that are not required to train. In fact, it is a sign of having reached a certain level within their professions that they are finally above having to report for training. This makes them not only uncomfortable with training but reluctant to come to training, period.

There is a prevailing culture of "it will not happen on my watch" among many. They are reluctant to spend time training for something that they hope and can reasonably assume will not happen during their tenure. Disasters are still rare occurrences, so it is easy for someone whose job has nothing to do with disaster response to be reluctant to spend time on such a rare occurrence.

Another hurdle to developing a regular and accepted training program is the fear of making mistakes. Many of the participants in any training will be very uncomfortable about appearing not to know what to do under the stress of a training exercise. Given that they have a reputation of competence in their particular departmental silo, it will be a threat to them to appear incompetent in front of their peers. What will the others say when they all go back to their jobs after training? Will a mistake or confusion in training translate into a change in their hard-won reputation? Adding to the mix and an even more powerful incentive not to appear confused or in need of guidance, many of these people are appointed officials, which means that they "serve at the pleasure of" an elected or a higher appointed official. How will a poor or confused performance affect their promotion or even their reappointment to their current position?

Finally, the teamwork required in an EOC is foreign to many of the people in the room. Unless they come from a public-safety background where teamwork is essential to the job, many have worked in environments where it is every person for himself. Everything is seen through the prism of self-interest, the "what's in it for me" syndrome. I like to call it the survivor attitude, referring to that TV show that celebrates a sophisticated game of "screw your neighbor to get to the top." Too many corporate cultures are exactly like that, despite all of the management consultants' teamwork rah-rah seminars. Yet if a disaster response is going to work, that type of attitude cannot exist in the EOC; it will simply slow operations to a stop.

How do you overcome these obstacles so that you can train the people that you need? There is no magic formula, I am afraid. As I suggested in Chapter 1, the roles of trusted agent and facilitator will go a long way in establishing your reputation as being competent and fair. If their bosses accept your leadership when they assign task members to come to the training session, it will go a long way to opening the door to your acceptance. But you will still have to earn that respect with good training. Establish some ground rules at the beginning:

- In a disaster response the people in this room right now will determine how well we, as a community will fare. You and everyone here will make a difference.

- Each one of you is a subject-matter expert whose knowledge is needed during a response. The objective of these training/ classes is to expose you to the policies, procedures, and types of problems you can expect so you can learn to apply your expertise to them.

- You are here to learn how to work in a very different and difficult environment that is entirely new for almost everyone in the room.

- We want to make mistakes here and now so we don't make mistakes when property and lives are on the line after a disaster.

- Make it as enjoyable as possible by setting the right tone. I used to say. "When was the last time you got to call in the helicopters?". It always drew a laugh and people seemed more open to the situation.

If you establish these ground rules up front, it will go a long way toward helping you over the hurdles previously mentioned. It does not mean that this is all you will have to do to win team members over, but it will set the right tone for the training.

REALITY-BASED TRAINING

Adults learn best in small, easy-to-absorb doses. They do not have only the training on their minds; they are thinking about the jobs they just left and the deadlines competing for their attention. Children put their full attention to learning; adults simply have more on their minds. So set your training goals to make a few important points that can be absorbed easily by those attending. Do not overwhelm them with long lectures. Develop short, easily repeatable exercises into an overall training plan.

Training for emergency response is about changing normal day-to-day behaviors by changing how someone reacts to situations and information. The training should be incremental in nature, one step at a time, with the long-term goal of changing how team members view and respond to information in the environment of an EOC. Remember that this is a new way to make decisions in a stressful environment; a single training session is not going to accomplish such a significant change. Your goal should be a long-range one—you cannot have the attitude of "one and done." View it as a process of exposing them to the whole range of new challenges they will face in a disaster response.

Adults can only absorb about 20 to 25 percent of what they are exposed to learn in a training day. Develop your training around short and easily absorbed lessons that can be repeated several times with different details. Adults can only abosorb two to three hours of meaningful content in any single training day. Plan your training around these parameters.

Adults do not learn by being lectured to. They learn best by talking about the subject so they can discover their own take on it; they learn best by doing. If you want them to learn something, then let them "do" it and the lesson will stick.

People accomplish more difficult tasks best through teamwork. Training therefore must be highly interactive and comprise more doing than listening. Involve the learner in "real life" exercises, case studies, and discovery exercises. Interactive training works best with a class of about 35 people, large enough for the students to break into manageable groups.

Scientists in the military and the aviation industry have been studying how teams react to stress and make decisions for years. They studied airline cockpit crews for behaviors that contributed to crashes and military command teams as they made decisions in battle. To train a team, they found that you need to train on two different tracks. One is learning the skills related to execution of the procedures that must be accomplished. The other track is learning how to function effectively as a team member and as a team. They found that good teams monitor each others' performance to see if a member needed help, not to correct behaviors. They developed a shared mental model through training and responding to outside inputs. A mental model is simply the way that the team sees the problem and understands the tasks that must be accomplished to manage the issue. Members have a Common Operating Picture with a shared situational awareness. This allows them to adapt to meet the challenges in a highly stressful and rapidly changing environment.

First learn and practice the procedural skills necessary; then you can begin to address more sophisticated training to incorporate those procedural skills into decision making.

> "If you are going to train someone to make decisions in a pressure time-sensitive environment, then they must train in similar circumstances. Create time-sensitive information-starved situations, then ask for their responses."
>
> —Gary Klein, *Sources of Power*

To accomplish the type of training you need, you must develop it with the following goals in mind:

- Students should be in their respective roles when they train. This means staffing their designated ESF or other role where they will be assigned during a response.
- The time frames they have to accomplish the tasks should be similar to the real-life time frames.
- The problems have to be realistic.
- Train for the most likely disasters. You can lose a class by using an earthquake scenario in a jurisdiction where earthquakes simply don't occur. Use the type of disaster most likely to occur.
- Use real disasters as a source for the lessons. Use real timelines and actual problems to design your classes.

As you design your classes select a specific operational element such as a Common Operating Picture, Visualization, or Situational Awareness for emphasis. Provide information about the situation in the same timeline and through the same technology that they would normally receive the information.

Allow mistakes and include consequences of those mistakes in training. Seeing the consequences as they train will help reinforce the proper behaviors. There are no single correct answers—there may be several ways to solve the problem—so build into the training the ability to allow participants to find unique answers.

Train often, and make the training short and to the point. At the end of a session, without warning, tell them a disaster has just occurred or a hurricane or flood warning has just been issued. Ask the class to answer the three questions for their department on that specific day:

- What have you got?
- What do you need to do?
- What do you need to do it?

The objective is to teach a constant awareness of their departmeantal COP at all times. If there is an unexpected event, they will be thinking about specific problems that are current and timely. Produce a map of the jurisdiction with a tornado path, earthquake damage, or a flood outline and ask the same question. This is a simple, repeatable exercise that will emphasize the importance of having a good COP and situational awareness at all times.

EXERCISE DEVELOPMENT

The following steps will help you develop a well thought-out and realistic scenario that will meet your training goals:

- Determine the exercise objectives and types of exercise that will meet your training needs.
- Select the general scenario type, location, and size.
- Consider the general sequences of events.
- Examine your training objectives to identify those factors that have a bearing on the course of action.
- Determine how your jurisdiction's geography and characteristics will affect the exercise's specific problems and sequence of events.
- Select a feasible sequence of events that can accomplish your training objectives.
- Select the final scenario objective and the final event that will end the exercise.

- Develop control measures for intervention guidelines to evaluate the progress of the exercise.

Conduct of the Exercise

To properly conduct an exercise, you would ideally have an instructor and a controller. The instructor's job is to make sure the learning objectives are met and that the participants learn the proper lessons from the exercise. The controller is more concerned with the mechanics of the exercise—for example, if you were using computers for a messaging exercise, he/she would make sure that the messages were delivered as designed and that the participants understood the program and were using it properly. The following guidelines assume that when conducting an exercise you will be able to partner with someone who will act as your controller:

- The instructor and the controller monitor the players to make sure that everyone is ready for the exercise and has the needed materials—i.e., briefing paper, computer, etc.

- The controller initiates and conducts the exercise.

- The participants employ the procedures according to the situation, standard operating procedures, and EOC protocols.

- The instructor monitors all players' activity to ensure opportunities for accomplishment of the learning objectives. The instructor should make notes of actions, both positive and negative, to aid them in conducting the postexercise debriefing.

- The controller assists the instructor in these monitoring activities in addition to conducting the exercise. The controller maintains the pace of the exercise.

- The instructor must decide whether or not to interrupt play or let the exercise continue when they observe actions that can affect the accomplishment of the learning objectives or results in negative learning if not corrected.

- The controller and instructor coordinate their activities to determine whether learning objectives have or have not been accomplished during the exercise.

- The instructor must decide when to terminate the exercise. The controller should be consulted prior to making this decision.

Monitoring an Exercise

The conduct of an exercise requires cooperation between the controller and the instructor. The controller is responsible for the mechanics of the exercise itself. The instructor is responsible for the learning activity. These responsibilities overlap. The controller must be aware of the learning objectives and alert the instructor to events that may preclude the development of a situation that provides the opportunity to accomplish the learning objectives.

The instructor is also concerned with the conduct of the exercise. Gamesmanship must not be allowed to occur, as it could result in situations or actions that promote negative learning. Gamesmanship occurs when a participant becomes more concerned with successfully completing by any means the steps that will let them and those around them meet the learning objectives than by learning from them. There are two major concerns for the instructor and controller during an exercise:

- The conduct of the exercise must provide opportunities to accomplish the learning objectives.

- Actions and situations that result in negative learning must be avoided.
    - Negative learning is defined as learning that results in inappropriate behaviors on the part of the participants, behaviors that would lead to significant negative consequences in the real world. Negative learning has to be critiqued.

The instructor must ensure, prior to the start of an exercise, that the controller has prepared the exercise components properly and that the players have been provided with the briefings, papers, and other materials necessary for them to be able to participate in the exercise.

During the exercise preparation, the controller and the instructor work together in developing the lesson. This same coordination must be maintained during the conduct of the exercise. The instructor and controller must have their own game plan worked out prior to the start of the exercise—the learning objectives, expected time of occurrence during the exercise, and accomplishment of the objectives. If not met, they must be prepared to step in.

The controller has the primary responsibility to conduct the exercise; however, he must remain alert to incidents or actions that will prevent the accomplishment of the learning objectives. The controller must work closely with the instructor to prevent or correct negative learning. The necessity for maximum instructor-controller coordination cannot be overstated; the successful conduct of an exercise requires a well-coordinated instructor/controller team effort.

Control of Learning

The instructor has the responsibility to control learning. She must ensure that the learning objectives are accomplished and negative learning is prevented or corrected. The instructor, with the assistance of the controller, must monitor the preparation activities of the players and the use of their assets. The instructor must decide when they or the controller should intervene, if necessary, to maintain control of learning.

Participants in an exercise must maintain an awareness of the purpose of the exercise. Regardless of outside influences and individual attitudes, the participants should keep the purpose of the training in mind—to learn from experience. It does not matter that the experience is "artificial" in the sense that it is just training. The experience will translate into needed behaviors during a real response. The proper attitude must be developed and maintained to prevent an attitude among participants of simply going through the motions without meeting the learning objectives.

Making mistakes should be encouraged during an exercise. In fact, it is preferable that mistakes be made in the training context rather than during actual disaster conditions. If a particular training goes poorly with multiple mistakes by many in the class, the instructor should praise the effort and discuss how successful their efforts were for learning. Explain that the more mistakes are made in training, the fewer will be made during a response. Reinforce just how much they learned because of the mistakes and how that will translate into the correct actions during a disaster.

It is the mission of an emergency-management team to perform successfully during a disaster. It is much more helpful to make mistakes in an exercise and learn an important lesson than to "beat" the exercise and lose during a real event.

Intervention

When players' actions during an exercise result in a situation that prevents the accomplishment of the learning objectives, the instructor has the responsibility to step in and maintain control of the learning. The intervention can take several forms:

- They can give an instruction to one of the participants that corrects a negative-learning point. For example, in a information-flow exercise one of the participants does not pass on a piece of information that needs to be shared with everyone. Since one of the main purposes of the exercise is to practice just such a situation, if the participant does not pass on the information, a important learning point will be lost. The instructor could quietly sit down next to the participant and explain what they should have done and make sure they pass on the information. The exercise continues as planned, and a strong learning point is made with the participant without pointing out the mistake out to the whole class.

- A break or halt in the exercise can be taken while information and/or detailed instructions are given to the group as a whole. If the instructor sees not just one or two of the participants missing the point or not performing as needed in the exercise, stop the exercise for a course correction. Explain what is going wrong and make sure everyone understands the right way to manage their portion of the exercise. This immediate reinforcement of the correct action allows the instructor make sure that the learning objectives are being met.

- Additional issues or messages can be injected into the exercise to bring the class back on track to accomplish the learning objectives. If chosen carefully, the new injects can compensate for the imbalance brought on by bad decisions or failure to follow protocols.

- It is important to evaluate the probable consequences of any of these interventions prior to implementing them. The instructor and controller should have built into the exercise some consequences to mistakes made. These consequences can lead to more learning than an intervention. It will be up to the instructor and controller to discuss their options before major changes in the exercise are made.

Feedback

There are three possible sources of critique and feedback that can occur in a exercise:

- exercise originated—the exercise itself reacts to the decision made and provides the proper feedback immediately
- instructor originated—this type of feedback can occur before, during, or after an exercise, most likely occur during the debriefing
- player originated—this occurs after the exercise and during the debriefing and results from a student discussing specific details of the exercise that were critical decision points within the scenario

When critique and feedback are provided is critical to learning from an exercise. Deciding critique or provide feedback during the exercise can be more damaging than allowing the exercise to run its course. Remember, critique or feedback is very different from issuing orders to correct a negative-learning incident. The orders issued by the instructor to correct a negative-learning incident do not comment on a student's decision; they simply correct the situation. A comment on an improper decision should come in the debriefing. All instructor critique and feedback should be provided at the end of the exercise.

Critique and feedback are the backbone of learning from exercises. The exercise itself will provide feedback to the trainee as she makes decisions during play. The instructor must provide not only the feedback that the exercise itself does not provide but also put into context the feedback the student received from the exercise. The instructor must make explicit the connection between raw exercise feedback and the learning objectives established in the development of the exercise:

- The instructor monitors and notes critical incidents that occur during the exercise.
- The instructor monitors the exercise itself to assure that it reacts in a realistic way to the decisions made by the trainees.
- The instructor ensures that gamesmanship does not take over the trainees' decision-making process.

- The instructor intervenes when necessary during the exercise, providing corrective action within the exercise.
- The instructor provides postexercise debriefing and critique.

Critique of EOC personnel performance is very delicate. Participants who qualify in an EOC exercise bring years of experience to the training. They have passed promotional exams and performed well in their fields as managers. Critiques of their decision making must be done with respect and professionalism, or any learning will be lost. Instead of calling it critique, it may be better to describe it as feedback for the participant.

Post Exercise Actions

The specific post exercise actions that must be accomplished by the instructor, with assistance from the controller and participation by the players are debriefing, critique, feedback, feedback assessment, and development of training recommendations:

- Critique is the responsibility of the instructor with assistance from the controller and is a structured part of the postexercise activities. The critique comments by the instructor should be organized chronologically as they occurred in the exercise. They should emphasize the accomplishment or nonaccomplishment of learning objectives, and they should correct negative learning.
- Feedback assessment is the next step in maximizing the effectiveness of an exercise. The instructor and controller should evaluate what occurred during each of the three periods:
  - pre-exercise
  - during the exercise
  - post exercise

The feedback must be evaluated by the instructor and other participants to identify training needs. The process is a simple but important one. The instructor evaluates the participants' performance by answering these questions:

- Did the players successfully achieve the learning objectives of the particular exercise? If so, why?

- Which tasks were not performed?
- Did the participants successfully perform all the tasks and skills required in the exercise?

The instructor, by evaluating the results of the critique and feedback activities, is able to identify training deficiencies. Once these deficiencies have been identified, additional training exercises can be designed to address them.

TRAINING RESOURCES

The following training documents are meant to be used as both examples of training and as finished training exercises. The reader can utilize them to provide the type of training just discussed in the chapter or change them as needed to meet the needs of a particular jurisdiction.

EXERCISE RESEARCH

The following exercise research examples are included to provide readers with ideas on how they might approach the research for an exercise before developing the training. The briefing papers included can be used to develop exercises in and of themselves, but they were also included as examples of the type of research that needs to be done prior to the development of any good exercise. Depending on the size of the exercise, this could be just the start of the research needed.

I used the National Planning Scenarios tables for each of the events as a starting point for the development of the impact figures. My intention was to simply scale to fit the exercise needs based on the size of the community affected. These were developed for a state EOC exercise but they can be scaled down by simple arithmetic until they fit the size of the community. The National Planning Scenarios are a rich source of detailed material, statistics, and estimates that will add realism to almost any exercise. The idea is to simply scale the numbers down to the size community, county, or state affected and use those figures. Remember, in developing this type of training the numbers you use do not have to be exact to produce good training. There are too many variables to produce the exact event, but by doing the best research possible you can develop training that will give participants skills to face a real disaster with all its complexities. The rest of the details were gathered from the Internet through Internet research into the type of event and digging through press briefings, damage reports and lessons learned.

Tornado Outbreak

Casualties	150 fatalities; 750 hospitalizations, 2500 injuries not requiring hospitalization.
Infrastructure damage	Extensive power outages in large areas of the state.
Evacuations/displaced persons	Approximately 5000 throughout the state with homes destroyed, apartment and condo complex's damaged. The number will vary according to the county.
Contamination	From hazardous materials whose storage facilities were damaged or destroyed, overturned rail cars.
Economic impact	Hundreds of millions
Potential for multiple events	There are twenty tornado touchdowns reported across the state.
Recovery time	Months to years

DETAILS

In late spring a large cold front coming into the state from the west interacts with a warm moist air from the gulf to produce a large squall line that produces multiple tornados across the state. This line of severer thunderstorms produces multiple Super Cells, which spawn multiple tornados ranging in severity from F2s to F4s. These are severe and long lasting storms that stay on the ground for long periods of time. The outbreak affects several neighboring states but the impact on the specific state participating in the training will be the following.

There were seven major destruction paths out of the 20 tornados to touch down.

Tornado	Deaths	Injuries (hospitalized)	Property damage in millions	Length in miles on the ground
1F4	24	432	50+	25
1F3	2	54	10+	8
2F3	5	49	10+	19
3F3	17	370	50+	17
4F3	1	34	5+	36
2F4	45	700	60+	121
3F4	33	650	45+	22

The rest of the dead and injured were distributed among the other 13 tornados. These seven tornados (F3s and F4s) would cause the most damage and deaths during the outbreak. F3s would have winds between 156 and 206 mph, tear off roofs, with some walls torn off of well-constructed houses, overturning trains, and uprooting most trees. F4s have winds between 207 and 260 mph and will level well-constructed houses, blow structures with weak foundations some distance, throw cars and generate large missiles from debris.

Damage reports to infrastructure:

1. F4 Railroad bridge blows apart and rests in river
2. F3 Blows over a train carrying a hazardous materials car
3. F4 State hospital severely damaged and needs evacuation
4. F4 Loading docks destroyed at railroad yard
5. F3 Power plant off line for 2 weeks
6. Schools damaged (see below)

School	Damage Estimate
Morgan Twp. Elementary (1–5) Enrollment (258)	Roof deck damage Estimated loss $20,000
E.O. Muncie Elementary School (K–6) Enrollment (779)	Roof/windows Estimated loss $500,000 Covered by insurance
Michigan Road Elementary School (K–6) Enrollment (239)	Estimated loss $500,000 Future uncertain Covered by insurance
Southwestern High School (9–12) Enrollment (464)	Estimated loss $300,000 Gymnasium $100,000 Repairable
Southwestern Elementary–Jr. High School (K–8) Enrollment (1266)	Estimated loss $1,500,000 Will be rebuilt
South Decatur High School (7–12) Enrollment (739)	60% of gym roof damaged Water damage to gym floor Water damage to lobby Water damage to the music area Cafeteria wall caved in Estimated loss $100,000

School	Damage Estimate
Kennard Elementary School (K–6) Enrollment (176)	Total loss Estimated loss $720,000 Insurance covers 90% of the cost
Blue River Valley High School (7–12) Enrollment (582)	Roof damage, glass damage, and water damage Estimated cost <$20,000 Fully covered by insurance
Monroe Central High School (7–12) Enrollment (565)	Estimated loss $1,900,000 Insurance available $1,500,000 Some equipment salvageable
Attwood Elementary School (K–6) Enrollment (179)	Roof/windows Estimated loss $11,000
Leesburg Elementary School (K–6) Enrollment (410)	Roof on gym and top of school Estimated loss $14,000
Sqayzee Elementary School (K–6) Enrollment (393)	Gym roof damage Estimated loss $30,000
Riddle Elementary (K–5) Enrollment (559)	60–65% of building damaged. Roof, wall, and 3/4 glass Estimated loss $300,000
Talma Middle School (6–8) Enrollment (279)	Total loss no estimate
Bellmont High School (9–12) Enrollment (1082)	Auditorium roof moved—with water damage. Roof on high school damaged; also, window and water damage. Estimated loss $50,000
Bellmont Jr. High School (5–8) Enrollment (422)	Steeple of church next door fell through roof and floor Estimated loss $100,000
Eastern High School (7–12) Enrollment (572)	Nominal roof damage Estimate unavailable
Polk Elementary School (1–6) Enrollment (146)	Roof damage Estimated loss $5,000
Perry Central Elementary (K–6) Enrollment (404)	Roof of auditorium blown off. Gym cannot be rebuilt, classroom damage Estimated loss $1,000,000+
Wilkinson Elementary School (1–6) Enrollment (350)	Gym roof damage Estimated loss $10,000

School	Damage Estimate
Charlottesville Elementary School	Estimated loss $3,000
Twin Lakes High School (10–12) Enrollment (669)	Total loss Estimated loss $3,300,000
Roosevelt Jr. High School (7–9) Enrollment (713)	Building can be utilized with repairs Estimated loss $1,900,000
Meadowlawn Elementary School (K–6) Enrollment (508)	Total loss Will be rebuilt Estimated loss $1,000,000
Total students affected 11,754	
Damages $13,283,000+	
Number of students moved until further notice 6,000	
Number of school districts reporting 25	

TIMELINE/EVENT DYNAMICS

The outbreak begins in the late afternoon and continues through the night. In the participating state the outbreak begins at 2 p.m. and continues until the last touchdown in recorded at 11 p.m. The 20 tornados occur in various parts of the state as the line of storms moves through the state. The seven causing the most damage and deaths are spaced throughout the outbreak.

SECONDARY HAZARDS/EVENTS

Natural gas and oil hazard: Leaks are caused by the storms with some significant damages to specific oil and gas storage facilities.

Damage to infrastructure and critical facilities: See above for schools. In addition, transportation lines (railroads and buses) are damaged, power plants are damaged, hospitals and other medical facilities are damaged. Essential services in the storms' paths both emergency and utilities, are severely impacted.

Debris: Debris is a huge problem, blocking roads and denying access to incoming assistance as well as on-scene responders. The amount of debris poses large problems for long-term disposal, as well as its initial removal.

SERVICE DISRUPTION

Medical services: Hospitals have been damaged in each of the paths of the seven worst tornados in the outbreak. Each needs assistance from the outside to continue to provide care to the community.

Fire and emergency medical services: Have both been impacted severely in the paths of the worst storms and need outside assistance to continue to provide services to their communities.

Transportation: Traffic lights throughout a large part of the affected area are out creating a grid lock of emergency vehicles, press, volunteers and the curious. The airport is out of service until the air traffic control facilities can be repaired.

Energy: Large-scale power outages will last for at least 10 days until the substation damaged in the storm can be repaired.

Homeless: Approximately 5,000 people are homeless because their homes or apartments were damaged by the storm.

Communication: All local emergency communications centers in the affected communities are on emergency power due to power outages. One has been damaged in the storm.

FEDERAL RESPONSE

Environmental Protection Agency is responding to coordinate the hazardous materials response.

American Red Cross has committed to opening shelters to aid the 5000 displaced by the storms.

Two **Urban Search and Rescue** teams have been put on alert and two are being initially deployed. Incident Support Team will be activated.

All FEMA **National Emergency Response Teams** and Emergency Support Team will be activated.

Department of Defense has issued a warning order for activation of a Task Force for the delivery of mass care and health and medical services should it become necessary.

NDMS, DMATS, and DMORTS have all been placed on alert. Three DMATS are in route to assist local hospitals with the casualties.

NATIONAL GUARD REQUESTS CATEGORIES

There would be a number of missions under each of these categories.

1. Security
    a. A very large presence is requested. Because of the scope of the damage to the state, the National Guard will be needed in a number of different communities.
2. Search and rescue teams in the local communities are overwhelmed and need assistance from the National Guard.
3. Distribute of generators to hospitals.
4. Assistance with patient care at hospitals.
5. Assistance with hazardous materials incidents. Many of the local hazmat teams were impacted by the storms.

Great Flood

Casualties	50 fatalities
Infrastructure damage	Multi-state event. Infrastructure in many communities completely wiped out. 75 towns completely inundated. Hundreds more partially flooded. Bridges out in a number of cities. Railroad traffic in the area halted causing shortages of vital supplies. 20 of the 275 federal levees have been over topped. 700 of the 1000 private levees have been overtopped.
Evacuations/displaced persons	85,000 people either temporarily or permanently evacuated from their homes at one time or another during the event.
Contamination	Extensive contamination of drinking water because of sewage plants flooded and hazardous materials facilities flooded.
Economic impact	Billions
Potential for multiple events	Evacuations needed in one area while levee assistance needed downstream.
Recovery time	Months to years

DETAILS

In April, the river had crested 6 to 10 feet (2 to 3 m) above flood stage and once again approached nearly the same levels during the month of May. At the beginning of June, the rivers dropped below flood stage and were receding. During the second week of June, river levels rose to near flood stage before yet again beginning their slow recession. By the end of June, the river was 4 feet (1.2 m) below flood stage at the major metropolitan community on the river in the state of the participating National Guard, while many other river locations in the region were near flood stage. In July the heavy rains started and the serious flooding began

TIMELINE/EVENT DYNAMICS

Areas will either be partially or completed flooded for the next 150 days. 6.6 million acres will be flooded and close to 400 counties will be impacted from one extent to another. Over half the damages caused by the flood will impact agriculture, including live stock, crops, fields, levees, farm buildings, and equipment. The floodplains along the main stem Mississippi and Missouri Rivers and the major tributaries that will be inundated generally are used for agriculture and most areas are sparsely populated. Throughout most of the area, river towns are protected by urban levees, or they are located primarily on a bluff. A few communities that will be completely flooded. Floodwaters will inundate neighborhoods rather than entire communities. Residences, businesses, and industries receive extensive damages in bottomland areas and along tributaries. Development in these urban areas, however, is largely in the uplands or is protected by urban levees. The remaining damages are primarily to residences, businesses, public facilities, and transportation. Much of the agricultural damage occurs in upland areas as the result of wet fields and a short growing season rather than inundation by floodwaters. Similarly, a portion of residential and business damages will be caused by basement flooding due to high groundwater and sewer back-up in areas outside the floodplain.

SECONDARY HAZARDS/EVENTS

Natural gas and oil hazards: Both types of facilities are flooded and put out of commission in various locations along the river. Some of the flooding produces leaks and fires at a few of the facilities. Some very large propane tanks are carried by the flood for miles and deposited in other towns.

Damage to infrastructure and critical facilities: S,chools in addition to transportation lines (railroads and buses) are flooded out and not usable, power plants are flooded causing power outages, hospitals and other medical facilities are flooded in some communities. Essential services both emergency and utilities, are severely impacted in the floods.

Debris: A huge problem, debris. It is blocking roads and denying access to incoming assistance. Debris from towns and cities up rivers is deposited in new towns and bridges that managed to survive the flood. The amount poses large problems for long-term disposal as well as its initial removal.

SERVICE DISRUPTION

Medical services: Hospitals will be damaged where the flooding is the worst. They are either damaged enough to restrict their ability to provide care or completely flooded out. Assistance from the outside will be needed to continue to provide medical care to the communities affected by the floods.

Fire and emergency medical services: Both have been impacted severely where flooding is the worst and need outside assistance to continue to provide services to their communities.

Transportation: Flooded interstates and major and minor state highways are closed until after the flood. Railway traffic is stopped as floods move through the area. Airports are closed due to flooding.

Energy: Large-scale power outages will last until the floodwaters recede and the stations have been repaired. This could mean weeks or months before complete service is restored.

Homeless: Approximately 70,000 people are homeless because their homes or cities were flooded. Some will never return to their homes, while others will return to rebuild.

Communication: Local emergency communications centers operations will be affected by floodwaters. In cities that are completely flooded the centers are non-functional. In other cities they are able to carry out some of the previous duties in a limited way.

FEDERAL RESPONSE

Environmental Protection Agency is responding to coordinate the hazardous materials response.

American Red Cross has committed to opening shelters to aid the 70,000 displaced by the storms. But they are stretched to the limited and need assistance from the National Guard.

All FEMA **National Emergency Response Teams** and Emergency Support Team will be activated.

Department of Defense has issued a warning order for activation of a task force for the delivery of mass care, health, and medical services should it become necessary.

NDMS, DMATS, and DMORTS have been placed on alert. Three DMATS are in route to assist local hospitals with the casualties.

NATIONAL GUARD REQUESTS CATEGORIES

There would be a number of missions under each of these categories.

1. Movement of planes, vehicles, and other equipment out of the path of the flood. Additionally, the movement of National Guard armory equipment and supplies to higher ground.
2. A number of communities request equipment and manpower for sandbagging activities.
3. Water works treatment facility supplying large metro area is flooded. A water station will be needed for large the metropolitan area for the foreseeable future. It will take over a month for the portable water to be certified as drinkable.
4. Air assets are needed for missions to aerially inspect gas lines and utility lines.
5. Equipment is needed to assist in the evacuation of nursing homes and hospitals in the path of the flood.
6. 6,500 national guardsmen needed for levee work of all types.
7. Air assets are needed to rescue a number of people in floating cars, including police officers when a levee breaks and a town is flooded suddenly.

Earthquake Outline

Casualties	1,400 fatalities; 100,000 injured, 18,000 require hospitalization; 20,000 missing and presumed to be trapped
Infrastructure damage	150,000 buildings destroyed, 1 million damaged
Evacuations/displaced persons	300,000 households (average 3 per)
Contamination	From hazardous materials
Economic impact	Hundreds of millions
Potential for multiple events	After shocks, fires, people trapped
Recovery time	Months to years

DETAILS

- Winter, middle of the week work day.
- 7.5 magnitude occurs. Damage in 15 to 20 states.
- Area approximately 25 squares miles around the epicenter sustains considerable damage to ordinary buildings and great damage to poorly built structures. Soil liquefaction has occurred, causing destabilization and collapse of numerous buildings no matter what the construction, transportation structures, and utilities. Some tall buildings collapse or "pancake" as floors collapse down on one another.
- Beyond the epicenter damage is spread over several hundred square miles.
- Several hours after the initial earthquake an after shock of 8.0 occurs. Additional aftershocks occur in the 7.0 to 8.0 range.
- Large waves overwhelmed barges and boats, also damaged river side building.
- 2,000 fires are currently burning.
- Flooding is severe in some areas due to levy breaking.

SERVICE DISRUPTION

Medical services: Only 11% of the hospitals in the area are functioning at greater than 50%. Backup generators are running out of fuel. There is a desperate need for additional hospital beds.

Fire and emergency medical services: Only 16% are functioning at greater than 50%. Dozens of trucks were damaged to the point of no longer being functional.

Transportation: Bridges have collapsed and caused significant obstructions on major highways. Damages to several major freeways are hampering incoming assistance. Railways and airport runways have buckled and sustained moderate to sever damage. All airports in the region are closed because of communication disruptions and moderately damaged runways and instrument landing systems and will be closed for at least 10 days before repairs can be made.

Energy: Large scale power outages will last for at least 10 days. Numerous ruptures to underground fuel lines, oil lines, and natural gas lines are straining repair crews.

Water: More than a million people are without water due to ruptured water mains and power outages. It will be 10 days before service can be returned.

Wastewater treatment: Wastewater primary interceptors were broken in the vicinity of the epicenter and will be inoperable for close to 10 days before a return to near normal. Over 300 have been damaged or are without power.

Homeless: Two-thirds of the 300,000 displaced victims need temporary housing. That is 200,000 needing temporary housing. Half of the existing pre-designed shelters have been damaged and cannot be used.

Military facilities: Military facilities are reporting moderate building damage, temporary loss of utilities, and access is difficult due to bridge/overpass damage.

Port facilities: Port cranes have fallen and been dislodged due to ground liquefaction, leaving ports completely non-functional. Damaged and sunken vessels litter adjacent piers and in some cases block the channel. The port will be out of service for a month.

Communication: Damage to microwave dishes and other vital parts of the communications infrastructure have resulted in limited communications capabilities. Cellular towers have also been damaged and the high cellular traffic after the earthquake has saturated what is left of the system. It will be a week before 90% of the infrastructure can be returned to normal.

FEDERAL RESPONSE

Environmental Protection Agency is on the scene to coordinate the hazardous materials response.

American Red Cross has committed thousands of volunteers from surrounding states since those volunteers in the impacted area are not capable of responding. So normal Red Cross shelters are not being manned.

All 28 **Urban Search and Rescue** teams have been put on alert and six are being initially deployed. An Incident Support Team will be activated.

All FEMA **National Emergency Response Teams** and Emergency Support Team will be activated.

Department of Defense has issued a warning order for activation of a Task Force for the delivery of mass care and health and medical services.

NDMS, DMATS, and DMORTS have all been activated and deployed.

NATIONAL GUARD REQUESTS CATEGORIES

There would be a number of missions under each of these categories.

- temporary hospital beds.
- debris removal on highways
- construction of temporary bridges over some critical waterways

- Clean up/restoration of airports
- Helicopters and fixed wing aircraft for supplies and personnel transportation
- Temporary airport operations, i.e., air traffic control
- Portable water transportation
- Security
- Search and rescue
- Commodities distribution generators
- Support and security for large tent cities (25,000 to 50,000 population at each location) that are set up for the homeless
- Evacuation of special needs population out of the area to other states
- Evacuation of homeless to shelters in other states, ala Katrina

Wildfires

Casualties	20 fatalities
Infrastructure damage	500,000 acres were burned, 1350 homes destroyed.
Evacuations/displaced persons	600,000 people either temporarily or permanently evacuated from their homes at one time or another during the event. 40 counties declared disaster areas.
Economic impact	400 million
Potential for multiple events	Several fire complexes merged to create a large enough threat to force the evacuation of a county during the height of the event.
Recovery time	Months to years

DETAILS

Drought conditions brought on by a strong El Nino began in early May and continued to increase in severity and area throughout May. Conditions turned critical in June as continued dry conditions and wind began to produce hundreds of fires. By mid-June major fires were burning throughout the state and would continue to stress the firefighting capabilities of the state as well as the nation. At the peak of the event more than 10,000 firefighters from around the country and a majority of the firefighting equipment from around the country will be in the state trying to control the event.

TIMELINE/EVENT DYNAMICS

The demand for resources, both civilian and military, will begin in June and escalate dramatically as the fires grow from large individual wildfires to large complexes. The demand for National Guard equipment and manpower will grow with the escalation of the size of the fires and the scarcity of equipment to fight the fires.

Day 1

First fire reported near small town. Fire moves so quickly the initial engine crew that responded to the fire had to be evacuated by helicopter. The first fire grows to 8,000 acres by the end of the day.

Second fire reported north of first fire rapidly expands in dry brush close to 20,000 acres by the end of the day. High winds are preventing air support for firefighters.

Day 2

0630   Major football stadium is opened to house as many as 100,000 evacuees.

0658   20,000 homes have lost power, 650 firefighters are on the first fire, that is less than five percent contained. New fires are igniting around the second fire creating additional demand for firefighters and equipment. High winds are preventing air support from firefighters.

1200   The second fire has jumped the Interstate, and businesses, government offices, and schools are shut down.

1300   College cancels all classes. School district closes classes for the rest of the week.

1800   Governor visits football stadium and promises additional support from the National Guard and the military in support of firefighters.

Day 3

0800   Second fire has rapidly grown unchecked to 145,000 acres due to weather conditions. It has caused the evacuations of close to 300,000.

0900   Fire reported on military base. It grows to 17,000 acres. Military crews are unable to contain it.

1000   Weather conditions permit air operations in support of firefighting efforts. National Guard air assets are requested. Weather conditions are favorable for firefighting efforts.

2300   300,000 acres in the state have been burned. 1300 building have been destroyed. 500,000 residents have been evacuated. Schools remain closed across the affected counties.

Day 4

Fires have been slowed but are not contained. 30,000 more acres are involved.

Day 5

Winds have died to the point that crews begin to contain all fires. More than 1400 acres have burned.

Day 6

Most evacuees have been allowed to return to their homes.

SECONDARY HAZARDS/EVENTS

Natural gas and oil hazards: Various facilities will be threatened by the wildfires.

Damage to infrastructure and critical facilities: Some schools, nursing homes, and isolated power sub-stations will be threatened during the height of the fires.

Debris: Debris will not be much of a problem.

SERVICE DISRUPTION

Medical services: Hospitals and the medical community will be faced with increased usage due to the increase in the smoke and other irritants produced by the fires.

Fire and emergency medial services: Firefighting manpower and equipment will be stretched to the limit. Departments will need assistance with both manpower and equipment. Coordination between structure firefighting crews and wildland firefighting crews will be difficult.

Transportation: Interstates and major and minor state highways will be closed periodically as smoke and fire conditions warrant.

Energy: Energy production and delivery should not be significantly affected.

Homeless: Approximately 70,000 people are will be evacuated at one time or another during the fires as their homes are threatened.

Communication: Local communications will continue to operate in support of the firefighting efforts.

FEDERAL RESPONSE

Environmental Protection Agency is responding to coordinate the hazardous materials response.

American Red Cross has committed to opening shelters to aid the 70,000 displaced in the counties and locations affected by the fires.

FEMA Emergency Response Teams

FEMA has responded to the state's emergency needs by coordinating the federal response in the following ways:

- Within hours after the state requested them, FEMA approved seven requests for firefighting grants. Under those grants, FEMA pays for 75 percent of the state's eligible fire-fighting costs. Some of those eligible costs include costs for equipment, supplies, and emergency work like evacuations, shelters, and traffic control.

- FEMA opened a Joint Field Office to coordinate federal, state, tribal and local response operations throughout the state.

- FEMA has identified and established a staging area in order to mobilize necessary federal assets as identified for emergency operations across the state.

- A federal Emergency Response Team has been identified and staged to deploy as necessary to assist the state as needed.

- FEMA opened its Regional Response Coordination Center on a 24/7 basis to support state operations. The interagency center is comprised of federal agencies including the Department of the Interior, Department of Transportation, United States Forest Service, United States Army Corps of Engineers, Department of Health and Human Services, and The Department of Homeland Security's Infrastructure Protection.

- FEMA's National Response Coordination Center was activated to coordinate the national federal interagency response in support of regional and statewide activities.

FEMA has sent a liaison to the State Emergency Operations Center to work with the state's response and recovery staff to compile information on the fires and ensure that any request is expedited and the right resources are sent to the right places. A FEMA liaison is also coordinating response efforts with the Wild Land Fire Services in the affected county.

Department of Defense has issued a warning order for activation of a Task Force for the additional aircraft and manpower should it become necessary.

> The Department of Defense (DoD) has deployed Defense Coordinating Officers (DCO) and Defense Coordinating Elements to the State, and to Boise, Idaho. A Command Assessment Element was deployed to the affected area to support emergency response efforts. Each DCO will provide command and control of any responding active-duty forces, should they be requested, and will facilitate requests for any additional DoD support through U.S. Northern Command (USNORTHCOM).
>
> USNORTHCOM has also designated Air Forces North as the Joint Force Air Component Commander (JFACC) that will provide command and control coordinating authority over Modular Airborne Fire Fighting System equipped C-130 aircraft. The JFACC's intent is to rapidly and effectively support USNORTHCOM's efforts to the National Interagency Fire Center (NIFC) in order to mitigate the effects of wildland fires.

The Department of the Interior

Department of the Interior (DOI) wildland firefighters have been assisting with suppression efforts throughout the area for the past several days. Specifically, the National Interagency Fire Center (NIFC) in Boise, Idaho, dispatched federal firefighters and firefighting equipment to assist state firefighters in suppressing the wildfires. NIFC is made up of trained wildland firefighters from DOI agencies and the USDA Forest Service. The DOI agencies include the Bureau of Land Management, National Park Service, U.S. Fish and Wildlife Service, and Bureau of Indian Affairs. The NIFC is working closely with state and other federal responders to coordinate the deployment of more firefighters and firefighting equipment to the affected areas.

The American Red Cross

Red Cross activities are focusing on sheltering efforts, with shelters open in five counties across Southern California. The number of shelters has been fluctuating as additional evacuations occur and the fires change direction. Thousands of Red Cross cots, blankets and toiletry kits are being moved from warehouses in the western United States into the affected areas.

The Red Cross is partnering with the Southern Baptists to move two church kitchens into the area, and 75 mobile feeding vehicles will be moving into the area over the next two days to provide food for the shelters and emergency personnel on the scene.

National Guard Requests Categories

There would be a number of missions under each of these categories.

1. Requesting command and control units to assist the Red Cross at the stadium being used as a shelter. These units should include military police.

2. 1500 soldiers under Title 32 from the Guard's Brigade Combat Team requested to conduct patrols to prevent looting, man traffic control points, and prepare to assist people at football stadium and the fairgrounds, where thousands of people are waiting out the fires.

3. State requesting as many helicopters and fixed wing aircraft as can be provided be assigned to assist with water drops and transportation of personnel and equipment and reconnaissance of the fire.

4. State Emergency Management is requesting four bulldozers and tractor-trailers from Engineer Brigade to assist operations.

5. Three out-of-state fixed wing cargo aircraft and 50 airmen have been assigned to assist in operations within the state.

6. Sheriff's department is requesting four helicopters to assist their operations with two of them capable of water drops. The others will transport equipment and personnel.

7. Three out-of-state UH-60 Black Hawk helicopters with 18 crew members have been assigned to assist operations.

8. Twelve guardsmen with two HUMVEEs, three 2.5-ton trucks, and one water buffalo have been requested from out-of-state to assist operations from out of state.

9. Two out-of-state UH-60 Black Hawk helicopters have been assigned to assist operations within the state.

10. Fourty-two out-of-state troops have been assigned to assist firefighting and evacuation operations within the state.

11. A heavy expanded mobility tactical truck fueler has been requested to assist firefighting operations.

12. Units to support interoperable communications between civilian and military with personnel and equipment to state EOC as well as various locations around the state.

13. The National Guards Modular Airborne Firefighting System have been requested. To include 145th Airlift Wing, Charlotte, N.C., the 146th Airlift Wing, Channel Island, CA, and the 153rd Airlift Wing of Cheyenne, WY.

14. Rescue Wing with pararescue personnel requested to assist in rescues of civilians and firefighters during the wildfire.

15. Requesting maintenance personnel capable of working on bulldozers and firefighting equipment to assist civilian maintenance units and free up firefighters.

16. Requesting 1,200 guardsmen to be used for firefighting.

17. Requesting bulldozers and personnel to man them to assist in the construction of firebreaks.

Table Top Exercises

The following are two examples of how to approach table top exercises in very different ways. Each has it own strengths and weaknesses, but both are designed to encourage teamwork and decision making among EOC personnel.

WEAPONS OF MASS DESTRUCTION TABLE TOP EXERCISE
TRAINING GOAL
SITUATIONAL AWARENESS AND INFORMATION FLOW

The following is a simple table top exercise designed to facilitate communication and situational awareness for EOC staffs. Read the two entries Situational Awareness and Visualization for ideas that will help you facilitate this exercise. The objective of the exercise is not to solve the problem, but increase the awareness of information flow and sharing in an EOC environment.

At a minimum you will need participants to play the emergency manager, law enforcement, fire/hazardous materials, EMS, and PIO. Other ESFs can take part, including someone from public health.

The basic scenario is there is a large community event (football game, community celebration, concert—choose one that fits your community) being held in your community. There is a large presence of fire, police, and EMS at the event because of its size and importance in the community. Using the event as a training opportunity you have gathered some of your EOC staff together to monitor the event and practice communications with field units. Have a map of the scene up and ready. Place law enforcement, EMS, and fire units on the map. The event is occurring without incident when the following messages are received.

The following abbreviations stand for the corresponding roles:

- LE—law enforcement
- FD—fire department
- Haz Mat—hazards materials
- EMS—emergency medical services
- PH—public health

Hand the following messages to the roles in the following order, giving a minute or two for the person to read the card before you give out the next one:

- Field LE to EOC: LE there has been an explosion in the stands. Many people are down. (Choose a location for the explosion on the map.)
- Field LE to EOC: LE officers down. Repeat we have officers down. We need EMS down here.

- Field EMS to EOC: EMS we are responding to the explosion site.
- Field LE Command to EOC: We have had a large explosion here with numerous causalities. It occurred just as the fireworks show was starting. It appears to be a fireworks accident.
- Field FD to EOC: FD have requested a Mass Casualty response. We are responding to the explosion site to assist EMS.
- Field EMS to EOC: EMS we have approximately 25 people down now. Request as many ambulances as possible to respond.
- Field LE to EOC: LE the media was broadcasting live from the event. They are now covering the explosion live.
- Field FD to EOC: FD we have extinguished a small fire with a can fire extinguisher.

Choose a point of the map and begin to chart the event. Talk about the kinds of information that might be included on the map and what symbols or information might be used to represent them.

At this point ask.

- What do we know?
- What are the informational priorities?
- What do we need to know that we don't know?
- Is this a terrorist attack or an accident?
- Does it matter?
- What should the EOC be doing at this point?
- Who should be notified?
- What should the public be told?

Do no limit the discussion to just these questions; open up to any discussion that concerns situational awareness and communication. Write your answers on flip charts or white boards so everyone can see them. When you are satisfied with the discussion, hand out the next set of messages.

- Field LE to EOC: LE we are setting up a perimeter around the site. (Use the map to draw a perimeter around the event let the class discuss where the perimeter should be.)

- Field EMS to EOC: EMS we have established a triage area at _____, treatment at _____ and transportation is to stage at _____. (Fill in the blanks with real intersections around your selected site. Let the EMS participant choose the sites.)
- Field LE to EOC: LE requesting additional officers to assist with crowd control.
- Field EMS to EOC: EMS be advised we have approximately 100 BLS patients. Advise hospitals to expect a mass casualty flood of patients. A number of the walking wounded have left the scene and will be heading for the hospital.

Give some time for discussion before handing out the next card. Some questions you might ask are:

How many additional officers will be needed?

Which hospitals and who should be notified?

Now hand out the next card.

- Field FD to EOC: FD there has been a second explosion. I repeat there has been a second explosion.
- Field EMS to EOC: EMS we had people down. We need additional units immediately.
- Field LE to EOC: LE we officers with difficulty breathing and blurry vision.
- Field FD to EOC: FD we are also experiencing symptoms. This is some sort of chemical attack.
- Field FD to EOC: FD we have requested the hazardous materials team for decontamination.

Update the map and discuss the event.

Stop and ask.

- What do we know?
- Does anyone know what type of chemical was used?
- How do you find out?

- Have our information priorities changed?
- Should some be added?

Discuss the fact that the first report of the event indicated it was some sort of accident.

- What should the EOC be doing now?
- What are implications of a chemical attack outside the incident scene?
- Do we know enough to know if we need to order evacuations?

Finish the exercise with a discussion of the information flow and situational awareness.

TRAINING EXERCISE

Decision Point
Livingston, Louisiana

The following is an example of training that teaches teamwork and decision-making under difficult circumstances. I've chosen this training as an example of the type of training that can be developed directly off a lessons learned document. This is a good example of boiling a long and complex response to a single very difficult decision that needs input from a whole team of people with varying expertise. The answer is not clear-cut and can be argued both ways. The use of a real incident adds complications and reality to the training.

The participants are to be broken into small groups of interdisciplinary experts. Someone trained in hazardous materials response should be a part of each group or available to move from group to group to assist in their decision-making. The object of the exercise is to present the participants with a real and difficult decision that has no correct school answer. It is meant to create discussion of the various long-term impacts of their decisions. It in many ways mimics the types of difficult decisions that may have to be made after a major disaster.

Training Notes

Break the class into smaller multidiscipline groups of four or five at each table. Ask them to choose a spokesman/leader for their group before they know what the problem and decision they will have to make.

Hand out the initial briefing paper and the map of the train derailment. Using Power Point slides 1 through 9 brief the participants on the incident. They will be able to follow along using their briefing paper and graphic. Slide 10 explains the decision they are to make. Now hand out the answers you want from each group.

Decision Handout for Participants

1. Identify your options.
2. Estimate the likely harm these options could have on the community at this point in the event.

3. Choose your actions.

4. Set objectives for those actions over the next 72 hours.

At this point in the training the small groups should be given a fixed amount of time to answer the questions. The objective is to let them work through the issues and come up with their own solutions. There are no correct answers—the objective is to give the opportunity to work together. Given the various subject matter experts in each group, there should be a vigorous discussion of the options.

Once the time limit is up, ask each of the group's leaders to answer the questions. After they have all given their answers encourage discussion between the groups. If one has a question about the others' decisions, that is fine but do not let them deteriorate into arguments. When the instructor determines that enough discussion has occurred, stop the discussion and reveal what decisions the real life team that was actually facing this challenge made by going through the slides.

Now that the actions of those who actually faced the decision have been revealed along with some of the lessons learned lead a discussion of what the participants think of the decisions made and if they would have changed their decision.

Initial Briefing Paper for Participants

At 0512 on the morning of September 28, a 101-car train derails in Livingston, Louisiana. The train includes 47 hazardous materials cars, 43 of those cars have derailed. When they derailed an explosion and fire around the hazardous materials cars immediately occurred.

One of the hazardous materials cars contains metallic sodium, but the car's location within the wreck is unknown. This chemical reacts explosively with water, so the fire department is unable to use water to try and control the leaks and fires until the metallic sodium car has been located within the wreck. Efforts to locate the car have been hampered by the fires and leaking hazardous materials.

Livingston, Louisiana, a town of 2,000, is completely evacuated. The railway line runs through the heart of Livingston and the state road that runs through the town is also shut down. Explosions and fires continue over the next several days as efforts to locate the metallic sodium car continue. On the fifth day after the event, the metallic sodium car is located intact among the other hazardous materials cars. Fires and leaks are almost under control. Railroad crews begin to re-rail some of the hazardous materials cars, and as a styrene car is lifted a fire ensues. The fire is extinguished. It is found that the car is leaking fumes that will eventually find an ignition source and ignite, making further clean up of the site too dangerous to proceed.

Decision Point

State police explosive experts are suggesting the styrene car be detonated and its fumes burned off in a planned explosion. This is very dangerous given the number and type of hazardous materials involved, and the effect the explosion could have on those materials.

In addition, there is a car filled with a carcinogenic product that is leaking into the ground water. The town of Livingston obtains most of its drinking water from the local wells. Various products are contaminating the ground at the site and eventually will find their way into the drinking water if the leads are not stopped soon.

Hazardous Materials Involved

Tetraethyl Lead (TEL)

Fire or Explosion

- Highly flammable; easily ignited by heat, sparks, or flame
- If rail car involved in a fire, isolate for 800 meters (1/2 mile) in all directions.
- Caution: this product has a very low flash point. Use of water spray when fighting may be ineffective.

Health

- Toxic: may be fatal if inhaled, ingested or absorbed through skin.

Runoff

- Causes pollution.

Vinyl Chloride

Fire or explosion

- Extremely flammable
- Will form explosive mixture with air

- Vapors may travel to a source of ignition and flash back
- Containers may explode when heated
- If tank care involved in a fire isolate for 1600 meters (1 mile) in all directions.

Health

- Vapors may cause asphyxiation without warning
- Inhalation, ingestion, or skin contact may cause severe injury or death.

Ethylene Glycol

Fire or explosion

- May form explosive mixture with air.
- May polymerize explosively when heated or involved with fire.
- Use water spray, fog, or alcohol-resistant foam.

Health

- May cause toxic effects if inhaled or absorbed through skin.

Styrene monomer

Fire or explosion

- Vapors form explosive mixtures with air
- Vapors may travel to ignition source and flash back
- Vapor explosions a possible hazard indoors, outdoors, or in sewers
- Containers may explode when exposed to heat.

Health

- Inhalation or contact with material may irritate or burn skin and eyes
- Fire may produce irritating corrosive and/or toxic gases

Toluene Disocyanate

Fire or explosion

- Combustible material may burn if ignited
- Substance will react violently with water releasing flammable toxic, or corrosive gas and runoff

Health

- Toxic inhalation, ingestion, or contact with skin with vapors, dusts, or substances may cause severe injury, burns, or death

Perchloroethylene

Fire or explosion

- Some of these materials may burn

Health

- Substance determined to be carcinogenic

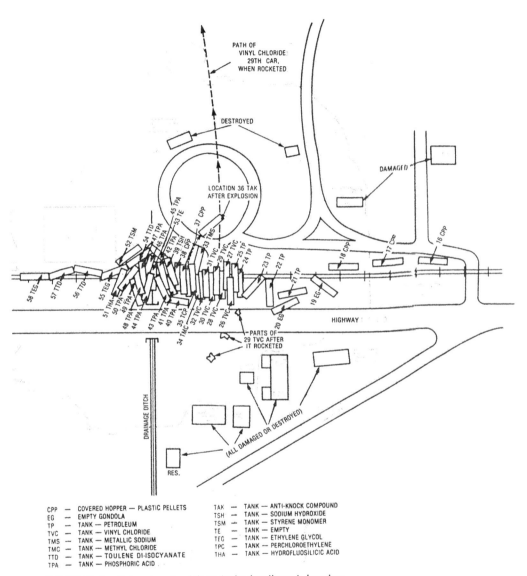

FIGURE 10.1   Livingston, Louisiana train derailment drawing.

POWER POINT SLIDES FOR THE DECISION POINT LIVINGSTON, LOUISIANA TRAINING

Slide One

- Decision point
- Livingston, Louisiana

Slide Two

- September 28
- 05:12 the extra 9629 derails
- 101 car train
  - 47 hazardous materials cars
    - 43 cars are derailed
      - 36 tank cars
      - 27 non-regulated hazardous materials cars
      - 5 flammable liquid cars
      - 20 breached or punctured

Slide Three

- A metallic sodium cars is involved in the derailment
- Its location within the derailment is unknown
- Metallic sodium reacts violently with water

Slide Four

- The following slides give a day-by-day account of events
- September 29
  - 0005 the TEL car explodes
  - 1500 fires still burning
    - 3 TEL cars involved
    - 4th and 5th plastic pellet cars involved

Slide Five

- September 30
- 14:00 #3 VCM (vinyl chloride) relief valve lifted and venting increases in intensity
- 1412 #3 VCM car venting decreased to a continuous burn

Slide Six

- October 1
- 1500 forward observation post reports an increase in and change in venting sounds
  - 1522 #4 VCM BELEVE's
  - 1523 #3 VCM venting increases in intensity
  - 1530 #3 VCM venting decreases in intensity

Slide Seven

- October 3
  - Metallic sodium car located
  - Assessment team makes entry to determine the stability of the products involved.
  - Team reports products are stable

Slide Eight

- October 4
  - Hole plugged in styrene car
  - Re-railing of cars on west end of wreck begins
    - □ Last three cars re-railed
  - Efforts to re-rail styrene car ignites product
  - Firefighters bring fire under control
  - Styrene car releasing vapors

Slide Nine

- Decision point
  - Because the vapors from the styrene will eventually ignite, the state police explosive experts suggest a planned explosion of the car to vent and burn off the product under controlled conditions
  - 14,000 gallons of perchlordothelene is leaking into the ground water and is a carcinogenic. Rains are spreading the product.

Slide Ten

- Decision point questions:
  - Identity your opinions

- Estimate the likely harm these options could have on the community at this point in the event.
- Choose your actions
- Set your response objectives for these actions over the next 72 hours.

Begin class discussion here.

Slide Eleven

- Outcome
  - October 5th the tank car was successfully detonated and the product was burned off
  - October 10 six vinyl chloride cars too badly damaged to be moved were detonated and their products were burned off
  - October 12 at 0800 the residents were allowed to return to the town.

Slide Twelve

- Aftermath
  - Clean up costs $15 million dollars
  - Incident lasts 14 days
    - Impact on the community lasted much longer

Slide Thirteen

- One year later
  - U.S. highway and railroad line still closed
  - 60,000 cubic yards of contaminated soil removed
  - Several families were displaced
  - 700 lawsuits were pending

Slide Fourteen

- Remember, your initial decisions can affect the outcome of the situation. If those decisions are wrong, you may make the situation worse instead of better.
- Gather information before you act.

- This is a perfect example of the need for a continuous size up to keep an accurate situational awareness of the event.
- Certain types of events will change and continue to change until actions are taken to stop the event.
- Remember the OODA Loop and use it
  - Observe
  - Orient
  - Decide
  - Act
  - Repeat

Slide Fifteen

- Any attempt to confront an incident without adequate knowledge of its potential dangers can be more work than simply evacuating the area, withdrawing, and taking no action.

Slide Sixteen

- Lessons learned
  - Detecting hazardous materials presence early is critical to proper handling
  - Estimating likely harm and then choosing response objectives
  - Identify action options
  - Continuously observe the sequence of events

Slide Seventeen

- Operational decisions have political consequences
- Political decisions have operational consequences

FUNCTIONAL EXERCISE

Hurricane Patricia

This exercise is designed to be used as a series of Table Top Exercises or a Full Functional Exercise. The exercise is broken into pre-storm preparation issues and post-storm problems. So an instructor can break the problem sets into either two or three different Table Tops held at different times.

There are briefing messages and Incident Action Plans that can be used to begin each section of the exercise. The assumption with each Incident Action Plan is the participants are an incoming shift and the IAP was designed to give them a shift change brief. The briefs are bare bones so a user can add jurisdiction exclusive details should they want to make the exercise more specific. I did not include exact hourly timing for the problems, leaving that up to the users, discretion. If used as a Table Top exercise, the messages can be delivered on 3x5 cards or a Power Point presentation. While a Functional Exercise would require the messages to be delivered to the participants by controllers or through a message system. The Expected Actions are general in nature and the user can adjust them to be more specific to match their specific individuals or roles.

Abbreviations

EM—Emergency Manager
LE—Law Enforcement
PW—Public Works
PIO—Public Information Officer
ESF—Emergency Support Function

URGENT - WEATHER MESSAGE
NATIONAL WEATHER SERVICE
446 AM EDT FRI AUG 13 2004

AT 11 AM...1500 UTC...THE NATIONAL HURRICANE CENTER
HAS ISSUED A HURRICANE WARNING FOR ALL OF THE EAST
COAST OF THE STATE. A HURRICANE WARNING MEANS
THAT HURRICANE CONDITIONS ARE EXEPECTED WITHIN
THE WARNING AREA WITHIN 24 HOURS. PREPARATIONS TO
PROTECT LIFE AND PROPERTY SHOULD BE RUSHED TO
COMPLETION.

...HURRICANE FORCE WINDS LIKELY OVER INLAND
COUNTIES BORDERING COASTAL COUNTIES BY LATE
TODAY...
...TROPICAL STORM FORCE WINDS LIKELY ACROSS THE
REMAINDER OF THE STATE THIS AFTERNOON AND
TONIGHT...

INTENSE HURRICANE PATRICIA LOCATED JUST OFF THE
COAST EARLY THIS MORNING IS FORECAST TO MOVE WEST
ALONG THE EAST COAST TODAY THEN INLAND ACROSS THE
STATE TONIGHT. PATRICIA IS LIKELY TO BECOME A MAJOR
HURRICANE PRIOR TO LANDFALL...WITH WINDS WELL OVER
HURRICANE FORCE NEAR THE CENTER. STRONG WINDS
WILL OVERSPREAD MUCH OF THE COASTAL AREAS OF THE
STATE FROM SOUTH TO NORTH BEGINNING LATE THIS
AFTERNOON...WITH DAMAGING WINDS EXPECTED FROM
SUNSET INTO THE OVERNIGHT HOURS...ESPECIALLY WELL
INLAND.

...INLAND HURRICANE WIND WARNING IN EFFECT
THROUGH TONIGHT...

THE INLAND HURRICANE WIND WATCH HAS BEEN
UPGRADED TO AN INLANDHURRICANE WIND WARNING. AS
PATRICIA APPROACHES LANDFALL OVER THE EAST COAST
LATE TODAY OR EARLY THIS EVENING...SUSTAINED WINDS
WILL INCREASE ABOVE 40 MPH DURING THE AFTERNOON.

PEAK WINDS ARE EXPECTED TO REACH HURRICANE FORCE...75 MPH WITH HIGHER GUSTS... FOR SEVERAL HOURS DURING THE EVENING AS THE CIRCULATION CENTER PASSES. WINDS WILL GRADUALLY LESSEN DURING THE EARLY MORNING HOURS...LIKELY FALLING BELOW 40 MPH TOWARDS DAYBREAK SATURDAY.

OUTER RAINBANDS ASSOCIATED WITH PATRICIA WILL SPREAD INTO THE REGION EARLY TODAY WELL IN ADVANCE OF THE CENTER...WITH SCATTERED SHOWERS AND STORMS CONTAINING TORRENTIAL RAINS AND GUSTY WINDS LIKELY. A THREAT FOR ISOLATED TORNADOES WILL ALSO EXIST TODAY.

FINAL PREPARATIONS FOR THE DAMAGING WINDS SHOULD BE RUSHED TO COMPLETION THIS MORNING. DRIVING WILL BECOME DANGEROUS THIS AFTERNOON AS WINDS PICK UP AND DEBRIS BEGINS TO BE BLOWN ABOUT.

IF YOU LIVE IN A MOBILE HOME...OR A HOME THAT AFFORDS LITTLE PROTECTION FROM FLYING GLASS AND DEBRIS... EVACUATION TO AN ALTERNATE SHELTER SHOULD BE COMPLETED THIS MORNING.

MANY INLAND MOBILE HOMES WILL EXPERIENCE SIGNIFICANT DAMAGE FROM 75 MPH SUSTAINED WINDS. DAMAGE TO SHINGLES...SIDING...AND POOL SCREENS WILL OCCUR TO MANY PERMANENT HOMES. MANY LARGE BRANCHES WILL SNAP... AND WATER LOGGED TREES WILL BECOME UPROOTED. LOOSE ITEMS WILL BECOME AIRBORNE...AND WILL RESULT IN ADDITIONAL DAMAGE AND POSSIBLE INJURIES. POWER LINES WILL BE BLOWN DOWN AND EXTENSIVE LOCAL POWER OUTAGES CAN BE EXPECTED.

FOR ADDITIONAL PREPAREDNESS INFORMATION
CONCERNING HURRICANE PATRICIA REFER TO THE
HURRICANE LOCAL STATEMENT ISSUED BY THE NATIONAL
WEATHER SERVICE AND THE RECOMMENDATIONS FROM
YOUR LOCAL EMERGENCY MANAGEMENT OFFICE.

HURRICANE PATRICIA

Incident Action Plan 1
Pre-Storm Preparations

Mission: To initiate county actions as necessary to respond to all emergency operations, protective measures, and local evacuations associated with Hurricane Patricia and to provide information to the public on protective actions.

Areas of operation: County-wide operations

Activation level: 1 (24 hrs)

Situation: Hurricane Patricia is expected to make landfall as a Cat 4+ hurricane on the coast in the vicinity of the county to the south of us in the next 36 hours.

Weather update: Hurricane Patricia is presently a Cat 4 hurricane with maximum sustained winds of 150 mph moving WNW @ 15 mph. Storm surge is expected to be 10+ feet above normal tide, with rainfall in excess of 6 inches.

General operating objectives:
1. Open shelters and support sheltering operations
2. Order and coordinate evacuation of areas
3. Coordination of public information

Planning assumptions: Seven percent of the population in the affected areas are elderly or below the poverty level and may need assistance in evacuating the area.

Issues and constraints: Assuring all departments within county government have prepared their staffs, equipment, and facilities for the impact of the storm and are ready to respond after the storm effects have subsided.

Objective 1: Sheltering operations

Task	Responsible/Status
Special needs populations	ESF 8
Shelter operations	ESF 6
Identify medical and transportation dependent populations	ESF 5 and 8
Provide law enforcement support	ESF 13

Objective 2: Order and coordinate the evacuation of affected areas

Task	Responsible/Status
Order the evacuation	ESF 5
Monitor evacuation	ESF 5 and ESF 13
Assist special needs populations and transportation dependant populations	ESF 5 and ESF 8

Objective 3: Coordination of public information

Task	Responsible/Status
Coordinate with all ESFs on message content	ESF 14
Support hot line operations	ESF 14

Initial Planning Meeting for ESFs

Current Situation by ESF 5

- Hurricane Patricia to make landfall as a Cat 4+ in the next 36 hours.

- We can expect to experience some impact by the storm. Unclear at this point the extent of the impact. It could be a direct hit with Cat 4+ winds and storm surge or it could be less.

Future Actions by ESF 5

- Actions
  - Develop the number of shelters to be opened and when based on the National Weather Service forecast.
  - Develop an evacuation plan according to the expected impact.

Future Actions by ESF 6

- Actions
  - Notify the Red Cross of the number and location of the shelters to be opened.
  - Coordinate with ESF 16 and ESF 8 for personnel to assist Red Cross with the shelter openings.
- Issues
  - When will we be able to determine the number and location of shelters? What is the lead time needed to open shelters?
  - Will there be enough personnel to man all shelters? If not, where will the additional personnel come from?

Future Actions by ESF 16

- Actions
  - Once evacuation size and scope are identified, execute the appropriate evacuation plan for the evacuation.
- Issues
  - When will the evacuation decision need to be made and still have enough time to complete the evacuation?

Future Actions by all ESFs

- Actions
  - Notification of personnel who will ride out storm at facilities or in the EOC.
  - Implement plan to shutter and protect all facilities prior to tropical storm force winds affecting the area.
- Issues
  - Time needed to implement shutter and facility protection plan. How long will it take to accomplish that plan?

PRE-STORM INJECTS

36 Hours to Landfall

From	To	Message	Expected Actions
USA Today reporter	ESF 14	What preparations is the county taking? How many visitors does the county have at this time of year? Will the visitors be able to get out?	Press release answering the questions
Local radio station calls	ESF 14	Have any shelters been opened in the county yet? What are the shelter locations? We have received numerous calls from the public.	Press release answering the questions
Local TV station	ESF 14	I need to talk with someone from county emergency management, we would like to take some footage in one of the shelters. We would like to ride out the storm in one of the shelters. Who should I talk to?	Forward to ESF 5 and ESF 6 for answer
Local radio station	ESF 14	We just received a call from a local grocery store manager. They have 2000 1-gallon jugs of water they would like to donate to be placed in shelters. Who should we talk to?	Forward to ESF 6 and ESF 15
TV station from out of state	ESF 8	We would like to do a live interview with you. We would like to talk to you about the preparations you are making for people with special needs during the hurricane. Can you help us out?	Forward to ESF 14
TV station from unaffected part of the state	ESF 3	We are attempting to interview someone from a utility company on how they are preparing for the hurricane. Can you spend a few minutes with us discussing what you are doing?	Forward to ESF 14

From	To	Message	Expected Actions
TV station from unaffected part of the state	ESF 5	Could you spend a few minutes with us discussing the hurricane preparations the county is doing?	Forward to ESF 14
Local radio station	ESF 14	If people need assistance in evacuating their homes who should they call?	Forward to law enforcement for draft press release
Utilities	ESF 3	Rain over the past 24 hours has caused an increased flow throughout the county. There have been a few minor problems with sewers running full and pump stations failures due to power outages for short periods of time. (1–2 hours). All preparations are being completed and equipment is being readied for severe weather operations.	
Local TV reporter	ESF 14	We have had some complaints about the evacuation not being ordered in time. I would like to visit a shelter and interview some evacuees to find out their take on this. Can you arrange a visit?	
Citizen phone call	ESF 3	There are a lot of limbs down on my street. The last thunderstorm did the damage. When are you going to get out here and clean this up?	
Law enforcement field ops	ESF 13	Flooding in the _____ block of _____ street has forced homeowners and residents of the _____ apartments out of their homes. Residents have been advised local shelters are full. There are approximately 100 people in need of temporary shelter.	Forward to ESF 6

From	To	Message	Expected Actions
Law Enforcement field ops	ESF 13	Road update I-___ and I-___ solid traffic. State road exits at I-___ and _____ closed.	Forward to all ESFs
Law enforcement field ops	ESF 13	_____ High School did not have enough Red Cross volunteers show up. The deputies are helping staff to run the shelter. They need more Red Cross volunteers so the deputies can be relieved.	Forward to ESF 6
Local reporter	ESF 4	We understand that fire departments from all over the state will be sending help. Something called a mutual aid agreement. Can I speak with someone who can tell me about this agreement and who will pay for all of this equipment and manpower.	Forward to ESF 14
Law enforcement field ops	ESF 13	The _____ and _____ shelters are full and people are standing in the parking lot. Transportation is needed to other shelters.	Forward to ESF 6
Radio reporter calls	ESF 14	How many shelters are open in the county? What are the shelter locations? We have received numerous calls from the public inquiring about the shelters.	Prepare press release
Local food bank	ESF 6	Just wanted to let you folks know that we are attempting to find a couple of warehouses for donated goods so we can be a staging point.	Forward to ESF 15
Law enforcement field ops	ESF 13	Field units are reporting a tornado sighting near _____.	

From	To	Message	Expected Actions
Special needs shelters	ESF 6	We do not have enough medical personnel here. We needed additional help. Can we have fire department or EMS paramedics assigned to the shelter before the storm?	
Local businessman	ESF 15	We have 250 porta potties available for use after the storm. I understand the _____ grounds are going to be used as a staging area. Who should I talk to about getting them there and staged.?	
Fire department communication	ESF 4	We have units responding to reports of damage caused by tornado in the area of _____.	
Public works field ops	ESF 3	Water station 249 lost power.	
Red Cross	ESF 6	_____ special needs shelter is reporting the breakers are constantly being tripped by the oxygen machines that many of the patients are bringing with them. They need some assistance.	
Utilities field ops	ESF 3	We have received a number of calls from concerned citizens in the _____ area. Sewage is coming out of manholes on Lake _____ blvd and _____. The citizens want to know what to do. What about hepatitis and other diseases? Will the lake be unsafe for them? If so, for how long?	Forward to ESF 14 for press release
Local humane society	ESF 6	Do you have access to a list of the local hotels and motels that take animals? We are getting a lot of calls and would like to be of help but we do not have our list available.	Forward to ESF 14 for a press release.

From	To	Message	Expected Actions
Local TV reporter	ESF 5	I just attended a Homeland Security class for the media. They suggest that local agencies create a joint information center. Are you going to do this?	
Local reporter	ESF 5	Can you tell me the total number of people in shelters in the county?	Forward to ESF 6
Red Cross	ESF 6	_____ high school is reporting they have no deputy there and are requesting that one be assigned as soon as possible. The shelter is at capacity and people are getting argumentative.	
Law enforcement field ops	ESF 13	Three commissioners have requested additional law enforcement presence in their neighborhoods to protect their families when they are at the EOC. What should we tell them?	
CNN Reporter	ESF 14	We would like to do a live interview with someone there about the preparations. This storm looks to be almost as bad as Katrina and we would like to discuss the preparations the county made to take care of the evacuees.	

HURRICANE PATRICIA

Incident Action Plan
7 Hours After Landfall

Mission: To initiate county actions as necessary to respond to all emergency operations, protective measures, and local evacuations associated with Hurricane Marina and to provide information to the public on protective actions.

Areas of operation: County-wide operations

Activation level: 1 (24 hrs)

Situation: Hurricane Patricia made landfall in the overnight hours. Winds have diminished. Extensive damage has been reported overnight.

Weather update: Hurricane Patricia is now a Category 1 hurricane well inland and moving in a northerly direction.

General operating objectives:

1. Support open general and special needs shelters.
2. Damage assessment of entire county.
3. Coordination of public information.

Planning assumptions: Large-scale damage to homes and businesses expected. Significant disruption of communication, power, and other basic services expected for foreseeable future.

Issues and constraints: Need for mutual aid and National Guard resources need to be identified. The amount and extent of damage is constraining the damage assessment and the identification of exactly how much and what type of mutual aid is needed.

Objective 1: Sheltering operations

Task	Responsible/Status
Special needs populations	ESF 8
Shelter operations	ESF 6
Identify medical and transportation dependent populations	ESF 5 and 8
Provide law enforcement support	ESF 13

Objective 2: Damage assessment

Task	Responsible/Status
Field damage assessment	ESF 1, 3, 4, and 12 ongoing
County-wide damage assessment	ESF 5
Search and rescue	ESF 4 and ESF 9

Objective 3: Coordination of public information

Task	Responsible/Status
Coordinate with all ESFs on message content	ESF 14
Support hot line operations	ESF 14

7 Hours Post Storm Injects

From	To	Message	Expected Actions
Law enforcement	ESF 13	State road _____ is flooded under 2 feet of water. Road is closed.	Forward to all ESFs
Law enforcement communications	ESF 13	We received a call from _____ County. They have dispatched approximately 100 officers to our area. They want to know if assistance is needed.	Email with instruction of where to stage officers.
Public works	ESF 3	Electricity out in vicinity of _____ and _____. Fuel pumping station out, fire stations in area are on generator power.	Forward to all ESFs
National media	PIO	What preparations were taken before the storm hit given the lessons learned from Hurricane Katrina? What did you do differently?	Develop press release
Red Cross	ESF 6	_____ High School. Shelter is cut off due to road flooding.	Forward to all ESFs
Law enforcement field office	ESF 13	Flooding in _____ area. Roads are closed.	Forward to all ESFs
Law enforcement field office	ESF 13	Interstate _____ flooded and closed at _____.	Forward to all ESFs
Public work field	Public works	Several treatment plant operators from plant #1 have had their homes damaged and their families are without shelter. They will report to work if their families can be housed at the plant. Can we put them up there?	Reply to email
Public works field	Public works	Our crews have not eaten. Where can they get food?	Forward to logistics

From	To	Message	Expected Actions
State police	LE	_____ is closed at _____ due to debris in the intersection. It appears to be a large structure. It will be closed for some time.	Forward to all ESFs
Public works field	Public works	Some of our employees have sustained minor injuries while repairing equipment. Where do they go for treatment?	Forward to EM
Field LE	EOC LE	_____ and _____ intersection is flooded up to the hospital and into emergency room.	Forward to all ESFs
Reporter	PIO	We have received a report from a shelter that one of the people in the shelter has meningitis. We are going to carry the story and we would like a comment from you about the story.	Forward to EM and public health for development of press release
Law enforcement communications	Law enforcement	_____ County is requesting communications support personnel. Requesting operators with radio and complaint desk experience only, police teletype is non-functional. They are a bordering county, can we send them any help?	Reply by email—no
LE field	LE	There is a large fishing boat across _____ road along the beach. It is completely blocking the road. _____ road will be closed until further notice.	Forward to all ESFs

From	To	Message	Expected Actions
Bell South representative	EM	The telephone status of the switching stations in the county is unknown at this time. Long distance service is out. Local service is disrupted. We need to urge everyone to stay off the lines until we can do some repairs.	Forward to all ESFs Work with PIO to develop a press release.
Logistics field	Logistics	Which of the POD sites do you want to activate? I will need to organize the personnel to man them before the ice and water is delivered.	Develop list and forward to all ESFs
Parks office	Logistics	We have two two-man crews with chainsaws available. Where would you like us to send them? What priority streets need to be cleared?	Forward to transportation
Local public works field	Public works	Our repair crews are trying to get to stations in damaged areas. Unruly citizens are throwing rocks at their trucks and making threatening gestures. What kinds of support can we get to protect our workers?	Forward to law enforcement
County commissioner	EM	I have about 35 people in my neighborhood who are willing to volunteer their services for search and rescue or clean-up. Can we use them?	Forward to volunteers
LE field operations	LE	Several employees have not yet reported to work and it is time to do payroll. What pay status are the employees in? How do we report their time?	Forward to EM

From	To	Message	Expected Actions
Local hospital	Public health	We are on emergency power. We have had some walk-in injured, but not many. Normal access to the hospital is blocked. We have extremely low water pressure, which is proving to be a problem throughout the facility.	Forward to EM and public works
Message center	EM	A large oak tree has fallen over and pulled up a water main. Water is washing out the road at _____ and _____. Somebody needs to get out here and control this.	Forward to public works
Citizen	Volunteers	I just moved from Tennessee and I have been trained as a shelter manager. Is there some way I can help now? My house was undamaged and I would like to help.	Reply by email
Message center	EM	The _____ cemetery has been flooded and the coffins are floating out of the ground and down the street. We need someone out here to sort out which is which and get them back into the ground.	Forward to LE and public health
Parks department	Public works	What kind of clothing or markings should be worn by county employees so they can be identified as hurricane assistance crews? No one has enough uniforms to last until the power is back on and they can clean their clothes.	Reply by email

From	To	Message	Expected Actions
Waste water field	Public works	We have at least a third of our waste water pumping station without power and we are just beginning to do our assessment.	Forward to all ESFs
Public works field	Public works	Our teams in the field are reporting a roof off and a partial collapse of the community college. We need someone out here to inspect the damage.	Forward to EM
LE field	LE	Our units are unable to get to the beach because of washed out roads, downed power poles, and debris. From what they can see there are numerous houses along the beach that have been completely destroyed. A number have floated off their foundations and are now in the middle of _____, the main beach road.	Forward to all ESFs
Firefighting field operatioins	Firefighting	The stations are experiencing a number of people walking up with all manner of requests. Everything from minor injuries to requests for supplies. Should we have supplies brought to the stations to take some of the pressure off the POD's.	Forward to EM and logistics
LE field	LE	We have a large chlorine tank leaking at the _____ public swimming pool. We need to get a team out here to take care of this.	Forward to EM, fire, Hazmat
Local media	PIO	We have heard rumors of looting. Can you tell us if they are true?	Develop press release

From	To	Message	Expected Actions
Waster water field ops	Public works	We have a 100% failure of our telemetry system. The antenna was blown down.	Forward to all ESFs
CNN Atlanta	PIO	Could you spend a few minutes with us discussing the damage and what you are doing to manage the evacuees?	Answer with email
Logistics field	Logistics	We expect the first mutual aid units in the next few hours. We need to establish the staging area for them. We are requesting law enforcement on site to assist in keeping out citizens looking for supplies.	Forward to LE
Corrections	LE	The jail has lost all power and the generator is not providing enough power to run the whole facility. The circuits that run the gates to enter the facility and the sally port were not put on the emergency circuits. Do not bring any more prisoners to the facility and be prepared for a possible transfer of those still being housed.	Forward to all ESFs
LE field	LE	The large cross interstate sign is down and blocking the interstate. I____ is completely closed both ways.	Forward to all ESFs
LE field	LE	The small civilian airport has been badly damaged by a tornado during the storm. We have a number of planes turned over and leaking. There is heavy damage to all structures. We need someone to come out here and inspect the damage.	Forward to EM, Fire and Hazmat

From	To	Message	Expected Actions
LE field	LE	The _____ apartments have collapsed and we have reports of people trapped. We need fire rescue out here to do some search and rescue.	Forward to EM, Fire, search and rescue, hazardous materials
LE field	LE	In the _____ neighborhood we have residents pulling up manhole covers in an effort to speed up the drainage of the flooding on their streets. It is a danger to anyone walking, as well as to cars. We need someone out here from public works to try and manage this flooding or talk to the residents.	Forward to public works
Message center	Public health	We are receiving a lot of calls about the water and whether it is safe to drink. What should we tell them?	Develop a statement for the message center
Power company	Public works	_____ substation is down and lines out. _____ substation access is blocked. Several hours before a report can be given. _____ appears undamaged but not receiving a feed. _____ substation is down. Lines are down.	Forward to EM

HURRICANE PATRICIA

Incident Action Plan 8
24 Hours Post Landfall

Mission: To initiate county actions as necessary to respond to all emergency operations, protective measures, and local evacuations associated with Hurricane Patricia and to provide information to the public on protective actions.

Areas of operation: County-wide operations

Activation level: 1 (24 hrs)

Situation: Hurricane Patricia made landfall 24 hours ago. Damage assessment and search and rescue operations are ongoing.

Weather update: Hurricane Patricia has dissipated to the north.

General operating objectives:

1. Damage assessment of entire county.
2. Search and rescue operations.
3. Support long-term sheltering operations.

Planning assumptions: Widespread damage to houses, businesses and infrastructure. Sheltering operations will be long-term. Sections of the county will remain restricted to public safety personnel only until they can be cleared as safe. Widespread power outages throughout the county will last for weeks. Communication disruption will last for weeks. POD operations will continue for some time to come.

Issues and constraints: Need for mutual aid and National Guard resources need to be identified. The amount and extent of damage is constraining operations and additional resources are needed to speed up the recovery and return to normal.

Objective 1: Sheltering operations

Task	Responsible/Status
Special needs populations	ESF 8
Shelter operations	ESF 6
Identify medical and transportation dependent populations	ESF 5 and 8
Provide law enforcement support	ESF 13

Objective 2: Damage assessment

Task	Responsible/Status
Field damage assessment	ESF 1, 3, 4, and 12 ongoing
County-wide damage assessment	ESF 5
Search and rescue	ESF 4 and ESF 9

Objective 3: Coordination of public information

Task	Responsible/Status
Coordinate with all ESFs on message content	ESF 14
Support Hot Line operations	ESF 14

Post Storm Injects
24 Hours Post Landfall

From	To	Message	Expected Actions
Law enforcement field	Law enforcement	Last night we did not have enough personnel to enforce the curfew. There were a number of incidents of looting. We need assistance from the National Guard as soon as possible. We need at least a company to support our officers. When can they get here?	Forward to EM to forward to state
Field logistics	Logistics	We should be receiving the first shipment of ice and water today. We need to coordinate with the PIO to make sure the public knows when and where the supplies will be available.	Forward to PIO
Public works field	Public works	We would like to request a 2 Debris Clearance Task Force from the state to assist with major street clearing. (See request assistance form I sent you if you want to use a form as an attachment for this)	Forward to EM to forward to state
Public works field	Public works	The senior citizens home on _____ has noticed that there are several vans in our yard on _____. They are requesting permission to use those vans to transport some of their residents to shelters.	Answer by email

From	To	Message	Expected Actions
Public works field	Public works	Excess water from the hurricane demands we pump 40 to 50 million gallons into the plant in order to keep the water off the civilian populace. The only problem is we can only handle 36 million gallons through our filters to be discharged at the distribution center. What do we do?	Answer
Message center	Public health	We are receiving calls from the public reporting dead animals along roadways and in empty fields. What should we tell them they should do with the corpses?	Forward answer to PIO for press release
Fire field	Fire	Our units are having a hard time finding their way around, even as well as they know the streets. Most of the street signs are down or gone. Can public works get to work on this problem? LE is also having problems.	Forward to PW
Local hospital	Public health	Because of low water pressure, our labs cannot process tests (along with other problems). Can we get a fire department pumper truck to help increase the pressure in the building?	Forward to FD

From	To	Message	Expected Actions
Fire field	FD	We would like to request two Type 2 Fire/Rescue Task Force teams to assist with search and rescue from the state. (See request assistance form I sent you if you want to use a form as an attachment for this.)	Forward to EM to forward to state
Fire field	Fire	Our units are running into a large number of homebound people with significant medical problems, including all manner of chronic respiratory problems. Can you work with public health to provide some sort of alternative so they do not tie up our units.	Forward to PH
Public works field	Public works	Due to the hurricane all of the fields where sludge is hauled are flooded, the digesters are full and there is no room to store sludge. What can be done with the sludge? Can more room be made so operations can continue?	Answer by email
Message center	Public health	We are getting calls from people who did not stock up on their medications before the storm and are now running low. There are almost no pharmacies open. Where can they get refills for their medications?	Forward to PIO with wording for press release

From	To	Message	Expected Actions
Message center	Public health	We are receiving calls from people who want to know what to do about their pools. Without power they going bad quickly and they are starting to become breeding places for mosquitoes that can carry diseases.	Develop press release
Fire field	Fire	Are there identified optional locations for fuel? A number of our stations' pumps are no longer working and our units are having difficulty going from station to station to get fuel.	Forward to EM for answer
Public works field	Public works	A convoy of 10 trucks and 20 people have arrived from South Carolina with emergency pumps and generators. Where can they be housed?	Forward to volunteers
LE field	LE	We are encountering a large number of non-English speaking people. We need assistance with translating.	Forward to volunteer to develop a press release asking for volunteers
Local media	PIO	We have heard reports of price gouging. Has an anti-gouging law been passed? If so can you give us details?	Develop press release
LE field	LE	We need to request two Type 2 LE special response teams from the state. (See request assistance form I sent you if you want to use a form as an attachment for this.)	Forward to EM to forward to state

From	To	Message	Expected Actions
Local hospital	Public health	Our emergency generator has not be able to keep up with demand. The air conditioning is not working well enough to keep the humidity down, so we have lost our ORs because of high humidity. Our emergency departments are packed with all manner and type of injuries.	Forward to all ESFs
Public works field	Public works	A sanitary mainline was damaged and is surcharging wastewater into homes and yards. Crews have set up bypass hoses and pumps to make a point repair on the mainline. Angry homeowners are requesting that we pump wastewater out of their homes and yards. What should we do?	Answer by email
LE Field	LE	We have had two units discover bodies in cars that were killed during the storm. They are requesting guidance on how to handle them until the ME can begin to collect them.	Forward to EM and public health
Public works field	Public works	The _____ beach road is completely washed out for almost a quarter of a mile in two different places. It will be closed indefinitely.	Forward to all ESFs
Local media	PIO	Can you give us the locations of the water and ice distribution sites and their hours of operations?	Forward to logistics

From	To	Message	Expected Actions
Public Health field	Public health	We would like to request two Type 3 Disaster Community Health Assistance Task Force teams to assist with the recovery operations.	Forward to EM to forward to state
Public works field	Public works	A crew working in the _____ neighborhood was approached by a resident. He saw a gas can on their trucks and is asking if he can buy some gas from them. His generator is running low and he is in danger of losing his food. What should we tell him?	Answer by email
Wastewater field	Public works	We are going to need to work crews 16 hours a day due to the flooding. How will we feed them? Can we work them this long?	Forward to EM for answer
Message center	EM	We are getting a lot of people demanding to know when they will be allowed back into areas we have blocked off so they can see their homes. What should we tell them.	Develop press release for PIO
Wastewater field operations	Public works	The street department is requesting two 6-inch pumps with 80 feet of hose to help control flooding. Should we fill this request?	Answer by email

From	To	Message	Expected Actions
Fire field	FD	Station _____ found a homeless man hiding in their outbuilding behind the station. He says he does not have anywhere to go. Can we get someone out there to transport him to a shelter?	Answer by email
FD field	FD	Emergency repairs have been made to station _____ and _____. The units are now responding out of their stations.	Forward to all ESFs
Wastewater field ops	Public works	Generator at _____ station is running rough and unable to deliver stable power loads. We are going to have to shut down the station until we can fix the generator or get a new one in here.	Forward to EM
State PIO	Local PIO	The governor wants to tour the damaged areas later today. She will need a law enforcement escort of about 10 officers as well as briefing by the EOC staff. She should arrive around 1500 today. Please coordinate these needs and advise when they are completed.	Forward to LE and EM
Message center	PIO	We are getting a lot of people from out of state asking how they can check on their family here. What should we tell them?	Develop a press release

Field Reports

The following reports can be used on-going, posting either through an EOC software or on white boards in an EOC. Adjust the numbers, the names, and any other details to fit your particular jurisdiction.

POST STORM REPORTS

Public Works Report

Plant #1	Plant flow at 3.2 mgd. rate. All equipment OK. Roads from administration building to plant covered with water nearing impassible conditions. Plant staff on duty for day shift.
Plant #2	Plant flow 12 mgd. rate. All equipment OK. _____ creek flowing at top of banks. Plant staff on duty for day shift.
Plant #3	Due to intermittent power losses, plant on 100% generator power as of 5 a.m. _____ River out of banks, back entrance flooded, flows approaching 40 mgd rate, all equipment on line and operating normal. Plant staff on duty for day shift. Chief operator on vacation out of state and unable to return.
Lift stations	All scheduled day personnel on duty with exception of one operator, and two laborers, and one assistant supervisor.
Collection section	All scheduled personnel on duty.
Office staff	All scheduled personnel on duty with the exception of one dispatchers that is on vacation out of state.

Shelter Report

Shelter	Population	Needs
_____ High School	Capacity 350 Population 370	
_____ High School	Capacity 585 Populations 456	Requesting additional porta potties. Need relief personnel for shelter managers.
_____ High School	Capacity 1000 Population 1100	Need personnel help in all areas. Getting overloaded with information inquires about family members.
_____ High School	Capacity 100 Population 250	Request relief personnel. Food for meals. We are too small and getting lost in the shuffle.
_____ Middle School	Special needs shelter Capacity 200 Population 230	Need additional medical personnel.
_____ Middle School	Capacity 556 Population 700	People are seeing our shelter from the Interstate and getting and coming here. We need to move these people to another shelter immediately. We also need more sheriff deputies to man the Interstate exit to prevent people from coming here.
_____ Middle School	Capacity 700 Population 600	
_____ Middle School	Special needs shelter Capacity 150 Population 130	

CHAPTER 11

Resources: Decision Aids and Worksheets

The following checklist, decision aids, and forms are meant to be a source of both usable documents as well as ideas for the readers use. The documents are meant to be copied should they meet the reader's needs or copied and changed to meet those needs. None of these documents are meant to replace any of the official Incident Command System (ICS) or National Incident Management System (NIMS) forms, rather they are meant to be used as tools to organize the information needed to fill out those documents and carry out the goals identified in them.

Immediate Actions and Personal Planning Checklists
for Emergency Managers and Elected Officials

PERSONAL IMMEDIATE ACTIONS FOR THE EMERGENCY MANAGER
AND EMERGENCY OPERATIONS CENTER STAFF

An emergency manager will have to make personal preparations prior to an event. As the leader of the response, he cannot be worried that he has not prepared himself or his family for the demands of a disaster. He should develop a personal "go kit." This kit will contain personal items he will need to be as comfortable as possible for a period of at least 72 hours. This kit should be put together and ready to pick up with little notice. It should be kept in your car so you will have it with you at all times. It should contain everything except perishable items such as medicines:

- change of clothes that can be worn in the emergency operations center (EOC)
- pillow, blanket, and other sleeping needs
- folding cot or sleeping bag if not available at EOC
- reference materials
- phone lists in a folder
- other necessities
- medications and personal-hygiene supplies

Once an event occurs, there will be little chance to go home to rest. In fact, you may not be able to go home even if you have some time available because of debris in the streets and road closures. A manager must plan to move into the EOC at any time and have considered sleeping arrangements for himself as well as staff, as many as can be accommodated. During the 2003 hurricane season I spent several nights in someone's office cubicle. The room had been designated as a dorm, with cots in each cubicle. It was kept dark and as quiet as possible so people could sleep when they had a chance. Not the ideal situation but it worked.

You will have to make plans to feed yourself and those in the EOC. There will be no open fast-food places and, unless you have designed a full-size commercial kitchen in your EOC, arrangements will have to be made. In our case they used a foodservice company initially, then relied on county personnel who brought in their barbecues to cook three meals a day.

You must have a plan in place for your own family. I have sent family members away throughout the event so I did not have to worry about them. I found it easier if they were gone and I was not worried about them. Whatever you decide, have a plan in place, because they will not see you very much for an extended period of time.

In the event of a sudden and unexpected tornado, earthquake, or terrorist strike have a plan so you can contact one another to make sure that everyone is all right. It can be a distraction from your responsibilities to worry about your family while trying to organize the response for your jurisdiction. On 9/11 I was responsible for opening an EOC for the city to brief our mayor. We were not directly involved and my story pales in comparison to those involved, but I think it is instructive. While I was in Florida my oldest son was going to college just outside of New York and went to the city often. It was a very long shot that he would be in the city that day, but until I talked to him directly it was a real distraction. Multiply that by several magnitudes if you had family in the city that morning, and you can begin to understand that the safety of your family can be a real issue. It is a two-way street—remember that they will want to hear that you are safe too.

Remember that every member of your staff will be leaving their families. Many of them will not be used to leaving their families during a crisis. Firefighters and police officers are used to it, but it never gets easier. Make sure there is some sort of plan that allows these people the opportunity to contact their families.

IMMEDIATE ACTIONS FOR ELECTED OFFICIALS

Prepare a kit for elected officials to give them what amounts to a checklist of actions that should be taken during a disaster. This incident could very well make or break a political career. It is critically important that elected officials be seen as being on top of the situation and in a leadership role with the responders. This kit will give them a basis for taking the actions needed to understand the incident and the decisions that need to be made. It gives them references and starting points for their initial actions until they are able to gain a real understanding of the situation. The kit should include:

- basic emergency plan with checklists
- notebook with pencils and pens
- identification with photo and title
- contact lists of all senior officials with cell and home numbers
- personal comfort items

Unless they have been involved in disaster training, they will not be prepared for the sudden change in the normal political and business environment. This checklist is meant to give officials the information they need to understand the gravity of the event:

- Begin a personal log—in this log they should record what they knew and when they knew it and when they a made major decisions and why. With this log they can recreate a timeline of information and their decisions for the inevitable questions that will be asked after the event. Items to note:
  - notified by
  - time notified
  - type of emergency
- There are questions elected officials should ask to understand the magnitude and scope of the incident:
  - type of incident
  - size of incident
  - known damage
    - injuries/deaths
    - area affected

o amount of property affected

o resources committed

o if outside resources are needed and have been requested

o EOC status

There are immediate actions public officials should take:

- Establish contact with the office of emergency management as soon as possible if for no other reason than to let them know that you are aware of the event and plan to go to the EOC.

- Direct all senior staff within the community to report problems, resource availability, and any issues that might affect their ability to continue to do their jobs.

- Once at the EOC, chair an assessment meeting with emergency management staff and department heads.

- In consultation with the emergency manager consider issuing emergency declarations when and if they are needed.

- Set reporting schedules for everyone. Early on in the event every hour or two may be appropriate until the extent of the event can be determined.

- If needed, in consultation with the emergency manager discuss when the next highest level of government should be advised of the incident and given the pertinent details.

- If necessary, establish contact with surrounding officials within your county, state, or region to advise them of the situation and if mutual aid from their jurisdictions may be needed.

- Remind senior staff members to keep their own logs of their actions and begin tracking expenses associated with the event so they can identify the specific costs allocated to their departments.

- In consultation with the emergency manager set a senior policy meeting schedule. Keep in mind the fluidity of information early in the incident and the importance of an accurate situational awareness.

- In consultation with the emergency manager and the designated public information officer set a schedule for the first and subsequent press conferences. This should be done as early as possible, as soon as enough information has been gathered to share with the public.

- Contact the jurisdiction's legal advisors about planned steps and need for:
  - emergency declarations
  - chain of succession
  - intergovernmental aid
  - social controls (curfews)
  - price controls
  - other possible restrictions
- Be aware of perceptions within the community about the response to the disaster, especially any perceptions that it is not being responded to equally in all neighborhoods.

SUGGESTED COMMUNITY ACTIONS

The following suggested actions can be used for pre-event development of actions to be taken should a disaster strike the community. They encompass a wide range of actions both pre and post events.

SUGGESTED COMMUNITY PROFILE INFORMATION

A formal community profile identifies all critical infrastructure, both response and civilian facilities. This list will become the starting point of any postevent damage assessment. The facilities on this list should be on the expected actions lists for the closest first responders to check after a event.

Critical community facilities include:

- hospitals
- nursing homes
- retirement centers (group homes)
- assisted-living facilities
- shelters/special-needs shelters
- schools
- tourist/recreational attractions
- major office complexes
- shopping centers/malls
- marinas
- airports
- ports
- railway terminals or yards
- mobile-home or manufactured-home parks
- RV sites

Essential service facilities include:

- police/sheriff stations and substations
- fire stations
- EMS stations
- 911 center
- public-works yards and facilities
- sewage-treatment and pump stations
- fueling facilities

- electrical stations and substations
- telephone switching/control stations
- animal shelters
- communication towers
- bridges

Resource locations include:

- bulk-fuel storage
- ice plants
- food storage
- construction-equipment marshaling yards

DISASTER FACILITY AND VEHICLE IMMEDIATE ACTION KITS

Each public-safety and public-works facility and vehicle should have essential information in a three-ring binder or some other type of easily accessed folder or book. This disaster immediate-action kit lists the first actions that should be taken in the event of a disaster. These actions should be taken with or without direction from the supervisors or leaders of that department. The actions and why the information that is collected is vital should be taught to all individuals who might be on duty when a disaster strikes. By preparing individuals all the way down to street-level personnel for expected actions to be taken, you ensure that the first information to flow into an EOC will be the essential elements of information needed to begin to estimate the impact of the disaster on the community. If each of the response departments within a community—law enforcement, fire, and public works—are assigned different parts of the critical infrastructure to survey, a clearer overall picture can be compiled more rapidly. For example, law enforcement would survey streets, intersections, and jails; the fire department could inspect hospitals, nursing homes, and hazardous-materials sites; public works could survey the electrical grid and water and sewer facilities. To make the proper decisions, the emergency-management team must have an assessment of the community from its own trained personnel. The team cannot depend on calls for help or reports from individuals or the media. This list of actions is by no means complete, and users should feel free to add or subtract elements to reflect their community needs.

Facility Immediate Actions

A facility administrator should be designated as soon as there are enough supervisors at the facility. It will be the administrator's responsibility to keep track of the facility personnel and actions taken during the response to the disaster. Because of the unusual activities and staff assignments it is critical to have someone whose responsibility is to document all of the various actions. Many of these actions are reimbursable by FEMA if they are properly documented. This supervisor or officer does not respond to the field. It is her responsibility to be in charge of that facility: to document personnel, equipment, supplies, and operations during the disaster, to order more supplies, and to ensure that the units in the field have the necessary logistical support. At a minimum they should record the following information:

- facility damage
- vehicle or equipment damage
- personnel injuries
- measures taken to secure the facility
- unusual actions taken by personnel to make repairs or solve other problems at the facility
- crew rosters and hours worked including all call-ups and off-duty personnel reporting for duty

Facility reports include the following:

- facility damage and condition
  - doors
  - roof
  - windows
  - electricity—working or running from backup generator
  - water
  - sewer
  - gas
  - other
- communications equipment
  - radios
  - telephones
  - Internet
- vehicles/equipment
  - damage
  - capabilities affected

Activity reports include:

- roster of on-duty personnel and other personnel who report in for duty
- problems or alarms personnel responded to with addresses, times, and disposition

- overtime status board for all personnel (very important because only overtime is reimbursable)
- radio or telephone watch sheet
- facility report to department for overall green-light rating
  - collate all snapshot assessments of the units in the station and report to the next higher authority within the chain of command
  - overall station green-light rating for facility
  - special personnel qualification list (any special skills individuals might have that could prove useful during the emergency)
  - unmet needs at the facility and with the personnel

Vehicle or Unit Immediate Actions

Each unit or vehicle should immediately tour its area of responsibility after the disaster to assess damage to the area and any target facility deemed critical. These assignments should be established before the disaster and be kept on the vehicle in the form of a three-ring binder or book. Each critical target facility should each have a page assigned to it with the information needed so there is no confusion. The crews on these vehicles should be trained as to how the survey should be filled out, and the survey should be on the vehicle at all times. Should an unexpected disaster occur, crews have a set of immediate actions to take and can begin gathering critical information without orders. The following is an example of such a report.

Area of Responsibility Critical Facility Snapshot Damage Assessment Survey

- unit or vehicle
- date/time
- facility name
- name of person contacted
- % operations affected
- degree of damage (heavy, moderate, light)
- power (yes/no)

- water (yes/no)
- access (blocked/open)
- operational
- immediate actions taken by personnel at the facility
- immediate threats to the facility

Highway and Street Assessment

- street/highway name
- direction of travel
- traffic signals
- street signs still intact or not
- equipment needed to open roadway
- exact location: nearest intersection, mile marker, or block number

HOSPITAL STATUS REPORT

	# Staffed Beds	Normal % of Occupancy	*Immediately Available Beds	**Available Bed + 1 hour	***Available Beds + 4 hours
Medical					
Surgical					
Orthopedic					
Pediatrics					
Adult intensive care unit					
Pediatric intensive care unit					
Isolation beds					
Operating suites					
Burn beds					
Emergency department beds					
Auxiliary emergency department beds					
Auxiliary inpatient beds					

* **Immediately available** = auto calculation from difference between number of staffed beds versus number of beds of normal occupancy.

** **1 hour available** = beds available due to early release, cancellation of elective procedures, emergency staff call backs (cleared beds).

*** **4 hour available** = same as 1 hour available (these figures do not include backfilling of beds with MCI victims).

Auxiliary emergency department beds = beds or chairs in areas opened during MCI's (i.e. physical therapy, conference rooms).

Auxiliary inpatient beds = beds in areas opened during overflow conditions due to emergency conditions.

	# Immediately Available	# Available + 1 hour	# Available + 4 hour
Respiratory therapists			
Pharmacists			
Surgeons			
Pediatricians			

+1 hour may be all available personnel

+4 hour may be reduced to scheduled staff for following shifts

DECONTAMINATE

Yes/No   hospital based decontaminate capacity

	Immediate	+1 hour	+2 hour
Estimated # of ambulatory patients per hour			
Estimated # of non-ambulatory patients per hour			

Yes/No   Repertory protection for decontaminate personnel

EMERGENCY SYSTEM SUPPORT

	Full Operations	Limited Operations	None
Emergency power			
HVAC on emergency power			
Chillers on emergency power			

FACILITY SHELTER IN PLACE CAPABILITY

Yes/No

Time to implement	<15 minutes	15–30 minutes	+30 minutes

SUGGESTED ACTIONS FOR PREPOSITIONED RESOURCES TO SUPPORT REGIONAL EVACUATIONS

All regional evacuations should be coordinated through the state governor's office to assure that, when several counties evacuate, they do not overload the evacuation routes. A sequenced evacuation must be coordinated by the counties and the state to avoid delays because of traffic overloads. To support these mass movements of people, resources must be prepositioned prior to the order. The following are some suggestions:

- programmable electronic public-information signs/displays
  - changes in road status
  - public-shelter locations and status information (full/still accepting evacuees)
  - hotel/motel availability
- local/small-area radio broadcast stations to provide updated information
- wreckers, tow trucks, and other heavy equipment for clearing roadways
- gasoline tankers for replenishing fuel supplies at gas stations on regional routes
- ambulances, medical personnel
- shelter-management personnel and supplies
- buses for transport of evacuees without other means of travel
- sampling/testing equipment and personnel

SUGGESTED ACTIONS FOR CONTAMINATED PUBLIC WATER SUPPLY

Should the contamination be widespread and long term, consider contacting military for assistance in water purification and expertise in field sanitation. They are the best resource because of the large number of people affected and the austere setting. Utilize local public-health officials as the point people for this operation. Until the situation is under control, use public-service announcements to keep public informed:

- Advise public that water is contaminated.

- Use public-service announcements and social media to describe how best to sanitize tap water if used for cooking and the locations of water points of distribution (POD).

- Military and public-health officials should consider spraying all standing water for control of mosquitoes to prevent diseases early on.

- Use public service announcements (PSAs) and social networks to advise on sanitation. If toilets are not working, the public-health department can help develop recommendations for the construction and use of waste-disposal facilities outside of homes.

SUGGESTED ACTIONS FOR LARGE SCALE SEARCH AND RESCUE OPERATIONS WITH OUTSIDE AGENCIES/VOLUNTEERS

Personnel sent into the field should be issued with personal health kits. There is no place to find any type of personal items for individuals serving in the field. Unless they are assigned to a fire station or other official facility, they will have nothing in the way of personal support. They will need:

- insect repellant if the event occurs during summer
- sunscreen if the event occurs during summer
- bottled water supply—enough for extended periods in the field under very hot and humid conditions
- Meals ready to eat (MREs) or other nonperishable food items
- Wound kits (bandages, water, Betadine®, moleskin, antibiotic cream, etc.)
- strings or rubber bands to close pants legs over tops of boots or shoes
- walking stick to control abandoned pets who are loose and can be aggressive

SUGGESTED ACTIONS VOLUNTEER MANAGEMENT

Designate a large staging area for all incoming resources and person-nel to report. Consider the closest stadium, fairground, or other large area capable of handling and organizing large numbers of people and equipment:

- Check credentials of all paramedics, firefighters, EMTs, law-enforcement officers, and any medical personnel including doctors and registered nurses
  - Have a procedure in place that allows medical and law-en-forcement personnel from out of state to practice in your state
- Officials running the staging area must be constantly informed by the EOC of any personnel and equipment needs so they can assign incoming assistance to priority needs. Assign personnel and resources in the following suggested order unless they are not needed.
  - relief of on-duty personnel who have been working since the storm struck so they can take care of their families and property
  - community fire and EMS needs
    - remove personnel in stages
      - one-third of local personnel to remain in the street at all times to assure that local knowledge is readily available to outside personnel
      - supervise or assign a liaison to outside crews or large teams of personnel
      - use 12-hour shifts for local and outside personnel
  - shelter needs
  - create shuttle service to and from staging area

SUGGESTED ACTIONS FOR USE OF MILITARY PERSONNEL

Initial uses for military personnel include:

- Security for fire and EMS personnel in the field frees up local law enforcement for other duties:
  - Show of force as protection for fire and EMS is good use of military resources. Additionally, they bring a communication system that can supplement the fire and EMS systems.
- Military can identify roads when street signs are down, paint street numbers and names, and team with local public works/ planning and development.
- Military can use air assets for quick aerial damage assessments with a local representative on board. They can develop survey teams to assess impact and conduct door-to-door and block-to-block surveys.
- Use military centralized command to assist in developing overall damage assessment:
  - The central collection point for this information should be a map that can be distributed to law-enforcement, fire, and EMS personnel as a new ground truth for response purposes.

SUGGESTED ACTIONS FOR WIDE SPREAD DESTRUCTION
FIRE STATION/POLICE SUB-STATION USE

Fires stations are the only public facilities strategically placed throughout the community. (Law-enforcement substations can also be used but they do not have the facilities, kitchens, generators and medical supplies that fire stations will have.) They will in all likelihood have emergency generators and power in areas where there is no power. People will flock to them. They should be used as decentralized assistance centers. Additional personnel will have to be assigned so units from that station are available for responses. Consider use of mutual aid or outside fire or law enforcement personnel:

- Set up tents adjacent to stations.
- Do not allow civilians inside of stations.
- Provide armed security through local law enforcement and eventually the National Guard.
- Provide medical care for minor injuries.
- Consider stations for points of distribution for certain supplies.
- Provide one hot meal at the station per day, coordinated through the National Guard or Salvation Army.
- Provide potable water.
- Establish bus transportation once a day and more often if necessary for citizens whose homes are destroyed and no longer habitable to be taken to established shelters.

Note: Law enforcement sub-stations can also be used but they do not have the facilities, kitchens, generators and medical supplies that fire stations will have.

SUGGESTED ACTIONS FOR POST DISASTER PRIORITIZATION OF HAZARDOUS MATERIALS CALLS

Hazardous-materials calls will increase during a hurricane or in other types of areawide events such as earthquakes. A prioritization of those calls should be established pre-event. It is necessary to facilitate the rapid removal of the most dangerous materials, limit unnecessary calls, and make the best use of the resources available.

- A hazardous-materials-qualified member should be assigned to the dispatch center to assist in the evaluation of the calls as they are received.
- Consider splitting the jurisdiction into quadrants and assigning specific hazardous-materials teams to each quadrant.
- Establish a supply center for materials and equipment needed for all incidents so teams can quickly and easily be resupplied.

Suggested criteria for prioritization of calls include:

1. life and safety first
   a. consider;
      i. toxicity
      ii. irritants
      iii. other health hazards
   b. ignore:
      i. minor outside spills or leaks
      ii. major spills or leaks not immediately threatening life or occupied structures
      iii. minor life-threatening spills that can be easily isolated by relocating people
   c. prioritize spills and leaks
      i. unstable reactive chemicals threatening life or occupied structures
      ii. major indoor flammable or explosive leaks or spills
      iii. outside leaks that threaten lives or occupied structures
      iv. minor indoor leaks
2. environmental
   a. threats to water supply, both surface and underground
   b. threats that would cause long-term environmental problems on the surface

SUGGESTED ACTIONS FOR POST DISASTER PRIORITIZATION OF EMERGENCY MEDICAL SERVICE CALLS

EMS calls can back up during events. A set policy for their prioritization should be established prior to the event. By prioritizing calls you will maximize the use of resources and handle the most critical calls first:

1. dispatch priority suggestions
   a. advanced life support/life-threatening
   b. major fire or life-threatening incident
   c. building or structure collapse with people trapped
   d. all other calls logged and response handled as resources become available

SUGGESTED ACTIONS FOR POST DISASTER DEMOBILIZATION MILESTONES

Milestones for demobilization should be established by all emergency services. These milestones will be used to determine when outside resources can be released and when normal work staffing and shifts can begin:

- Call-volume level has returned to normal or a level that normal staffing can manage.
- Enough roads are open to allow for near-normal response times and access to a majority of the areas within the city.
- All search and rescue of affected areas has been completed.
- All hospitals in the area are now back to providing full services.
- All personnel in the various departments have been relieved long enough to check on families and make temporary arrangements for shelter if needed.

SUGGESTED PRE-SCRIPTED PRESS RELEASES

There are certain types of press releases that can be pre-scripted prior to an event. These releases can then be on hand and ready for use should a disaster occur. These are by no means all of the press releases that can be pre-scripted and should be used to prompt a jurisdiction to develop their own list of scripts that will meet their individual needs.

SAMPLE NOTIFICATION OF OUTSIDE AGENCIES

Notification (FBI, CDC, ATF, Coast Guard, EPA, FAA, FBI, FEMA, National Guard, State Police, State EOC)

This is _____ . Be advised we have just experienced a _____ (explosion, hazardous materials release, possible terrorist event, suspected smallpox case, anthrax case, building collapse, evacuation in progress, shelter-in-place in progress, mass-casuality event).

We are requesting that you _____ (respond, stand by until we have more information, close air space, shut down waterways, request National Guard).

SAMPLE PRESS RELEASE

State of Emergency

This is _____ of the _____ _____ at the Emergency Operations Center. At _____ today the (proper elected official) declared a State of Emergency. This State of Emergency was declared in order for the City to be able to qualify for the outside help it needs to manage this emergency. By doing this the (proper elected official) will be able to request the Governor and the Federal Government for assistance in the days and weeks ahead. At this time it is unknown how long this Declaration will need to be in place but the (proper elected offical) would like to assure every citizen of _____ that this Declaration will only be in place until this emergency is under control.

SAMPLE PRESS RELEASE

Curfew

Whereas, the County/City of _____ has experienced a (incident type) resulting in the (wide spread damage, death or injuries) to our community.

Whereas the services to County/City residences, (power, water, utilities) have been disrupted; and

Whereas it is in the public interest and for the safety of the community, that a reasonable restriction be placed on the use of streets until such time as the consequences of the (event) have been stabilized; and

Whereas in order to protect, preserve and promote the general health and welfare and safety of the community and it citizens it is necessary that a curfew be established to restrict the use of the street of the County/City during this emergency.

Now therefore, I _____ _____ and chief executive officer of _____ in furtherance of public health, safety and welfare do hereby declare a state of emergency to exist and do further declare and require, in the interest of safety to persons and property that the streets of the County/City be hereby closed to the general public for travel both vehicular and pedestrian, for the hours of _____ to _____ .

SAMPLE PRESS RELEASE

Isolation

Whereas, the County/City of _____ has experienced an outbreak of _____ resulting in the death and illness of a number of it's citizens.

Whereas the health and well being of those not infected could be jeopardized by public contact.

Whereas it is in the public interest and for the safety of the community, that a reasonable restriction be placed on public contact until such time as the epidemic has been controlled and public contact is again without infectious risk; and

Whereas in order to protect, preserve and promote the general health and welfare and safety of the community and it citizens it is necessary that area of isolation be established to restrict travel into and out of the designated area (s) during this emergency.

Now therefore, I _____ (proper elected official) of the County/City of _____ in furtherance of public health, safety and welfare do hereby declare a state of emergency to exist and do further declare and require, in the interest of safety to persons in _____ and those within the State that all roads into and out of an area bounded by _____ and _____, _____ and _____ , _____, and _____ be closed to all modes of transportation both vehicular, pedestrian, rail or air are hereby prohibited until further notice.

_____

SAMPLE PRESS RELEASE

Public Gatherings

This is _____ of the _____

_____ at the Emergency Operations Center. At _____

today the (proper elected official) in consultation with the State and CDC have banned all public gatherings and are closing all business-es. Given the outbreak of _____ and it continued spread through the citizens of _____. The (proper elected official) have taken this step to try and stop the spread of this terrible disease. The Mayor and the City Council do not take this step lightly and under-stand the impact it will have on the community but it is an absolutely necessary step to stop the spread of this disease.

Anyone found to violate this ban will be arrested and placed in quarantine until it can be determined if they have been exposed to _____. The (proper elected offical) would urge everyone to heed this ban. It is the only way this terrible epidemic can be stopped. This is only a temporary measure and will be lifted as soon as possible. The (proper elected official) would urge every citizen to heed this ban.

SAMPLE PRESS RELEASE

Quarantine

This is _____ of the _____
_____ at the Emergency Operations Center. At _____
today the (proper elected official) have ordered the quarantine of the
County/City of _____. The epidemic of _____ that has
occurred here cannot be allowed to spread to other cities and counties in the State. In an effort to stem the tide of _____ cases the
(proper elected official) in close consultation with the Governor and
the Center for Disease Control have taken this step.

No one will be allowed to enter or leave the County/City by any
means of transportation. The roads in and out of the County/City
will be blocked. No bus traffic will be allowed in County/City or out
of the County/City. The airport is closed to all traffic immediately.
This quarantine will remain in effect until the epidemic is stopped.
The (proper elected official) would urge every citizen to remain calm
and to listen carefully to the media for updates over the next days.

SAMPLE PRESS RELEASE

Hurricane
Prestorm Instructions

Hurricane _____ is a Category _____ hurricane with winds up to _____ miles per hour and a storm surge of _____.

If you live in the following evacuation zones _____, _____, _____, you are ordered to evacuate. Consult your local newspaper, our web page, or the local media for the evacuation routes and traffic status of those routes.

The following areas are under a voluntary evacuation order and anyone living in those areas are urged to evacuate. Hurricane _____ is a dangerous storm.

Consult your hurricane guide in the local newspaper or on our Hurricane _____ web site. Sign up for hurricane updates from the Department of Emergency Management on our Twitter site _____.

The _____ office of emergency management has the following recommendations.

1. Have at least 7 days of non-perishable food.
2. Have at least 7 days of water, minimum of two gallons a day per person.
3. Have a portable radio with batteries.
4. Have a flashlight with extra batteries.
5. Gather all medications and keep them with you at all times even when you go to a shelter.
6. Have a first aid kit with you.
7. If you decide not to evacuate, move to an interior section of your house preferably an interior bathroom.
8. Make sure you have a full tank of gas in your car.

Please stay tuned to the Emergency Broadcast System on radio channel _____ for future updates.

SAMPLE PRESS RELEASE

Post Hurricane Landfall

Hurricane _____ made landfall in this area a short time ago. Fire, law enforcement and EMS crews are fully staffed and working. In order to insure the public safety, fire and EMS officials ask that you follow the following instructions:

1. Stay to tuned to any radio or TV station you can find still broadcasting.

2. Stay indoors until your receive an all clear from police, fire or community emergency management.

3. Do not drink water from the tap without boiling it for the next 72 hours or until you are told it is safe to drink by authorities.

4. Do not touch fallen or hanging wires of any kind under any circumstances, if on the ground, hanging free or attached to an object. Do not touch it.

5. Do not call to report individual interruptions in electric or phone service.

6. Do not call 911 for information on the storm instead call the Hurricane Hot Line at _____ for information. Only call 911 for life threatening emergencies.

Please stay calm. Local, state, and federal response teams are on the way.

ADDITIONAL PRESS RELEASE

Hurricane Language That May Be Considered if Your Jurisdiction Takes a Direct Hit From a Storm

If you or someone in your family or neighborhood is in need of emergency medical assistance it will be available at all shelters. If you need assistance removing victims from debris or reaching injured persons, go to the nearest major intersection. Police and fire department units are making their way to theses locations as quickly as possible.

Beware that after a storm there are many unusual hazards such as chemicals leaking from storage containers, downed power lines, broken water mains, or open sewage drains. Stay away from these hazards and report them to any police, firefighters or other city/county workers you see.

Use caution in filling portable generators, and small tools such as power saws. Be sure to allow the motor to cool before refilling with gasoline. The hot motor casing could ignite gasoline if not allowed to cool.

If you are relocating to an emergency shelter now because of damage to your home, be sure to take medications, toiletries, non-perishable food, and pillows, blankets and other items to make yourself comfortable. Bring enough of these supplies to be comfortable for up to 72 hours.

Public safety officials and other city/county vehicles will be in the streets doing damage assessment, clearing roads and doing other repairs, if you need assistance wave a towel or other article of clothing to signal them.

If you need police, fire, or emergency medical assistance call 911 or _____ should the 911 lines be down or busy.

SAMPLES OF INCIDENT INFORMATION TRACKING FORMS

These forms are meant as examples of the types of information that will need to be captured and the types of formats, which can be used.

EMERGENCY OPERATIONS CENTER

Incident Action Plan

00/00/00

Indicate the date the action plan was developed

Operational Period: 0000 hours through 0000 hours

New Operational Objectives
1.
2.
3.

Lead Functional Areas
1.
2.
3.

Continuing Operational Objectives	Percent Complete	Resources Needed

Completed Objectives

INCIDENT STATUS REPORT
Incident Essential Elements Of Information

This report should be updated as often as possible

Date		Time	

Information Element	Response
Local declaration issued	Date _____ Time _____
Public protective actions	Date _____ Time _____
• Evacuation	
• Shelter-in-place	
• Isolation	
• Quarantine	
• Area affected	
• Estimated # effected	
Sheltering (mass care)	
• Number of shelters open	
• Number of special needs shelters open	
• Total number of persons in shelters	
• Total shelter capacity	
• Shelter name and current population	Shelter name Population _____ _____ _____ _____ _____ _____
• Special needs shelter name and current population	Shelter name Population _____ _____ _____ _____ _____ _____
Public protective action cancelled	Date _____ Time _____
Victims	Injured _____ Dead _____
• Cases	Cases New cases Deaths _____ _____ _____

Medical facilities			
• Hospitals	Facility _____ _____ _____	Beds _____ _____ _____	Available beds _____ _____ _____
• Hospital closures	Date _____ _____	Facility _____ _____	
• Nursing home closures	Date _____ _____	Facility _____ _____	
Special medical facilities			
• Vaccination center	Facility name _____ _____	Number vaccinated _____ _____	
• Type C facility opened and current population	Facility name _____ _____	Population _____ _____	
• Type X Facility Opened and Current Population	Facility name _____ _____	Population _____ _____	
Schools			
• Public schools closed	Date _____ _____	Facility _____ _____	
• Private schools closed	Date _____ _____	Facility _____ _____	
Distribution sites			
• Medical goods	Date _____ _____	Facility _____ _____	
• Goods	Date _____ _____	Facility _____ _____	

ESF SHIFT CHANGE BRIEF

Incident name		Date	
Incident commander		Position (EMS, fire, etc.)	

Type of incident		Location	
Current known injuries/cases		Current death count	

Resources

Units assigned	Units available	Units in rehab

Mutual aid units assigned	Mutual aid units available	Mutual aid units in rehab

Situation

Actions taken and completed
Continuing actions
Current resource needs
Current supply needs

SITUATION REPORT

Date _____ Time _____

Transportation

(Functional area as in previous example)

Significant Events/Problems

Unit Status

Available	Committed

Mutual Aid Units

Available	Committed

PANDEMIC/ BIOTERRORIST INCIDENT STATUS REPORT

Date _____ Time _____

EOC Incident Essential Elements of Information

Information Element	Response
Local declaration issued	Date _____ Time _____ Date _____ Time _____
Public protective actions	
• Evacuation	
• Shelter-in-place	
• Isolation	
• Quarantine	
• Area affected	
• Estimated # effected	
Sheltering (mass care)	
• Number of shelters open	
• Number of special needs shelters open	
• Total number of persons in shelters	
• Total shelter capacity	
• Shelter name and current population	Shelter name Population _____ _____ _____ _____ _____ _____
• Special needs shelter name and current population	Shelter name Population _____ _____ _____ _____ _____ _____
Public protective action cancelled	Date _____ Time _____
Victims	Injured _____ Dead _____
• Cases	Cases New cases Deaths _____ _____ _____

Medical facilities			
• Hospitals	Facility	Beds	Available beds
	_____	_____	_____
	_____	_____	_____
	_____	_____	_____

	Date	Facility	
• Hospital closures	_____	_____	
	_____	_____	

• Nursing home closures	Date	Facility	
	_____	_____	
	_____	_____	

Special medical facilities			
• Vaccination center	Facility name		Number vaccinated
	_____		_____
	_____		_____

• Type C facility opened and current population	Facility name		Population
	_____		_____
	_____		_____

• Type X facility opened and current population	Facility name		Population
	_____		_____
	_____		_____

Schools		
• Public schools closed	Date	Facility
	_____	_____
	_____	_____

• Private schools closed	Date	Facility
	_____	_____
	_____	_____

Distribution sites		
• Medical goods	Date	Facility
	_____	_____
	_____	_____

• Goods	Date	Facility
	_____	_____
	_____	_____

EMERGENCY OPERATIONS CENTER REQUEST AND NOTIFICATION FORMS

The following forms are examples of the types of requests and notifications a local EOC may have to make during an incident. They also include the types of details needed for the requests or notifications to be met.

To: _____ (hospitals, medical examiner)

NOTIFICATION OF CONTAMINATED REMAINS

There has been a _____ (terrorist, hazardous materials, chemical, biological, radiological) incident involving _____ (anthrax, smallpox, plague, tabun, cyanide, sarin, mustard, radiation), causing _____ (1,2,3,...) deaths. The incident occurred at the _____ at approximately _____ hours. Their deaths were due to _____ (explosion, hazardous materials, chemical, biological, radiological exposures). The remains will _____ (need, not need) autopsies. Medical personnel capable of working on a crime scene and able to use _____ (Level, A, B, C) protection will be required to remove the remains.

To: _____ (hospitals, medical examiner)

NOTIFICATION OF CONTAMINATED PATIENTS

There has been a _____ (terrorist, hazardous materials, chemical, biological, radiological) incident causing _____ (1,2,3,...) deaths and _____ (1,2,3...) injuries. The incident occurred at the _____ at approximately _____ hours. It involved _____ (anthrax, smallpox, plague, tabun, cyanide, sarin, mustard, radiation). Expect a rush of injuries that may be contaminated. Be advised your facility should take appropriate steps to manage the patients.

REQUEST ASSISTANCE

Incident requiring assistance_____
(terrorist, hazardous materials, chemical, biological, radiation, explosives)

Type of assistance needed _____
(see following for the forms that should be used)

Type of resources needed _____
(see below for the forms that should be used)

Date _____ and **time**_____ resources will be needed.

Staging area location _____

Approximate **Date** _____ and **Time** _____ resources will be released.

STATE PUBLIC WORKS MUTUAL AID RESOURCE REQUISITION

Debris Clearance Task Force

1   Passenger van with supervisor and 2 support personnel
1   Crew cab pickup with a crew foreman
1   Front end loader with operator
1   Backhoe with operator
1   5 CY dump trucks with operators
6   8 CY dump trucks with operators
1   Service/maintenance truck with mechanic
2   Lowboy transports with 2 drivers
6   Chain saws and 4 operators
2   Chippers and 2 operators

Number task forces needed _____
Dates needed: from _____ to _____.

Additional Resources Available

Number needed:
_____ RV's self contained
_____ Generators portable
_____ Fuel truck with pump capacity
_____ Materials storage unit

Dates needed: from _____ to _____.

STATE FIREFIGHTING MUTUAL AID RESOURCE REQUISITION

Type 1   Firefighting strike team

Capabilities: mobile response to fire suppression or support of local fire service.

  5   Type 1 fire engines, each engine consisting of an officer, a driver and two firefighters
  1   Strike team leader with command vehicle

All units will have common communication capability.

Number of strike teams Needed:_____
Dates needed: from _____ to _____.

Type 2   Fire/rescue task force

Capabilities: mobile response to fire suppression, treatment and triage of victims, search and rescue efforts to support the local fire and rescue services.

  5   Any combination of type 1 fire engines, rescue, squad or aerial units
  1   Task force leader with command vehicle

All units will have common communications capability.

Number of task forces needed: _____
Dates needed: from _____ to _____.

Type 3   Fire/rescue specialized response task force

Capabilities: mobile response to specialized operations such as chemical, radiological, hazardous materials, explosions, aircraft crashes, train derailments, collapsed structures, confined space, urban search and rescue or any other large scale events requiring apparatus, equipment and specially trained personnel.

  2   Specialized operations teams, 5–7 members each trained for special operations
  3   Specialized response vehicles carrying needed specialized equipment to handle the specified event.
  1   Special operations officer with command vehicle

All units will have common communications capability.

Type or types of strike teams or task forces: _____

Number and type of task forces needed: _____

Dates needed: from _____ to _____.

STATE EMS/HEALTH AND MEDICAL RESOURCE REQUISITION

Type 1   Medical support strike team:

Capabilities: mobile response to multiple causality or evacuation support problems.

    5   Advanced life support (ALS) ambulances w/personnel
       Each unit with a minimum of 1 EMT/driver, 1 paramedic

Number of strike teams needed:_____
Dates needed: from _____ to _____

Type 2   Medical air response and transport unit

Capabilities: mobile helicopter response, treatment and transport of victims requiring pre-hospital medical services.

    1   Advanced life support certified air ambulance equipped with paramedic and 1 flight nurse paramedic

Number medical air response and transport units needed _____
Dates needed: from _____ to _____

Type 3   Disaster community health assistance task force

Capabilities: house to house assistance to victims, report health conditions, provide on-site treatment and referral to available services, coordinate provisions of higher level of medical care, provide comfort.

    1   RN/public health nurse with field experience
    1   Environmental health specialist
    1   Social worker with CISD experience/training
    1   Security person

Type or types of EMS/health and medical teams needed: ___ ___ ____

Number of each type of disaster community health assistance task forces needed: ____ ____ _____

Dates needed: from _____ to _____

STATE LAW ENFORCEMENT SPECIAL RESPONSE REQUISITION

Type 1   Law enforcement special response team

Capabilities: rapid response to intensive situations needing additional law enforcement resources such as hostage situations, barricaded suspects, or other types of incidents needing special weapons or tactics.

1   Vehicle w/supervisor
1   Van
8   Officers

Type 2   Law enforcement special response team

Capabilities: general law enforcement assignments such as traffic control, roving and fixed security assignments, crowd control, and response to calls for service.

1   Vehicle w/supervisor
4   Marked vehicles with 2 officers in each vehicle.

Type or types of teams needed _____ _____

Number of each type of law enforcement special response teams needed: ___ ___

Dates needed: from _____ to _____

SUGGESTED INCIDENT COMMAND
FIELD OPERATIONS WORKSHEETS

The following are examples of incident command field operations worksheets that can be used by incident commanders on a number of different types of incidents. These forms are meant as field work sheets and not replacement for the official ICS Forms.

INCIDENT COMMANDER
Tactical Worksheet

Safety	Significant Events	Staging
• Don PPE • Be alert for Haz Mat • Be alert for secondary device	Event Time FA	• LE staging • Fire staging • EMS staging • Haz Mat staging • Combined staging • Media staging • Mutual aid staging
Notifications	**Hazardous Materials Control Measures**	**Scene Control**
• EOC • State • FAA • Coast Guard • EPA • Hospital • Fatality management • ATF • FBI • Bomb squad • State police	**Chemical** _____ Initial isolation zone Protective action zone Hot zone Warm zone Cold zone Plume model **Decontaminate** Gross decontaminate Technical decontaminate Decontaminate corridor	• Security perimeter • Entry corridor • Exit corridor
Public Protective Actions	**Victims**	**EMS Operations**
• Evacuate • Shelter-in-place	Dead ALS BLS	• Triage • Treatment • Transportation
Units Assigned		
Law enforcement	Fire Haz Mat	EMS

HAZARDOUS MATERIALS INCIDENT COMMANDER WORKSHEET

Building and Unit Placement Sketch

Hazardous Materials Decision Making

	Detect hazardous materials presence
	Estimate likely harm without intervention
	Choose response options
	Identify action options
	Do best Options
	Evaluate progress
	Repeat 3–6 as operations progress

Assign Roles

Operations	Hazardous Materials	Emergency Medical Services	Firefighting	Law Enforcement	Public Information

Weather Information

Wind Velocity	Direction	Humidity	Temperature
Miles Per Hour	CP/Staging Upwind	Effect on Plume	Effect on Plume

Operational Considerations

Set up command post	Up wind, limited entry
Choose staging area	Up wind, limited access, good entry and exit access
Proper protective clothing	Determine the proper protective clothing necessary for incident. Normal bunker gear, disposable tyvek suits, full encapsulation.
Rescue strategy	Determine the rescue strategy if victims are involved (tape and go using bunker gear, disposable tyvek suits or full encapsulation entry)
Recon team	Protective clothing, SCBA, check all 4 sides
Establish required zones	Hot-warm-cold, secure perimeter, mark zones, limit access, work with law enforcement to eliminate intrusion by foot, highway, water, or air traffic
Forward observer post	If incident is large enough to warrant, upwind with good visibility
Evacuate/shelter in place considerations	Consult with Emergency Response Guidebook for initial evacuation and product characteristics. Determine best strategy evacuation or shelter in place. If evacuation chosen coordinate shelter and evacuation routes.

Public information considerations	Communicate evacuation/shelter in place decision through PIO, media, and EAS.
Mass causality	Establish triage, treatment and transportation areas with adequate entry and exit corridors. Establish casualty collections if needed.
Decontamination	Establish decontamination strategy for the incident technical or gross decontamination.
Planning considerations	• Rescue addressed • Runoff addressed • Enough vapor testers • Personnel adequate • Water supply adequate • Apparatus safety staged • Plume area addressed

External Resources Considerations

Mutual aid needs		Private hazardous waste disposal firm		Public works	
Absorbents needs		Human resources		Transportation (public buses/school buses)	
Railroad notifications		Risk management		Water department	
Bomb squad		Legal department		Personnel relief	
Chemtrac		Media (TV, radio, print)		Arson investigation	
Coast Guard		Medical examiner			
EPA		Law enforcement			
Electric company		FBI			
Gas company		ATF			
Health department		Relief and rehab			
Hospitals		Salvation Army			
Heavy equipment		Red Cross			

FIRE INCIDENT COMMANDER
Tactical Worksheet

Address _____

Building and Unit Placement Sketch

Safety	Significant Events	Units In Staging
• Don PPE • Be alert for Haz Mat	Event Time	
Notifications	**Weather**	**Units in Mutual Aid Staging**
EOC ATF FBI Bomb squad State police	Time _____ Wind direction _____ Speed _____	

Unit Assignments

Units Assigned to Firefighting	EMS	Hazardous Materials
Unit time	Unit time	Unit time

EMERGENCY MEDICAL SERVICES INCIDENT COMMANDER
Tactical Worksheet

Safety	Significant Events	Units In Staging
• Don PPE • Be alert for Haz Mat	Event Time	

Notifications	Number of Victims	Units in Mutual Aid Staging
• EOC Hospital • Mass causality • Contaminated remains	Dead ALS BLS	

Unit Assignments

Triage	Treatment	Transportation
Unit	Unit	Unit

Patients transported	Hospital _____	Hospital _____

LAW ENFORCEMENT INCIDENT COMMANDER
Tactical Worksheet

Tactical Drawing

Safety	Significant Events	Units In Staging
• Don PPE • Be alert for Haz Mat	Event Time	
Notifications	**Notes**	**Units in Mutual Aid Staging**
• EOC • ATF • FBI • Bomb squad • State police		

Unit Assignments

Security Perimeter	Facility Security	Evacuation
Intersection unit	Facility Unit	Unit

FEMA Glossary

A

Action Plan: See Incident Action Plan.

Agency: An agency is a division of government with a specific function, or a nongovernmental organization (e.g., private contractor, business, etc.) that offers a particular kind of assistance. In ICS, agencies are defined as jurisdictional (having statutory responsibility for incident mitigation) or assisting and/or cooperating (providing resources and/or assistance). (See Assisting Agency, Cooperating Agency, Jurisdictional Agency, and Multiagency Incident.)

Agency Administrator or Executive: Chief executive officer (or designee) of the agency or jurisdiction that has responsibility for the incident.

Agency Dispatch: The agency or jurisdictional facility from which resources are allocated to incidents.

Agency Representative: An individual assigned to an incident from an assisting or cooperating agency who has been delegated authority to make decisions on matters affecting that agency's participation at the incident. Agency Representatives report to the Incident Liaison Officer.

Air Operations Branch Director: The person primarily responsible for preparing and implementing the air operations portion of the Incident Action Plan. Also responsible for providing logistical support to helicopters operating on the incident.

Allocated Resources: Resources dispatched to an incident.

All-Risk: Any incident or event, natural or human-caused, that warrants action to protect life, property, environment, public health and safety, and minimize disruption of governmental, social, and economic activities.

Area Command (Unified Area Command): An organization established (1) to oversee the management of multiple incidents that are each being handled by an ICS organization, or (2) to oversee the management of large or multiple incidents to which several Incident Management Teams have been assigned. Area Command has the responsibility to set overall strategy and priorities, allocate critical resources according to priorities, ensure that incidents are properly managed, and ensure that objectives are met and strategies followed. Area Command becomes Unified Area Command when incidents are multijurisdictional. Area Command may be established at an emergency operations center facility or at some location other than an incident command post.

Assigned Resources: Resources checked in and assigned work tasks on an incident.

Assignments: Tasks given to resources to perform within a given operational period, based upon tactical objectives in the Incident Action Plan.

Assistant: Title for subordinates of the Command Staff positions. The title indicates a level of technical capability, qualifications, and responsibility subordinate to the primary positions.

Assisting Agency: An agency or organization providing personnel, services, or other resources to the agency with direct responsibility for incident management.

Available Resources: Resources assigned to an incident, checked in, and available for a mission assignment, normally located in a Staging Area.

B

Base: The location at which primary Logistics functions for an incident are coordinated and administered. There is only one Base per incident. (Incident name or other designator will be added to the term Base.) The Incident Command Post may be collocated with the Base.

Branch: The organizational level having functional or geographic responsibility for major parts of the Operations or Logistics functions. The Branch level is organizationally between Section and Division/Group in the Operations Section, and between Section and Units in the Logistics Section. Branches are identified by the use of Roman Numerals or by functional name (e.g., medical, security, etc.).

C

Cache: A pre-determined complement of tools, equipment, and/or supplies stored in a designated location, available for incident use.

Camp: A geographical site, within the general incident area, separate from the Incident Base, equipped and staffed to provide sleeping, food, water, and sanitary services to incident personnel.

Chain of Command: A series of management positions in order of authority.

Check-In: The process whereby resources first report to an incident. Check-in locations include: Incident Command Post (Resources Unit), Incident Base, Camps, Staging Areas, Helibases, Helispots, and Division Supervisors (for direct line assignments).

Chief: The ICS title for individuals responsible for functional Sections: Operations, Planning, Logistics, and Finance/Administration.

Clear Text: The use of plain English in radio communications transmissions. No Ten Codes or agency-specific codes are used when utilizing clear text.

Command: The act of directing and/or controlling resources by virtue of explicit legal, agency, or delegated authority. May also refer to the Incident Commander.

Command Post: See Incident Command Post.

Command Staff: The Command Staff consists of the Public Information Officer, Safety Officer, and Liaison Officer. They report directly to the Incident Commander. They may have an Assistant or Assistants, as needed.

Communication Unit: An organizational Unit in the Logistics Section responsible for providing communication services at an incident. A Communication Unit may also be a facility (e.g., a trailer or mobile van) used to provide the major part of an Incident Communications Center.

Compacts: Formal working agreements among agencies to obtain mutual aid.

Compensation/Claims Unit: Functional Unit within the Finance/Administration Section responsible for financial concerns resulting from property damage, injuries, or fatalities at the incident.

Complex: Two or more individual incidents located in the same general area that are assigned to a single Incident Commander or to Unified Command.

Cooperating Agency: An agency supplying assistance other than direct operational or support functions or resources to the incident management effort.

Coordination: The process of systematically analyzing a situation, developing relevant information, and informing appropriate command authority of viable alternatives for selection of the most effective combination of available resources to meet specific objectives. The coordination process (which can be either intra- or interagency) does not involve dispatch actions. However, personnel responsible for coordination may perform command or dispatch functions within the limits established by specific agency delegations, procedures, legal authority, etc.

Coordination Center: A facility that is used for the coordination of agency or jurisdictional resources in support of one or more incidents.

Cost Sharing Agreements: Agreements between agencies or jurisdictions to share designated costs related to incidents. Cost sharing agreements are normally written but may also be oral between authorized agency or jurisdictional representatives at the incident.

Cost Unit: Functional Unit within the Finance/Administration Section responsible for tracking costs, analyzing cost data, making cost estimates, and recommending cost-saving measures.

Crew: See Single Resource.

D

Delegation of Authority: A statement provided to the Incident Commander by the Agency Executive delegating authority and assigning responsibility. The Delegation of Authority can include objectives, priorities, expectations, constraints, and other considerations or guidelines as needed. Many agencies require written Delegation of Authority to be given to Incident Commanders prior to their assuming command on larger incidents.

Demobilization Unit: Functional Unit within the Planning Section responsible for assuring orderly, safe, and efficient demobilization of incident resources.

Deputy: A fully qualified individual who, in the absence of a superior, could be delegated the authority to manage a functional operation or perform a specific task. In some cases, a Deputy could act as relief for a superior and therefore must be fully qualified in the position. Deputies can be assigned to the Incident Commander, General Staff, and Branch Directors.

Director: The ICS title for individuals responsible for supervision of a Branch.

Dispatch: The implementation of a command decision to move a resource or resources from one place to another.

Dispatch Center: A facility from which resources are ordered, mobilized, and assigned to an incident.

Division: Divisions are used to divide an incident into geographical areas of operation. A Division is located within the ICS organization between the Branch and the Task Force/Strike Team. (See Group.) Divisions are identified by alphabetic characters for horizontal applications and, often, by floor numbers when used in buildings.

Documentation Unit: Functional Unit within the Planning Section responsible for collecting, recording, and safeguarding all documents relevant to the incident.

E

Emergency: Absent a Presidentially declared emergency, any incident(s), human-caused or natural, that requires responsive action to protect life or property. Under the Robert T. Stafford Disaster Relief and Emergency Assistance Act, an emergency means any occasion or instance for which, in the determination of the President, Federal assistance is needed to supplement State and local efforts and capabilities to save lives and to protect property and public health and safety, or to lessen or avert the threat of a catastrophe in any part of the United States.

Emergency Management Coordinator/Director: The individual within each political subdivision that has coordination responsibility for jurisdictional emergency management.

Emergency Operations Centers (EOCs): The physical location at which the coordination of information and resources to support domestic incident management activities normally takes place. An EOC may be a temporary facility or may be located in a more central or permanently established facility, perhaps at a higher level of organization within a jurisdiction. EOCs may be organized by major functional disciplines (e.g., fire, law enforcement, and medical services), by jurisdiction (e.g., Federal, State, regional, county, city, tribal), or some combination thereof.

Emergency Operations Plan (EOP): The plan that each jurisdiction has and maintains for responding to appropriate hazards.

Event: A planned, non-emergency activity. ICS can be used as the management system for a wide range of events, e.g., parades, concerts, or sporting events.

F

Facilities Unit: Functional Unit within the Support Branch of the Logistics Section that provides fixed facilities for the incident. These facilities may include the Incident Base, feeding areas, sleeping areas, sanitary facilities, etc.

Federal: Of or pertaining to the Federal Government of the United States of America.

Field Operations Guide: A pocket-size manual of instructions on the application of the Incident Command System.

Finance/Administration Section: The Section responsible for all incident costs and financial considerations. Includes the Time Unit, Procurement Unit, Compensation/Claims Unit, and Cost Unit.

Food Unit: Functional Unit within the Service Branch of the Logistics Section responsible for providing meals for incident personnel.

Function: Function refers to the five major activities in ICS: Command, Operations, Planning, Logistics, and Finance/Administration. The term function is also used when describing the activity involved, e.g., the planning function. A sixth function, Intelligence, may be established, if required, to meet incident management needs.

G

General Staff: A group of incident management personnel organized according to function and reporting to the Incident Commander. The General Staff normally consists of the Operations Section Chief, Planning Section Chief, Logistics Section Chief, and Finance/Administration Section Chief.

Ground Support Unit: Functional Unit within the Support Branch of the Logistics Section responsible for the fueling, maintaining, and repairing of vehicles, and the transportation of personnel and supplies.

Group: Groups are established to divide the incident into functional areas of operation. Groups are composed of resources assembled to perform a special function not necessarily within a single geographic division. (See Division.) Groups are located between Branches (when activated) and Resources in the Operations Section.

H

Hazard: Something that is potentially dangerous or harmful, often the root cause of an unwanted outcome.

Helibase: The main location for parking, fueling, maintenance, and loading of helicopters operating in support of an incident. It is usually located at or near the incident Base.

Helispot: Any designated location where a helicopter can safely take off and land. Some helispots may be used for loading of supplies, equipment, or personnel.

Hierarchy of Command: See Chain of Command.

I

Incident: An occurrence or event, natural or human-caused, that requires an emergency response to protect life or property. Incidents can, for example, include major disasters, emergencies, terrorist attacks, terrorist threats, wildland and urban fires, floods, hazardous materials spills, nuclear accidents, aircraft accidents, earthquakes, hurricanes, tornadoes, tropical storms, war-related disasters, public health and medical emergencies, and other occurrences requiring an emergency response.

Incident Action Plan (IAP): An oral or written plan containing general objectives reflecting the overall strategy for managing an incident. It may include the identification of operational resources and assignments. It may also include attachments that provide direction and important information for management of the incident during one or more operational periods.

Incident Base: Location at the incident where the primary Logistics functions are coordinated and administered. (Incident name or other designator will be added to the term Base.) The Incident Command Post may be collocated with the Base. There is only one Base per incident.

Incident Commander (IC): The individual responsible for all incident activities, including the development of strategies and tactics and the ordering and the release of resources. The IC has overall authority and responsibility for conducting incident operations and is responsible for the management of all incident operations at the incident site.

Incident Command Post (ICP): The field location at which the primary tactical-level, on-scene incident command functions are performed. The ICP may be collocated with the incident base or other incident facilities and is normally identified by a green rotating or flashing light.

Incident Command System (ICS): A standardized on-scene emergency management construct specifically designed to provide for the adoption of an integrated organizational structure that reflects the complexity and demands of single or multiple incidents, without being hindered by jurisdictional boundaries. ICS is the combination of facilities, equipment, personnel, procedures, and communications operating within a common organizational structure, designed to aid in the management of resources during incidents. It is used for all kinds of emergencies and is applicable to small as well as large and complex incidents. ICS is used by various jurisdictions and functional agencies, both public and private, to organize field-level incident management operations.

Incident Communications Center: The location of the Communications Unit and the Message Center.

Incident Complex: See Complex.

Incident Management Team (IMT): The Incident Commander and appropriate Command and General Staff personnel assigned to an incident.

Incident Objectives: Statements of guidance and direction necessary for the selection of appropriate strategy(ies), and the tactical direction of resources. Incident objectives are based on realistic expectations of what can be accomplished when all allocated resources have been effectively deployed. Incident objectives must be achievable and measurable, yet flexible enough to allow for strategic and tactical alternatives.

Incident of National Significance: Based on criteria established in HSPD-5 (paragraph 4), an actual or potential high-impact event that requires a coordinated and effective response by and appropriate combination of Federal, State, local, tribal, nongovernmental, and/or private-sector entities in order to save lives and minimize damage, and provide the basis for long-term community recovery and mitigation activities. (Source: National Response Plan)

Incident Types: Incidents are categorized by five types based on complexity. Type 5 incidents are the least complex and Type 1 the most complex.

Incident Support Organization: Includes any off-incident support provided to an incident. Examples would be Agency Dispatch centers, Airports, Mobilization Centers, etc.

Initial Action: The actions taken by resources that are the first to arrive at an incident site.

Initial Response: Resources initially committed to an incident.

Intelligence Officer: The intelligence officer is responsible for managing internal information, intelligence, and operational security requirements supporting incident management activities. These may include information security and operational security activities, as well as the complex task of ensuring that sensitive information of all types (e.g., classified information, law enforcement sensitive information, proprietary information, or export-controlled information) is handled in a way that not only safeguards the information, but also ensures that it gets to those who need access to it to perform their missions effectively and safely.

J

Joint Field Office (JFO): The JFO is a temporary Federal facility established locally to coordinate operational Federal assistance activities to the affected jurisdiction(s) during Incidents of National Significance. The JFO is a multiagency center that provides a central point of coordination for Federal, State, local, tribal, nongovernmental, and private-sector organizations with primary responsibility for threat response and incident support and coordination. The JFO enables the effective and efficient coordination of Federal incident-related prevention, preparedness, response, and recovery actions. The JFO replaces the Disaster Field Office (DFO) and accommodates all entities (or their designated representatives) essential to incident management, information-sharing, and the delivery of disaster assistance and other support.

Joint Information Center (JIC): A facility established to coordinate all incident-related public information activities. It is the central point of contact for all news media at the scene of the incident. Public information officials from all participating agencies should collocate at the JIC.

Joint Information System (JIS): Integrates incident information and public affairs into a cohesive organization designed to provide consistent, coordinated, timely information during crisis or incident operations. The mission of the JIS is to provide a structure and system for developing and delivering coordinated interagency messages; developing, recommending, and executing public information plans and strategies on behalf of the Incident Commander; advising the Incident Commander concerning public affairs issues that could affect a response effort; and controlling rumors and inaccurate information that could undermine public confidence in the emergency response effort.

Jurisdiction: A range or sphere of authority. Public agencies have jurisdiction at an incident related to their legal responsibilities and authority. Jurisdictional authority at an incident can be political or geographical (e.g., city, county, tribal, State, or Federal boundary lines) or functional (e.g., law enforcement, public health).

Jurisdictional Agency: The agency having jurisdiction and responsibility for a specific geographical area, or a mandated function.

K

Kinds of Resources: Describe what the resource is (e.g., medic, firefighter, Planning Section Chief, helicopters, ambulances, combustible gas indicators, bulldozers).

L

Landing Zone: See Helispot.

Leader: The ICS title for an individual responsible for a Task Force, Strike Team, or functional Unit.

Liaison: A form of communication for establishing and maintaining mutual understanding and cooperation.

Liaison Officer (LNO): A member of the Command Staff responsible for coordinating with representatives from cooperating and assisting agencies. The Liaison Officer may have Assistants.

Logistics: Providing resources and other services to support incident management.

Logistics Section: The Section responsible for providing facilities, services, and materials for the incident.

Local Government: A county, municipality, city, town, township, local public authority, school district, special district, intrastate district, council of governments (regardless of whether the council of governments is incorporated as a nonprofit corporation under State law), regional or interstate government entity, or agency or instrumentality of a local government; an Indian tribe or authorized tribal organization, or in Alaska a Native village or Alaska Regional Native Corporation; a rural community, unincorporated town or village, or other public entity. See Section 2 (10), Homeland Security Act of 2002, Public Law 107-296, 116 Stat. 2135 (2002).

M

Major Disaster: As defined under the Robert T. Stafford Disaster Relief and Emergency Assistance Act (42 U.S.C. 5122), a major disaster is any natural catastrophe (including any hurricane, tornado, storm, high water, wind-driven water, tidal wave, tsunami, earthquake, volcanic eruption, landslide, mudslide, snowstorm, or drought), or, regardless of cause, any fire, flood, or explosion, in any part of the United States, which in the determination of the President causes damage of sufficient severity and magnitude to warrant major disaster assistance under this Act to supplement the efforts and available resources of States, tribes, local governments, and disaster relief organizations in alleviating the damage, loss, hardship, or suffering caused thereby.

Management by Objective: A management approach that involves a four-step process for achieving the incident goal. The Management by Objectives approach includes the following: establishing overarching objectives; developing and issuing assignments, plans, procedures, and protocols; establishing specific, measurable objectives for various incident management functional activities and directing efforts to fulfill them, in support of defined strategic objectives; and documenting results to measure performance and facilitate corrective action.

Managers: Individuals within ICS organizational Units that are assigned specific managerial responsibilities, e.g., Staging Area Manager or Camp Manager.

Medical Unit: Functional Unit within the Service Branch of the Logistics Section responsible for the development of the Medical Emergency Plan, and for providing emergency medical treatment of incident personnel.

Message Center: The Message Center is part of the Incident Communications Center and is collocated or placed adjacent to it. It receives, records, and routes information about resources reporting to the incident, resource status, and administrative and tactical traffic.

Mitigation: The activities designed to reduce or eliminate risks to persons or property or to lessen the actual or potential effects or consequences of an incident. Mitigation measures may be implemented prior to, during, or after an incident. Mitigation measures are often informed by lessons learned from prior incidents. Mitigation involves ongoing actions to reduce exposure to, probability of, or potential loss from hazards. Measures may include zoning and building codes, floodplain buyouts, and analysis of hazard-related data to determine where it is safe to build or locate temporary facilities. Mitigation can include efforts to educate governments, businesses, and the public on measures they can take to reduce loss and injury.

Mobilization: The process and procedures used by all organizations (Federal, State, and local) for activating, assembling, and transporting all resources that have been requested to respond to or support an incident.

Mobilization Center: An off-incident location at which emergency service personnel and equipment are temporarily located pending assignment, release, or reassignment.

Multiagency Coordination (MAC): The coordination of assisting agency resources and support to emergency operations.

Multiagency Coordination Entity: A multiagency coordination entity functions within a broader multiagency coordination system. It may establish the priorities among incidents and associated resource allocations, deconflict agency policies, and provide strategic guidance and direction to support incident management activities.

Multiagency Coordination Systems (MACs): Multiagency coordination systems provide the architecture to support coordination for incident prioritization, critical resource allocation, communications systems integration, and information coordination. The components of multiagency coordination systems include facilities, equipment, emergency operation centers (EOCs), specific multiagency coordination entities, personnel, procedures, and communications. These systems assist agencies and organizations to fully integrate the subsystems of the NIMS.

Multiagency Incident: An incident where one or more agencies assist a jurisdictional agency or agencies. May be single or unified command.

Mutual-Aid Agreement: Written agreement between agencies and/or jurisdictions that they will assist one another on request, by furnishing personnel, equipment, and/or expertise in a specified manner.

N

National Incident Management System (NIMS): A system mandated by HSPD-5 that provides a consistent nationwide approach for Federal, State, local, and tribal governments; the private-sector; and nongovernmental organizations to work effectively and efficiently together to prepare for, respond to, and recover from domestic incidents, regardless of cause, size, or complexity. To provide for interoperability and compatibility among Federal, State, local, and tribal capabilities, the NIMS includes a core set of concepts, principles, and terminology. HSPD-5 identifies these as the ICS; multiagency coordination systems; training; identification and management of resources (including systems for classifying types of resources); qualification and certification; and the collection, tracking, and reporting of incident information and incident resources.

National Response Plan (NRP): A plan mandated by HSPD-5 that integrates Federal domestic prevention, preparedness, response, and recovery plans into one all-discipline, all-hazards plan.

O

Officer: The ICS title for the personnel responsible for the Command Staff positions of Safety, Liaison, and Public Information.

Operational Period: The period of time scheduled for execution of a given set of operation actions as specified in the Incident Action Plan. Operational Periods can be of various lengths, although usually not over 24 hours.

Operations Section: The Section responsible for all tactical operations at the incident. Includes Branches, Divisions and/or Groups, Task Forces, Strike Teams, Single Resources, and Staging Areas.

Out-of-Service Resources: Resources assigned to an incident but unable to respond for mechanical, rest, or personnel reasons.

P

Planning Meeting: A meeting held as needed throughout the duration of an incident, to select specific strategies and tactics for incident control operations, and for service and support planning. On larger incidents, the Planning Meeting is a major element in the development of the Incident Action Plan.

Planning Section: Responsible for the collection, evaluation, and dissemination of information related to the incident, and for the preparation and documentation of the Incident Action Plan. The Section also maintains information on the current and forecasted situation, and on the status of resources assigned to the incident. Includes the Situation, Resources, Documentation, and Demobilization Units, as well as Technical Specialists.

Preparedness: The range of deliberate, critical tasks and activities necessary to build, sustain, and improve the operational capability to prevent, protect against, respond to, and recover from domestic incidents. Preparedness is a continuous process. Preparedness involves efforts at all levels of government and between government and private-sector and nongovernmental organizations to identify threats, determine vulnerabilities, and identify required resources. Within the NIMS, preparedness is operationally focused on establishing guidelines, protocols, and standards for planning, training and exercises, personnel qualification and certification, equipment certification, and publication management.

Preparedness Organizations: The groups that provide interagency coordination for domestic incident management activities in a nonemergency context. Preparedness organizations can include all agencies with a role in incident management, for prevention, preparedness, response, or recovery activities. They represent a wide variety of committees, planning groups, and other organizations that meet and coordinate to ensure the proper level of planning, training, equipping, and other preparedness requirements within a jurisdiction or area.

Prevention: Actions to avoid an incident or to intervene to stop an incident from occurring. Prevention involves actions to protect lives and property. It involves applying intelligence and other information to a range of activities that may include such countermeasures as deterrence operations; heightened inspections; improved surveillance and security operations; investigations to determine the full nature and source of the threat; public health and agricultural surveillance and testing processes; immunizations, isolation, or quarantine; and, as appropriate, specific law enforcement operations aimed at deterring, preempting, interdicting, or disrupting illegal activity and apprehending potential perpetrators and bringing them to justice.

Procurement Unit: Functional Unit within the Finance/Administration Section responsible for financial matters involving vendor contracts.

Public Information Officer (PIO): A member of the Command Staff responsible for interfacing with the public and media or with other agencies with incident-related information requirements.

R

Recorders: Individuals within ICS organizational units who are responsible for recording information. Recorders may be found in Planning, Logistics, and Finance/Administration Units.

Reinforced Response: Those resources requested in addition to the initial response.

Reporting Locations: Location or facilities where incoming resources can check in at the incident. (See Check-in.)

Resources: Personnel and major items of equipment, supplies, and facilities available or potentially available for assignment to incident operations and for which status is maintained. Resources are described by kind and type and may be used in operational support or supervisory capacities at an incident or at an EOC.

Recovery: The development, coordination, and execution of service- and site-restoration plans; the reconstitution of government operations and services; individual, private-sector, nongovernmental, and public-assistance programs to provide housing and to promote restoration; long-term care and treatment of affected persons; additional measures for social, political, environmental, and economic restoration; evaluation of the incident to identify lessons learned; postincident reporting; and development of initiatives to mitigate the effects of future incidents.

Resource Management: Efficient incident management requires a system for identifying available resources at all jurisdictional levels to enable timely and unimpeded access to resources needed to prepare for, respond to, or recover from an incident. Resource management under the NIMS includes mutual-aid agreements; the use of special Federal, State, local, and tribal teams; and resource mobilization protocols.

Resources Unit: Functional Unit within the Planning Section responsible for recording the status of resources committed to the incident. The Unit also evaluates resources currently committed to the incident, the impact that additional responding resources will have on the incident, and anticipated resource needs.

Response: Activities that address the short-term, direct effects of an incident. Response includes immediate actions to save lives, protect property, and meet basic human needs. Response also includes the execution of emergency operations plans and of mitigation activities designed to limit the loss of life, personal injury, property damage, and other unfavorable outcomes. As indicated by the situation, response activities include applying intelligence and other information to lessen the effects or consequences of an incident; increased security operations; continuing investigations into nature and source of the threat; ongoing public health and agricultural surveillance and testing processes; immunizations, isolation, or quarantine; and specific law enforcement operations aimed at preempting, interdicting, or disrupting illegal activity, and apprehending actual perpetrators and bringing them to justice.

S

Safety Officer: A member of the Command Staff responsible for monitoring and assessing safety hazards or unsafe situations, and for developing measures for ensuring personnel safety. The Safety Officer may have Assistants.

Section: The organizational level having responsibility for a major functional area of incident management, e.g., Operations, Planning, Logistics, Finance/Administration, and Intelligence (if established). The section is organizationally situated between the Branch and the Incident Command.

Segment: A geographical area in which a Task Force/Strike Team Leader or Supervisor of a single resource is assigned authority and responsibility for the coordination of resources and implementation of planned tactics. A segment may be a portion of a division or an area inside or outside the perimeter of an incident. Segments are identified with Arabic numbers.

Service Branch: A Branch within the Logistics Section responsible for service activities at the incident. Includes the Communication, Medical, and Food Units.

Single Resource: An individual, a piece of equipment and its personnel complement, or a crew or team of individuals with an identified work Supervisor that can be used on an incident.

Situation Unit: Functional Unit within the Planning Section responsible for the collection, organization, and analysis of incident status information, and for analysis of the situation as it progresses. Reports to the Planning Section Chief.

Span of Control: The number of individuals a supervisor is responsible for, usually expressed as the ratio of supervisors to individuals. (Under the NIMS, an appropriate span of control is between 1:3 and 1:7.)

Staging Area: Location established where resources can be placed while awaiting a tactical assignment. The Operations Section manages Staging Areas.

State: When capitalized, refers to any State of the United States, the District of Columbia, the Commonwealth of Puerto Rico, the Virgin Islands, Guam, American Samoa, the Commonwealth of the Northern Mariana Islands, and any possession of the United States. See Section 2 (14), Homeland Security Act of 2002, Public Law 107-296, 116 Stat. 2135 (2002).

Strategy: The general direction selected to accomplish incident objectives set by the Incident Commander.

Strategic: Strategic elements of incident management are characterized by continuous long-term, high-level planning by organizations headed by elected or other senior officials. These elements involve the adoption of long-range goals and objectives, the setting of priorities, the establishment of budgets and other fiscal decisions, policy development, and the application of measures of performance or effectiveness.

Strike Team: A specified combination of the same kind and type of resources with common communications and a Leader.

Supervisor: The ICS title for individuals responsible for a Division or Group.

Supply Unit: Functional Unit within the Support Branch of the Logistics Section responsible for ordering equipment and supplies required for incident operations.

Support Branch: A Branch within the Logistics Section responsible for providing personnel, equipment, and supplies to support incident operations. Includes the Supply, Facilities, and Ground Support Units.

Supporting Materials: Refers to the several attachments that may be included with an Incident Action Plan, e.g., communications plan, map, safety plan, traffic plan, and medical plan.

Support Resources: Nontactical resources under the supervision of the Logistics, Planning, Finance/Administration Sections, or the Command Staff.

T

Tactical Direction: Direction given by the Operations Section Chief that includes the tactics required to implement the selected strategy, the selection and assignment of resources to carry out the tactics, directions for tactics implementation, and performance monitoring for each operational period.

Tactics: Deploying and directing resources on an incident to accomplish incident strategy and objectives.

Task Force: A combination of single resources assembled for a particular tactical need with common communications and a Leader.

Team: See Single Resource.

Technical Specialists: Personnel with special skills that can be used anywhere within the ICS organization.

Threat: An indication of possible violence, harm, or danger.

Time Unit: Functional Unit within the Finance/Administration Section responsible for recording time for incident personnel and hired equipment.

Type: A classification of resources in the ICS that refers to capability. Type 1 is generally considered to be more capable than Types 2, 3, or 4, respectively, because of size, power, capacity, or, in the case of incident management teams, experience and qualifications.

Tools: Those instruments and capabilities that allow for the professional performance of tasks, such as information systems, agreements, doctrine, capabilities, and legislative authorities.

Tribal: Any Indian tribe, band, nation, or other organized group or community, including any Alaskan Native Village as defined in or established pursuant to the Alaskan Native Claims Settlement Act (85 Stat. 688) (43 U.S.C.A. and 1601 et seq.), that is recognized as eligible for the special programs and services provided by the United States to Indians because of their status as Indians.

U

Unified Area Command: A Unified Area Command is established when incidents under an Area Command are multijurisdictional. (See Area Command and Unified Command.)

Unified Command: An application of ICS used when there is more than one agency with incident jurisdiction or when incidents cross political jurisdictions. Agencies work together through the designated members of the Unified Command, often the senior person from agencies and/or disciplines participating in the Unified Command, to establish a common set of objectives and strategies and a single Incident Action Plan.

Unit: The organizational element having functional responsibility for a specific incident Planning, Logistics, or Finance/Administration activity.

Unity of Command: The concept by which each person within an organization reports to one and only one designated person. The purpose of unity of command is to ensure unity of effort under one responsible commander for every objective.

Suggested Readings

I have drawn up a list of what I consider valuable books that help expand any emergency manger's knowledge. The first list of books does not include official histories or lessons learned; rather they are what I consider valuable social histories that can provide the reader with personal details and perspectives that an official history often lacks. I have found them to be a rich source of material for training and planning as well as perspective. I do not think an emergency manager can depend on official training manuals and histories alone to prepare for the realities of a disaster. These books will fill the gaps left after even the best training. The list is in no particular order and should be used according to the reader's interests. This list is by no means a complete one; there are any number of books that can provide the reader with helpful information. These are just some of the best in my opinion. The second list includes some of references that I have found to be particularly helpful in doing research for plans and exercises.

SOCIAL HISTORIES

John M. Barry: *The Great Influenza: The Story of the Deadliest Plague in History* (Viking, 2004). This is simply the best history of the influenza outbreak of 1918. It is filled with the type of details that should provide any emergency manager insights into the impact of the next pandemic on his community.

Bill Minutaglio: *City on Fire: The Forgotten Disaster That Devastated a Town and Ignited a Landmark Legal Battle* , (Harper Collins, 2003). The explosion of two ships containing millions of pounds of ammonium nitrate in Texas City Harbor is the subject of this book. It provides details of what the use of a tactical nuclear weapon in a modern city would look like.

Douglas G. Brinkley: *The Great Deluge: Hurricane Katrina, New Orleans and the Mississippi Gulf Coast*,)William Morrow, 2006). This is one of the seminal works on Hurricane Katrina, with a minute-by-minute account of the events on the Gulf Coast. A must-read for any emergency manager whose major threat is hurricanes. It is filled with details that should make you stop and make sure you have those problems covered in the plans.

Patrick Creed and Rick Newman: *FireFight: Inside the Battle to Save the Pentagon on 9/11*, (Ballatine, 2008). Simply the best account of the implementation of the ICS and NIMS in the midst of a major terrorist attack that I have read. This is a from-the-ground-up, minute-by-minute account of the confusion and chaos that accompanies such an attack and the struggle to gain control of the event and build an organized operation. It should be required reading for any emergency-response command officer or emergency manager who wants to understand what he is facing in a sudden terrorist attack. It should also be on every trainer's shelf because it includes a wealth of incident specifics that could easily be turned into "what if" scenarios.

Mark Levine: *F5: Devastation, Survival, and the Most Violent Tornado Outbreak of the Twentieth Century* (Miramax, 2007). If you live in Tornado Alley and you are responsible for emergency operations, this book is the one to read. Its detailed account of the confusion and chaos after an F5 provides a clear picture of the challenges you will face after such an event. Although set in the "dark ages" of emergency management, the 1970s, it nonetheless contains a level of detail that should provide a trained reader with "what would I do if?" moments through out.

Christopher Cooper and Robert Block: *Disaster: Hurricane Katrina and the Failure of Homeland Security* (Times Books, 2006). This well-researched and sourced book is a critical look at the intricacies of the Department of Homeland Security and its response to Hurricane Katrina. In addition, it goes into some depth about the state of FEMA before and after Katrina. It is a thought-provoking look at the nation's disaster-response organizations during the largest disaster to strike the United States. One of the biggest facts to strike me was that Katrina occurred well after 9/11, with all of its resultant time, money, and effort spent to improve our response capabilities.

REFERENCES

David E. Hogan, D.O., F.A.C.E.P, Jonathan L. Burstein, M.D., F.A.C.E.P (editors): *Disaster Medicine* (Lippincott Williams & Wilkinson, 2002). This is an excellent reference book filled with important statistics, details, and disaster-by-disaster breakdowns of the problems and types of cases each will produce. An excellent planning reference for anyone looking to understand the medical aspects of a disaster.

The 9/11 Commission Report, Final Report of the National Commission on Terrorist Attacks Upon the United States, Authorized Edition. While much of the report does not cover emergency management, Chapter 9, "Heroism and Horror," provides the most detailed account of the operations at the World Trade Center that I have read. There is a dearth of histories, official or unofficial, of the largest civilian response to a terrorist event. This chapter is one of the closest studies that exists and provides good detail.

Michael Riordan (editor):*The Day After Midnight: The Effects of Nuclear War* (Cheshire, 1982). The book, based on a government report by the Congressional Office of Technology Assessment, was originally created for government officials. Mr. Riordan has distilled the report into an important source of hard data on a subject where it is hard to find useful information. It is filled with the kind of data the will help any emergency manager understand the immediate and long-term effects of a nuclear detonation on the development of plans.

Erik Auf Der Heide: *Disaster Response: Principles of Preparation and Coordination* (Mosby, 1989). Recently in an online survey this was cited as the one book that every emergency manger should have on his or her shelf. It is a practical guide to disaster response with example after example from real disasters and practical lists of needed resources. A true classic.

Brian A. Jackson, D.J. Peterson, James T. Botris, Tom La Tourrette, Irene Brohmakulan, Ari Houser, Jerry Sollinger: *Protecting Emergency*

Responders: Lessons Learned from Terrorist Attacks (RAND Science and Technology Policy Institute, 2002). A conference was held in December 2001 of individuals who had experience at the World Trade Center, the Pentagon, Oklahoma City, and the anthrax letters. These individuals shared their lessons learned in how to protect the first responders to terrorist events. Their real-life experiences provide a valuable resource for policy development in any jurisdiction.

Index